Prosecutorial Misconduct

A Practical Guide for Criminal Defense Lawyers

NEAL J. STEPHENS
AND
AMANDA STEPHENS JAMES

AMERICAN BAR ASSOCIATION
Criminal Justice Section

Cover design by Carolina Martinez/ABA Design

Printed in the United States of America.

28 27 26 25 24 5 4 3 2 1

Library of Congress Cataloging-in-Publication Data

Names: Stephens, Neal, author. | James, Amanda Stephens, author. | American Bar Association. Section of Criminal Justice, issuing body.
Title: Prosecutorial misconduct : a practical guide for criminal defense lawyers / authors, Neal Stephens and Amanda Stephens James.
Description: Chicago : American Bar Association, Section of Criminal Justice, 2024. | Includes index. | Summary: "Throughout my career, I have defended clients in numerous matters where I needed to litigate issues related to every possible variety of prosecutorial misconduct - false statements in search warrant affidavits, improper conduct before the grand jury, improper closing argument, etc. While I continue to believe that the overwhelming majority of prosecutors are professional and ethical, our recent history demonstrates that there are far too many individuals serving prison sentences due to unchecked prosecutorial misconduct. This book aims to arm criminal defense attorneys with the tools needed to fight back against the minority of prosecutors who choose to use their immense power in the wrong way"--Provided by publisher.
Identifiers: LCCN 2024019917 (print) | LCCN 2024019918 (ebook) | ISBN 9781639055166 (paperback) | ISBN 9781639055173 (epub)
Subjects: LCSH: Prosecutorial misconduct--United States. | Public prosecutors--Professional ethics--United States. | Misconduct in office--Law and legislation--United States. | Criminal justice, Administration of--Moral and ethical aspects--United States. | Criminal defense lawyers--United States.
Classification: LCC KF9640.S725 2024 (print) | LCC KF9640 (ebook) | DDC 345.73/01262–dc23/eng/20240512
LC record available at https://lccn.loc.gov/2024019917
LC ebook record available at https://lccn.loc.gov/2024019918

To Kathy, the greatest wife and mom in the world.

Contents

Preface

In 1995, I left private practice in California and moved my young family across the country to join the U.S. Attorney's Office (USAO) in Miami. I was in my late twenties and eager to fight what I viewed as the most dangerous criminal organization in the world—the Medellin Cartel. Many of my peers in the Office had answered the same call and relocated to Miami from every corner of the United States. At the time, the USAO-Miami was the largest office in the country and well stocked with aggressive trial attorneys. Lee Stapleton, the First Assistant U.S. Attorney at the time, had the foresight to assign all the newbies to the Appellate Section before we could rotate into the trial sections. Lee knew that Linda Hertz, the legendary Chief of the Appellate Section, would make sure we appreciated the gravity of the decisions we would soon be making as prosecutors. Linda did not disappoint. On Day 1, I reported to Linda's office, and she delivered a simple, but very stern, message about the Office's expectations: "Be honest, be accountable, and always do the right thing." Over the course of the forty weeks I spent in the Appellate Section, Linda made sure that I understood how an ethical prosecutor responds to every possible factual scenario. For the rest of my career as a narcotics prosecutor, I would hear Linda's voice before I made any decision in my cases.

Upon returning to private practice in California, I received an immediate baptism as a criminal defense attorney when a prosecutor knowingly withheld critical *Brady* information in a matter. The prosecutor's approach to discovery caught me off guard and sparked the next phase of my career, which ultimately led to this book. Over the next twenty-five years I defended clients in numerous matters where I needed to litigate issues related to every possible variety of prosecutorial misconduct—false statements in search warrant affidavits, *Brady/Giglio* violations, improper conduct before the grand jury, *Napue* violations, improper closing argument, among others. These battles with the government generated the work product contained in this book and also inspired me to focus all my pro bono efforts on working Innocence Project cases, primarily with my good friends at the Northern California Innocence Project (NCIP). Those matters illustrated that indigent defendants often lack the resources to identify and oppose prosecutorial misconduct in their cases. One positive from working these challenging matters was the spark it ignited in my daughter and co-author, Amanda. My friends at the NCIP motivated Amanda to work with them after she graduated college and her experience at the NCIP led her to law school at the University of Michigan to study in Professor Eve Primus' highly regarded M-Defender program, an amazing incubator of the next generation of criminal defense attorneys.

While I continue to believe that the overwhelming majority of prosecutors are professional and ethical, our recent history demonstrates that there are far too many individuals serving prison sentences due to unchecked prosecutorial misconduct. This book aims to arm criminal defense attorneys with the tools needed to fight back against that minority of prosecutors who choose to use their immense power in the wrong way.

The chapters are presented chronologically and grouped around prosecutorial misconduct that occurs in the three core pillars of a criminal prosecution: the pre-indictment investigation, pre-trial discovery, and trial. We include favorable case law from the federal circuits so that you will have a solid starting point for any motions you may want to file in your cases. We also include relevant governing standards—such as the DOJ's *Justice Manual* and the *ABA Standards for Criminal Justice*—because those standards can help in pre-indictment discussions with prosecutors and may also influence a trial judge to look more closely at motions that challenge a prosecutor's misconduct.

PART I

Prosecutorial Misconduct During a Criminal Investigation

CHAPTER 1

Search Warrants

Prosecutors and their investigators may commit misconduct in several different respects related to search warrants. Common violations include misrepresenting material information in the search warrant affidavit, seeking an overbroad search warrant, failing to adequately protect your client's privileged information, failing to obtain appropriate internal approvals to search certain locations (e.g., a defense attorney's office), and pursuing a search warrant when U.S. Department of Justice (DOJ) policy dictates that the prosecutor should have used lesser intrusive means, such as a subpoena. These issues can be attacked pre-indictment or post-indictment.

The most common remedy sought will be the suppression of illegally obtained evidence based on a lack of probable cause in the search warrant affidavit. But misconduct related to other aspects of a search warrant provides other options to consider. For example, you might also seek to recuse a rogue prosecutor who appears hell-bent on prosecuting your client based on false information presented to the court in a misleading warrant affidavit. Getting that investigation rotated to a more ethical, objective prosecutor might ultimately result in a declination. You might also use the leverage you generate from exposing the misconduct to negotiate a more favorable resolution for your client because the government wants to avoid a judicial finding of bad faith against a prosecutor or detective who knowingly misrepresented material facts in a sworn affidavit to the court. A finding of bad faith against an agent or detective likely prevents them from serving as a lead agent/detective on future cases because defense counsel will severely impeach the agent in any cross-examination. A finding of bad faith against a prosecutor can also lead to state bar association sanctions and should also negatively impact any upward mobility in their office. In addition, a finding of bad faith against anyone on the prosecution team could spark a wave of habeas motions attacking prior convictions in other cases worked by the unethical member of the prosecution team. If members of the prosecution team intentionally lied in a warrant affidavit, they should suffer the consequences for doing so.

1.1 GOVERNING STANDARDS

The analysis of a search warrant should start with the DOJ's policies regarding how and when the prosecutor should pursue a warrant. Both 28 C.F.R. Part 59 and Section 9-19.200 of the DOJ's *Justice Manual* describe the methods law enforcement should use to obtain documentary evidence held by third parties. These policies describe how prosecutors should handle obtaining documents from lawyers, treating physicians, clergy, and other disinterested third parties who are neither a subject nor a target of the investigation but who may possess relevant information about the subjects and targets of the investigation. The guidelines recognize that using a search warrant in this scenario implicates three privacy issues: (1) the privacy of a person's home or office; (2) the search may require examination of private papers within the scope of the warrant but are not themselves subject to seizure; and (3) the search may intrude on confidential relationships where the privacy of other individuals is implicated. *See* 28 C.F.R. § 59.1(a). As a result, the DOJ expects its prosecutors to use the least intrusive means to obtain information from these disinterested third parties—subpoenas, summons, or formal or informal requests—before resorting to the far more invasive search warrant. *See* 28 C.F.R. §§ 59.1(b) and 59.4(a)(1). If the prosecutors do go forward with a search warrant, they must execute the search warrant "in such a manner as to minimize, to the greatest extent practicable, scrutiny of confidential materials." 28 C.F.R. § 59.4(b)(4). In other words, the prosecutors need to use a judicial neutral or an established Taint Team process to ensure that members of the prosecution team do not seize or review potentially confidential materials. The law related to the government's use of Taint Teams is described in further detail in Chapter 2.

Similarly, Section 9-13.420 of the *Justice Manual* covers searches of premises of attorneys. This section involves a search of a location used by a subject or target of the investigation where the prosecutors should expect to come across attorney–client privileged information. For example, a search of any corporate office will likely contain privileged documents related to communications between the company's executives and their in-house and outside counsel. In addition, using a search warrant against a corporation, particularly a publicly traded company, will generate devastating negative media attention that will destroy the company's reputation—possibly so severely that the company will fail, and innocent employees will lose their jobs and careers.

As a result, the DOJ again instructs its lawyers to take the least intrusive approach to obtaining potentially privileged material. *JM* Section 9-13.420(A). If the prosecutor uses a subpoena, the DOJ avoids the privilege issues as well as unnecessarily tainting a good company that the DOJ ultimately decides should not be charged after it reviews the information it subpoenaed. The DOJ also requires that prosecutors obtain approval by the relevant U.S. Attorney or Assistant Attorney General as well as the DOJ's Office of Enforcement Operations, Policy, and Statutory Enforcement Unit, before proceeding with a search warrant involving an attorney's office. *JM* Sections 9-13.420(B) and (C). The DOJ also expects its prosecutors to frame the search warrant as specifically as possible to minimize the need to search and review privileged material. Section 9-13.420. DOJ also describes specific protocols, including the use of a Taint Team to review the material seized. Sections 9-13.420(D) and (F).

The DOJ is careful to include a provision in its policies and regulations that expressly states that violations of these protocols for obtaining evidence cannot be used against the DOJ in a motion to suppress. *See* 28 C.F.R. § 59.6(b) and *JM* Section 9-13.420(F). Nevertheless, raising violations of these policies to either the DOJ or the court can help in a variety of other ways. First, raising the issue with the DOJ can provide a basis to seek the recusal of a rogue prosecutor from an investigation that an ethical prosecutor might decline to prosecute. *See* Chapter 7. Second, including violations of the DOJ *Justice Manual* in a motion puts the court on notice that the prosecutors are knowingly violating their own policies. While not dispositive, an objective trial judge will become more skeptical of the government's credibility on the warrant issue and subsequent issues in your case. Third, successful motions for terminating sanctions are often comprised of prosecutorial misconduct that permeates multiple aspects of a case. *See United States v. Preston*, 873 F.3d 829 (9th Cir. 2017) (the "cumulative impact" of prosecutorial errors—including commenting on the Defendant's decision not to testify and improperly vouching for the victim-witness warranted reversal of conviction). As a result, it is worth the time to try to identify and expose all aspects of prosecutorial misconduct to build the strongest possible case of cumulative impact in a pre-trial motion, a post-trial motion, or an appeal. Finally, violations of these policies form the basis of a complaint to the DOJ's Office of Professional Responsibility (OPR) against the prosecutor for violating DOJ protocols. *See* 28 C.F.R. § 59.6(a). If submitting an OPR complaint to the DOJ might help your client, a violation of these policies provides a basis for pursuing that action. Just be aware that the OPR exonerates its attorneys on approximately 99 percent of the complaints lodged and then those prosecutors may attempt to use that exoneration in support of their opposition to any motion you need to file with the court to challenge the same misconduct. Typically, you will get more traction with the OPR or the state bar if you have an order from the court where the judge found that the prosecutor acted in bad faith.

1.2 OBTAINING THE SEARCH WARRANT AFFIDAVIT BEFORE INDICTMENT

If the government executes a search warrant at your client's business or residence before charging your client, consider seeking a copy of the search warrant affidavit before the prosecutor files charges. Obtaining the affidavit will allow you to analyze the factual basis of the government's case so you can harness your best possible arguments for seeking a declination of any charges. Note that you will likely confront practical and legal roadblocks to obtaining the affidavit.

First, the government will likely have sealed the search warrant affidavit so you should expect that prosecutors will not simply hand you a copy of the affidavit before they are required to do so in post-indictment Rule 16 discovery. If the prosecutor rejects your request, you can still pursue a pre-indictment motion to unseal the warrant affidavit.

Second, as a practical matter, your client might not want to have the allegations in the search warrant affidavit made public via a motion. Depending on the underlying facts, it might be better to consider some sort of resolution with the government that keeps the expected probable cause allegations under seal.

As summarized below, the law on obtaining a sealed search warrant before the government files charges is mixed. Most courts will grant the defendant's request, but a few will not. However, if you suspect that the government may have misrepresented facts to the court to obtain probable cause for the search warrant, obtaining the search warrant affidavit before the government files charges allows you time to (a) move to recuse a rogue prosecutor, (b) proffer your strongest case for declination or a favorable resolution to the prosecutor's supervisors, and (c) make an informed analysis regarding whether you have that rare case where your client may testify before the grand jury to potentially head off an indictment that would be premised on false and misleading information.

There are three available grounds to invoke in a pre-indictment motion seeking access to a sealed warrant affidavit: (1) the common law right of access to judicial records, (2) the First Amendment, and (3) the Fourth Amendment.

The common law right of access is the strongest option. There is a general, common law right to inspect and copy public records and documents, including "judicial records," but the common law right is not absolute. *Nixon v. Warner Communications*, 435 U.S. 589, 597–99 (1978). It is well established that a search warrant affidavit qualifies as a "judicial record." *Baltimore Sun Co. v. Goetz*, 886 F.2d 60, 64 (4th Cir. 1989); *United States v. Sealed Search Warrants*, 868 F.3d 385, 396 (5th Cir. 2017); *United States v. Wecht*, 484 F.3d 194, 208 (3d Cir. 2007) (documents filed with the court are considered "judicial records").

The common law right of access is favored by courts because it promotes the trustworthiness of the judicial process, curbs judicial abuses, and provides the public with a better understanding of the judicial process, including its fairness. *SEC v. Van Waeyenberghe*, 990 F.2d 845, 849 (5th Cir. 1993). Courts also state that there is a presumption in favor of disclosure. *Id.* at 848. As a result, "the district court's discretion to seal the record of judicial proceedings is to be exercised charily." *Id.* The court should conduct a balancing test that weighs the public's common law right of access against the interests favoring non-disclosure. *Id.* at 393. The government will typically argue against disclosure to protect its investigation, protect its confidential informants and witnesses, and may even claim that publishing the search warrant affidavit will harm the reputation of the target(s) of their investigation. As a result, how long the search warrant affidavit has been under seal may be relevant to the court—the longer the matter has remained under seal, the less likely the government will suffer harm from the disclosure of the warrant affidavit. In addition, courts have emphasized that matters involving public officials and matters of legitimate public concern should be disclosed. *Bradley on behalf of AJW v. Ackal*, 954 F.3d 216, 229 (5th Cir. 2020). Courts also find that potential media interest in the matter weighs in favor of disclosure because the press guards against the miscarriage of justice by subjecting the police, prosecutors, and judicial process to extensive public scrutiny and criticism. *Id.* at 231, quoting *Sheppard v. Maxwell,* 384 U.S. 333, 350 (1966). Courts have also stated that the presumption of the public's right of access may alone outweigh any government interest favoring non-disclosure. *Id.* at 233.

The Fourth Circuit agrees with the Fifth Circuit's analysis regarding granting pre-indictment access to judicial records pursuant to the common law right of access. *Baltimore Sun Co. v. Goetz,* 886 F.2d 60, 64 (4th Cir. 1989); *see also Matter of Search of Office Suites for World & Islam Studies Enter.,* 925 F. Supp. 738, 740 (M.D. Fla. 1996) (district court recognizes common law right of access to search warrant affidavits once search warrants are executed). Other circuits seem inclined to follow the Fifth Circuit but have not yet been presented the same fact pattern involving a pre-indictment request involving a search warrant affidavit. *See In re Search of Fair Fin.,* 692 F.3d 424, 433 (6th Cir. 2012) (recognizing a common law right of access to warrant materials when denying motion grounded on First Amendment principles); *United States v. Corbitt,* 879 F.2d 224, 229 (7th Cir. 1989) (applying the common law right of access to presentence reports).

To date, the Second Circuit has recognized the general proposition regarding a common law right of access but has limited its application to post-indictment motions. *See Application of Newsday, Inc.,* 895 F.2d 74, 76 (2d Cir. 1990) (affirming release of redacted search warrant affidavit but emphasizing the investigation had been completed). A minority of courts have rejected the common law right of access related to a pre-indictment motion to obtain a search warrant. *See Times Mirror Co. v. United States,* 873 F.2d 1210, 1211 (9th Cir. 1989); *Sealed Search Warrants,* 1999 WL 1455215 at *8 (D. N.J. 1999).

As to a First Amendment challenge, the Eighth Circuit has recognized a qualified First Amendment right of access to documents filed in support of search warrant applications, even where the investigation remains ongoing. *In re Search Warrant for Secretarial Area Outside Office of Gunn,* 855 F.2d 569, 573 (8th Cir. 1988). The majority of circuits, however, have rejected a challenge based on the First Amendment. The Fourth, Sixth, and Ninth Circuits have rejected using the First Amendment as a basis to obtain access to search warrant materials pre-indictment while an investigation is ongoing. *See Times Mirror Co. v. United States,* 873 F.2d 1210, 1211 (9th Cir. 1989) (denying media access to search warrants and supporting affidavits relating to a pre-indictment investigation); *Baltimore Sun Co. v. Goetz*, 886 F.2d 60, 64–65 (4th Cir. 1989) (finding that a newspaper has no First Amendment right to unseal search warrant affidavit but may have a common law right); *In re Search of Fair Finance*, 692 F.3d 424, 433 (6th Cir. 2012) (affirming district court denial of a newspaper's motion to unseal search warrants and supporting documents).

As to the Fourth Amendment, a few district courts have recognized a right to access search warrant materials pre-indictment brought by the subject of the property searched. *See, e.g., In re Search Warrants Issued on Apr. 26, 2004*, 353 F. Supp. 2d 584, 587 (D. Md. 2004) (finding that a property owner had a Fourth Amendment right to examine a redacted version of a search warrant affidavit); *In re Search Warrants Issued Aug. 29, 1994*, 889 F. Supp. 296, 299 (S.D. Ohio 1995) (unsealing search warrant papers under search subject's Fourth Amendment right); *Matter of Up N. Plastics, Inc.*, 940 F. Supp. 229, 232 (D. Minn. 1996) (denying a government motion to continue sealing a search warrant application and affidavit). But the Seventh Circuit held that the Fourth Amendment confers no right of access to affidavits in support of search warrants. *In re EyeCare Physicians of America*, 100 F.3d 514 (7th Cir. 1996) (affirming district court denial of company's motion to have the search warrant application and affidavit unsealed because the Fourth Amendment does not recognize a right of access to sealed search warrant affidavits pre-indictment); *see also In re Searches & Seizures*, No. 08-SW-0361 DAD, 2008 WL 5411772, at *3 (E.D. Cal. Dec. 19, 2008) (denying the qualified Fourth Amendment right of access due to a compelling government interest).

1.3 *FRANKS* CHALLENGES: ATTACKING FALSE STATEMENTS IN WARRANT AFFIDAVITS

After obtaining a copy of the search warrant affidavit, the next step is to analyze the warrant affidavit to assess whether the prosecutor misled the court to obtain probable cause to search. A *Franks* hearing allows individuals to challenge the truthfulness of statements made in search warrant affidavits. *Franks v. Delaware*, 438 U.S. 154 (1978). The *Franks* doctrine extends to both false statements and material omissions. *United States v. Lull*, 824 F.3d 109 (4th Cir. 2016); *United States v. Glover*, 755 F.3d 811 (7th Cir. 2014); *United States v. Jacobs*, 986 F.2d 1231 (8th Cir. 1993). To qualify for a *Franks* hearing, an individual must make a "substantial preliminary showing" (1) that the affiant's statement "was made knowingly and intentionally, or with reckless disregard for the truth," and (2) that the "allegedly false statement (or material omission) is necessary to the finding of probable cause." *Franks*, 438 U.S. at 155.

If the defendant satisfies the *Franks* elements, the court should void the warrant under the Fourth or Fourteenth Amendment. The good faith exception should not apply to save the warrant. For example, the Fifth Circuit has stated that the good faith exception does not apply in four situations, including when "the issuing judge was misled by information in an affidavit that the affiant knew was false or would have known was false except for his reckless disregard of the truth." *United States v. Mays*, 466 F.3d 335, 343 (5th Cir. 2006); *United States v. Cavazos*, 288 F.3d 706, 709–10 (5th Cir. 2002).

To prevail on a *Franks* motion, the defendant bears the burden of showing by a preponderance of the evidence that a misstatement or omission was more than mere negligence. *United States v. Runyan*, 290 F.3d 223, 234 (5th Cir. 2002). The defendant's allegations "must point out specifically with supporting reasons the portion of the warrant affidavit that is claimed to be false" and "must be accompanied by an offer of proof," such as an affidavit. *Franks*, 438 U.S. at 154. If the defendant does not present affidavits or sworn statements with his or her *Franks* motion, their absence must be "satisfactorily explained." *Id.*

To establish that the officer or prosecutor acted with "reckless disregard for the truth," most courts require that the defendant establish that the affiant entertained serious doubts as to the truth of his or her allegations. *United States v. Whitley*, 249 F.3d 614, 621 (7th Cir. 2001); *United States v. Reed*, 921 F.3d 751, 756 (8th Cir. 2019) ("reckless disregard requires showing that the officer 'must have entertained serious doubts as to the truth of his statements or had obvious reasons to doubt the accuracy of the information'"); *Stonecipher v. Valles*, 759 F.3d 1134, 1142 (10th Cir. 2014) ("to establish reckless disregard in the presentation of information to a magistrate judge, 'there must exist evidence that the officer in fact entertained serious doubts as to the truth of his allegations . . . and [a] factfinder may infer reckless disregard from circumstances evincing obvious reasons to doubt the veracity of the allegations'").

Because the affiant's state of mind generally will be proved circumstantially, a fact finder may infer reckless disregard from circumstances evincing "obvious reasons to doubt the veracity of the allegations." *Whitley*, 249 F.3d at 621. The Seventh Circuit has further expanded this principle "to include the state of mind not only of the affiant, but also of those governmental agents from whom the affiant received false information incorporated into the affidavit." *Id.* In other words, the validity of the search is not saved if the affiant has incorporated an intentional or reckless falsehood passed on by another governmental agent. *Id.*; *see also Rhoten v. Stroman*, No. 116CV00648ADAJCM, 2020 WL 1536381, at *5 (W.D. Tex. Mar. 31, 2020) ("An agent can be liable when he deliberately or recklessly provides false information to another agent, who then includes the misinformation.").

Omissions can be more difficult to prove than false statements. As the Fifth Circuit stated, "[I]t will often be difficult for an accused to prove that an omission was made intentionally or with reckless disregard . . . unless he has somehow gained independent evidence that the affiant had acted from bad motive or recklessly in conducting his investigation and making the affidavit." *United States v. Martin*, 615 F.2d 318, 329 (5th Cir. 1980). Nevertheless, a defendant can meet the standard for establishing reckless disregard regarding an omission by showing that an officer withheld a fact that "[a]ny reasonable person would have known that this was the kind of thing the judge would wish to know." *Wilson v. Russo*, 212 F.3d 781, 788 (3d Cir. 2000); *United States v. Jacobs*, 986 F.2d 1231, 1235 (8th Cir. 1993). In addition, when the facts omitted from the affidavit are clearly critical to a finding of probable cause, some courts will allow the fact of recklessness to be inferred from proof of the omission itself. *United States v. Tomblin*, 46 F.3d 1369, 1377 (5th Cir. 1995); *but see United States v. Colkley*, 899 F.2d 297, 301 (4th Cir. 1990) (expressing doubts about the validity of inferring bad motive under *Franks* from the fact of omission alone, for such an inference collapses into a single inquiry of the two elements—intentionality and materiality—which *Franks* states are independently necessary). Moreover, there is a split in the courts regarding whether the defendant must show that the affiant intended to mislead the magistrate judge. *Compare Lombardi v. City of El Cajon*, 117 F.3d 1117, 1121 (9th Cir. 1997) ("we disagree that intent to mislead the magistrate is required to overcome a summary judgment on a claim of qualified immunity in a civil rights suit based on *Franks*") and *United States v. Torres*, 694 F. App'x 937, 944 (5th Cir. 2017) (an omission may amount to improper government conduct only if the omission is material and the defendant shows that the affiant excluded material information with the intent to mislead the magistrate).

1.4 *FRANKS* PROGENY: HELPFUL CASES

Our review of approximately 400 opinions regarding *Franks* challenges reveals that defendants win only about 10 percent of these challenges. Many of these challenges arise in 42 U.S.C. Section 1983 and *Bivens* litigation, but the legal principles in those matters should still apply to a challenge in a criminal case. Successful challenges often involve false statements or omitted information related to the source of the government's information—particularly where the government fails to disclose bias and credibility issues with their snitch. If you encounter a warrant affidavit based on a law enforcement source, hunt for any discrepancy that might allow you to build a *Franks* challenge. As described below, some courts have a fairly reasonable standard related to materiality, which suggests you might prevail if you can show some issue with the informant—either tied to bias or the accuracy of the information the informant provided to law enforcement.

Here is a summary of helpful circuit level opinions on *Franks* challenges:

First Circuit

Jordan v. Town of Waldoboro, 943 F.3d 532 (1st Cir. 2019) (court finds a *Franks* violation in a Section 1983 suit where the affiant falsely represented the facts surrounding a father providing his son a power of attorney to control the father's property).

United States v. Gifford, 727 F.3d 92 (1st Cir. 2013) (no probable cause where police omitted that a house used by the affiant to compare electrical usage rate against the target marijuana grow house was one third the size of the suspected grow house and police also failed to disclose their informant's basis of knowledge, credibility, and reliability).

Second Circuit

Walczyk v. Rico, 496 F.3d 139 (2d Cir. 2007) (court denies officer's motion for summary judgment in a civil action by finding that the officer omitted the undisputed fact that Plaintiff had not resided at one of the target residences in the warrant affidavit for seven years).

Third Circuit

United States v. Brown, 631 F.3d 638 (3d Cir. 2011) (*Franks* violation found and DNA sample suppressed where the affiant gave the "false impression of a continuous sequence of events observed by a number of witnesses" to connect Defendant with the crime but failed to check the affidavit's contents against the investigation reports or have the lead investigating officer confirm the accuracy of the affidavit).

Fourth Circuit

Humbert v. Mayor & City Council of Baltimore City, 866 F.3d 546 (4th Cir. 2017) (in Section 1983 litigation, Plaintiff successfully challenged an arrest warrant that stated the victim positively identified him as her attacker when the evidence actually showed that the victim could not identify Plaintiff as her attacker and DNA evidence exonerated him).

Osborne v. Georgiades, 679 F. App'x 234 (4th Cir. 2017) (in Section 1983 litigation, Plaintiff established material omissions that violated *Franks* where Plaintiff was falsely arrested for sexually abusing a minor and the warrant affidavit failed to disclose that the minor repeatedly denied any wrongdoing and the medical report showed no signs of physical abuse).

United States v. Lull, 824 F.3d 109 (4th Cir. 2016) (*Franks* violation found in narcotics buy-bust prosecution where affiant in search warrant omitted that their confidential informant stole money the police gave him to buy drugs and was arrested for that theft).

Miller v. Prince George's Cty., MD, 475 F.3d 621 (4th Cir. 2007) (in Section 1983 litigation against a police officer for making false statements and omissions in a warrant affidavit, the court found a triable issue of material fact where the lead detective investigating the case knew the suspect's name and his race, Caucasian, yet identified Plaintiff, an African American man, in his warrant affidavit).

In re Search Warrants Served on Home Health & Hospice Care, Inc., 121 F.3d 700 (4th Cir. 1997) (following the seizure of five million documents, court finds *Franks* violation where the affidavit falsely stated Defendants used Post-it notes to falsify medical records, changed their billing practices to avoid detection, and employed people to work after-hours to alter documents).

Fifth Circuit

Winfrey v. Rogers, 901 F.3d 483, 494 (5th Cir. 2018) (in Section 1983 litigation, *Franks* violation found where Defendant acquitted on murder charges established that warrant affidavit (1) omitted statements that contradicted the physical evidence, (2) misstated dog scent identification procedure, and (3) omitted inconsistences between witness statements).

United States v. Alvarez, 127 F.3d 372 (5th Cir. 1997) (court reverses order denying motion to suppress where affiant stated that that a minor's breasts were "genitals" under the relevant statute, which was a false statement of law).

Hale v. Fish, 899 F.2d 390 (5th Cir. 1990) (in Section 1983 litigation, Plaintiff establishes *Franks* violation where arrest warrant (1) omitted information that the affiant's informant had a motive to lie regarding Plaintiff thereby impacting the informant's bias and credibility, and (2) failed to include witness testimony contradicting the informant's allegations).

United States v. Namer, 680 F.2d 1088 (5th Cir. 1982) (*Franks* violation found where search warrant affidavit stated that Defendant's financial products were "*classified* as securities" under the state blue sky laws where the state's Securities Commission had no formal classification procedure for securities and one agency official had merely told the affiant that Defendant's transactions "*could* be securities").

Sixth Circuit

McCallum v. Geelhood, 742 F. App'x 985, 987 (6th Cir. 2018) (in Section 1983 litigation, *Franks* violation found where search warrant alleged an officer received confidential information from a reliable informant that Plaintiffs trafficked illegal narcotics from their home and the affiant subsequently admitted that she never actually received information from the informant described in her affidavit and never even knew the informant's identity).

United States v. Bennett, 905 F.2d 931 (6th Cir. 1990) (*Franks* violation found regarding motion to suppress where the warrant affidavit stated that (1) an informant saw several bags of marijuana in Defendant's residence, and (2) Defendant bought a shipment of marijuana and the affiant ultimately admitted that those statements in his affidavit were untrue).

Seventh Circuit

Rainsberg v. Benner, 913 F.3d 640 (7th Cir. 2019) (in Section 1983 litigation, *Franks* violation found where officer presented numerous false statements in arrest warrant regarding Plaintiff, who the officer suspected of killing his mother, including (1) misstating a time stamp in a phone record to place Plaintiff in her apartment during the murder; (2) mischaracterizing Plaintiff's behavior at a Kroger grocery store to suggest he disposed of a murder weapon in a trash can; (3) inaccurately describing Plaintiff as a "callous son"; and (4) representing that nothing was taken from the mother's apartment, when in fact other investigators discovered her purse and medication missing).

United States v. Glover, 755 F.3d 811 (7th Cir. 2014) (court reverses denial of *Franks* hearing where the search warrant affidavit omitted that affiant's informant worked with the police for six years, affiliated himself with a gang, and committed several crimes while working as an informant).

Betker v. Gomez, 692 F.3d 854 (7th Cir. 2012) (in Section 1983 litigation, *Franks* violation found where affidavit was based on an alleged statement from Plaintiff's estranged sister-in-law regarding the alleged location of firearms where Plaintiff subsequently presented testimony from the sister-in-law contradicting the statements in the officer's warrant affidavit).

United States v. Cortina, 630 F.2d 1207 (7th Cir. 1980) (*Franks* violation affirmed and evidence suppressed where FBI agent "deliberately lied . . . to support the search warrant" regarding alleged discussions between the agent and his informant. The district court characterized the FBI agent's statements as "intentional misrepresentations" that "show[ed] a reckless disregard for the truth." *Id.* at 1212. The Seventh Circuit affirmed finding the agent "willfully disobeyed the law in two ways: he lied in the affidavit, and he lied on the witness stand." *Id.* at 1214. The Seventh Circuit's scathing criticism of the agent's "abhorrent conduct" made clear that the court does "not allow or condone reckless or deliberate misrepresentations made to a magistrate.").

Eighth Circuit

United States v. Wells, 223 F.3d 835 (8th Cir. 2000) (*Franks* violation affirmed where a witness identified the suspect's car as either dark green or dark black but the affidavit stated that the witness saw "a dark colored" vehicle thereby leading to the Defendant's arrest, who was washing a dark blue car near the scene of the crime).

United States v. Jacobs, 986 F.2d 1231 (8th Cir. 1993) (court reverses denial of motion to suppress where affiant omitted that a drug sniffing dog failed to alert to the presence of drugs in a FedEx package addressed to Defendant that contained narcotics).

Ninth Circuit

United States v. Perkins, 850 F.3d 1109 (9th Cir. 2017) (court reverses denial of *Franks* hearing in child pornography prosecution where the agent's search warrant affidavit failed to disclose (1) that the Canadian authorities dropped charges against the Defendant because the images at issue were not pornographic; (2) important descriptions of the images by the Canadian officers; and (3) copies of the images at issue).

United States v. Hernandez, 135 F. App'x 97 (9th Cir. 2005) (*Franks* violation found and evidence suppressed where affiant's search warrant affidavit: (1) omitted that multiple witnesses could not positively identify Defendant in a photo lineup; (2) presented material facts in a false and misleading manner; (3) failed to state the police never saw Defendant during their surveillance; and (4) gave a false impression an officer positively identified Defendant).

Mendocino Envtl. Ctr. V. Mendocino Cty., 192 F.3d 1283 (9th Cir. 1999) (in Section 1983 litigation, Plaintiffs established a *Franks* violation where the warrant affidavit omitted the fact that one of the Plaintiffs, who was transporting explosives in his car, had received death threats).

United States v. Ippolito, 774 F.2d 1482 (9th Cir. 1985) (Ninth Circuit applies *Franks* to false statements and omissions in wiretap affidavits where the district court found that the affiant, to establish necessity for the wiretap intercepts, falsely asserted that an informant would not testify against Defendant out of fear of retaliation).

Tenth Circuit

Harte v. Board of Commissioners of County of Johnson, Kansas, 864 F.3d 1154 (10th Cir. 2017) (in Section 1983 litigation challenging a search warrant of Plaintiff's suspected marijuana grow, *Franks* violation found where affiant-based search warrant affidavit on two allegedly positive field tests for marijuana from trash pulls and one "suspicious trip" to a garden store. The search revealed that the target location was a tomato garden, and a retained expert showed the substance in the trash pulls was Teavana tea.).

United States v. Adams, 615 F. App'x 502 (10th Cir. 2015) (suppression of firearms seized from Defendant's residence affirmed on probable cause grounds where the search warrant affidavit inaccurately stated the expiration date for Defendant's firearm permits).

Stewart v. Donges, 915 F.2d 572 (10th Cir. 1990) (in Section 1983 litigation, the Tenth Circuit found that a triable issue of fact remained about whether an officer knew but omitted from a search warrant affidavit the fact that a theft victim had recanted his accusations).

Eleventh Circuit

Daniels v. Bango, 487 F. App'x 532 (11th Cir. 2012) (in Section 1983 litigation, *Franks* violation found where arrest warrant submitted by undercover officer who claimed he had accurately identified a suspected drug dealer following a conversation during an undercover buy with the drug dealer failed to disclose that (1) Plaintiff's jail release date did not match the dealer's statement to the affiant; (2) Plaintiff's court case concluded before the date the dealer provided to the affiant; (3) Plaintiff's case resolved with time served while the dealer told the affiant that he faced "fifteen years"; and (4) police spent twenty minutes closely observing the suspect during a controlled buy).

1.5 ATTACKING OVERBROAD SEARCH WARRANTS

The breadth of a search warrant is another potential area to seek to suppress evidence. In any seizure involving data stored on electronic devices—like computers, telephones, and email servers—the government typically seizes all the data on the device with no regard to the scope of the probable cause alleged in their warrant affidavit. The prosecution team then hunts for evidence of crimes by sifting through data that they had no probable cause to seize. Defense counsel can respond by filing a motion to suppress because the warrant itself was overbroad or the agents seized material that exceeded the scope of the warrant.

To assess whether you have a basis to file a motion to suppress due to overbreadth, there are three possible angles to analyze: (1) does the warrant authorize seizing records that fall outside the probable cause described in the warrant affidavit; (2) is the warrant an "all records" warrant that allows law enforcement to seize nearly every document at the target location; and (3) did the agents seize records outside the relevant time frame alleged in the warrant affidavit?

Black Letter Fourth Amendment law requires that a warrant be limited to the specific areas or things for which there is probable cause of criminal activity. *Maryland v. Garrison*, 480 U.S. 79, 84 (1987); *United States v. Sanjar*, 876 F.3d 725, 735–36 (5th Cir. 2017) (explaining that a warrant is "problematic" under the Fourth Amendment if it authorizes seizure of all of a mental health center's files where probable cause of fraud existed as to only certain aspects). Thus, the warrant affidavit must establish a nexus between the thing to be searched and seized and the evidence of criminal activity sought. *United States v. Payne*, 341 F.3d 393, 400 (5th Cir. 2003).

In *Center Art Galleries—Hawaii, Inc. v. United States*, for example, the target's business consisted of sales of works of art, 20 percent of which were created by Salvador Dali and 80 percent by other artists. 875 F.2d 747, 751 (9th Cir. 1989). In its search warrant affidavit, the government recited twenty-two instances of alleged misrepresentations regarding only Dali's work. *Id.* The court held that the warrants to search Defendant's businesses were overbroad because, among other things, the government failed to limit the warrants to items pertaining to the sale of Dali artwork despite the lack of probable cause of criminal activity unrelated to Dali. *Id.*

Likewise, when the government alleged fraud within specific investment funds in a large family of funds, the warrant needed to be limited to those specific funds. *United States v. Vilar*, No. S305CR621KMK, 2007 WL 1075041, at *20 (S.D.N.Y. Apr. 4, 2007). In *Vilar*, the warrant affidavit alleged wrongdoing involving three of the company's investment vehicles, two suspects, and two groups of alleged victims. *Id.* at *19. "Clearly, then, there was probable cause to conduct some form of search of [the Defendant-company's] U.S. offices." *Id.* at *20. But "[t]he search ultimately authorized by the Warrant . . . was more extensive than what was supported by the warrant application." *Id.* Instead of restricting the search to only those items supported by probable cause, "the very first paragraph of the Warrant Rider authorizes the seizure of, among other items, *all* client files, *all* investment advisory agreements, and *all* documents concerning communications with Amerindo clients, regardless of whether those documents had any relation to the funds, accounts, and individuals addressed by the Warrant application." *Id.* (emphasis in original).

Defense counsel should also challenge any "all records" warrant. The Fourth Amendment requires that search warrants "particularly describe the place to be searched, and the persons or things to be seized." U.S. Const. amend. IV. The Fourth Amendment recognizes that "those searches deemed necessary should be as limited as possible." *Coolidge v. New Hampshire*, 403

U.S. 443, 467 (1971). "[T]he specific evil" in the case at bar "is the 'general warrant' abhorred by the colonists," permitting "exploratory rummaging in a person's belongings." *Id.*; *United States v. Kimbrough*, 69 F.3d 723, 727 (5th Cir. 1995) ("The Fourth Amendment prohibits the issuance of general warrants allowing officials to burrow through a person's possessions looking for any evidence of a crime.") (citing *Andresen v. Maryland*, 427 U.S. 463, 480 (1976)).

The Fifth Circuit, for example, looks at the substance of a warrant—not the label—to determine whether it is an "all records" request that triggers close scrutiny under the Fourth Amendment. Thus, a warrant with an exhaustive list of every possible type of business record typically retained by the target company is considered an "all records" warrant even if not labeled that way by the government. *See United States v. Oglesby*, No. 4:18-CR-0626, 2019 WL 1877228, at *8 (S.D. Tex. Apr. 26, 2019) (citing *United States v. Humphrey*, 104 F.3d 65, 69 (5th Cir. 1997)).

In *United States v. Leary*, the Tenth Circuit rejected the government's argument that the warrant was constitutional because it limited the search via a detailed list of business records to be seized at a corporate office. 846 F.2d 592, 602 (10th Cir. 1988). The court reasoned: "Nor did the list of business records to be seized provide any meaningful limitations on the [] search. The warrant encompassed virtually every document that one might expect to find in a modern export company's office." *Id.*

In addition, proving that the government obtained an improper "all records" warrant can be established by the items actually seized by the agents who executed the search. *Voss v. Bergsgaard*, 774 F.2d 402, 405 (10th Cir. 1985) ("The insufficient particularity of the warrants is . . . illustrated by some of the items actually seized. . . . The warrants allowed precisely the kind of rummaging through a person's belongings, in search of evidence of even previously unsuspected crimes or of no crime at all, that the fourth amendment proscribes.").

Just as the failure to be specific with regards to subject matter invalidates a search warrant, "[f]ailure to limit broad descriptive terms by relevant dates, when such dates are available to the police, will render a warrant overbroad." *United States v. Abboud*, 438 F.3d 554, 576 (6th Cir. 2006) (internal citations omitted); *United States v. Cook*, 657 F.2d 730, 733 (5th Cir. 1981) ("Failure to employ the specificity available will invalidate a general description in a warrant."). Thus, in *Abboud*, when "law enforcement knew that the evidence in support of probable cause in the affidavit revolved only around a three-month period in 1999[,] the authorization to search for evidence irrelevant to that time frame could well be described as 'rummaging.'" *Abboud*, 438 F.3d at 576. Courts routinely invalidate warrants as overbroad on this ground. *See, e.g., Vilar*, 2007 WL 1075041 at *20 (holding search warrant overbroad when "the allegations of wrongdoing in the warrant application date back to no earlier than 2001," but "the Warrant itself contains no time limitations").

The government often opposes an overbreadth challenge by asserting that the warrant affidavit alleged a violation of a broad statute—like mail or wire fraud—that would bring the disputed material in scope. But numerous circuit courts have rejected this approach by reasoning that "limiting" the breadth of a search by referencing a general criminal statute is no limit at all. *See Roche v. United States*, 614 F.2d 6, 8 (1st Cir. 1980); *Leary*, 846 F.2d at 601–02; *United States v. Cardwell*, 680 F.2d 75, 77 (9th Cir. 1982); *Rickert v. Sweeney*, 813 F.2d 907, 909 (8th Cir. 1987); *see also United States v. Abrams*, 615 F.2d 541, 545 (1st Cir. 1980) (deeming warrant insufficiently particularized and noting, among other things, that "[a] time frame should also have been incorporated into the warrant"); *United States v. Jacobson*, 4 F. Supp. 3d 515, 526 (E.D.N.Y. 2014) ("a warrant's failure to include a temporal limitation on the things to be seized may, in certain circumstances, render a warrant insufficiently particular"); *United States v. Triumph Capital Grp., Inc.*, 211 F.R.D. 31, 58 (D. Conn. 2002) (recognizing a "temporal limitation" as "one indicia of particularity").

CHAPTER 2

Filter Teams

In recent years, the DOJ has increasingly relied on "Filter Teams" to review documents seized in searches to filter out potentially privileged documents before providing the remaining non-privileged documents to the members of the DOJ's prosecution team for use in their investigation. The increasing acceptance of this Filter Team option has made the DOJ much more aggressive in pursuing search warrants when it historically would have opted to use a less intrusive subpoena.

A Filter Team is sometimes referred to as a "Taint Team" or "Privilege Team." The Filter Team should be comprised of prosecutors and case agents who do not work on the underlying investigation. In the DOJ's eyes, Filter Team members act like an ethical screen to prevent the prosecution team members from being polluted or tainted by privileged information seized from the target location.

After executing a search warrant at a target location that possesses privileged information, the DOJ's standard approach is to reach out to defense counsel shortly after the execution of the search to request a list of attorneys who have provided legal services to the target of the search. The prosecutors tell defense counsel that the Filter Team will run electronic searches to identify documents that are to/from the attorneys on the list and will then screen out those documents to protect the privilege. "Trust us." What could possibly go wrong?

There are numerous flaws with the DOJ's approach. First, a Filter Team is an animal that the DOJ created for its own purposes. There is no principle in common law, no statute, and no regulation that permits an investigating prosecutor to raid a corporation, seize thousands of privileged communications, and then simply walk down the hall and hand over those privileged communications to another prosecutor to review. No one in the government, including any member of any Filter Team, should have access to those privileged communications. But the Filter Team concept has gained traction in recent years because defense attorneys have capitulated to the DOJ's proposed process. As a result, courts have grown increasingly comfortable with the practice. When a defense attorney does challenge a Filter Team, the government responds by reciting all the recent cases in that district where the use of a Filter Team was "approved" by defense counsel and argue that the government's proposed protocol is "routinely" accepted by courts.

Second, all Filter Teams present a classic "fox guarding the hen house" problem since any Filter Team will be comprised of federal prosecutors and agents who work in the same offices as their counterparts on the prosecution team. Thus, there is an inherent risk that the Filter Team will leak information to the prosecution team, or a rogue member of the prosecution team will find a way to access the privileged information. We have yet to work a matter with a Filter Team where there was not a breach of the ethical screen that involved prosecution team members obtaining access to some privileged material.

Third, a Filter Team represents a *per se* intrusion of your client's attorney–client privilege because the DOJ prosecutors and federal agents are still reviewing this privileged information—even though the reviewers are on a Filter Team.

As a result, consider challenging the Filter Team process with a motion that would force the government to turn the seized material over to a judicial neutral or special master to review. This area of law is loaded with opportunities to expose government misconduct because the government often fails to follow its own protocols regarding its Filter Team process—either intentionally or due to inexperience and incompetence.

2.1 GOVERNING STANDARDS

As noted in Chapter 1.1, Section 9-13.420 of the *Justice Manual* summarizes the protocols a prosecutor should use when conducting a search "of business organizations where such searches involve materials in the possession of individuals serving in the capacity of legal advisor to the organization." The *Justice Manual* states that a Privilege Team (i.e., a Filter

Team) should be established before the search that will include both Filter Team agents and prosecutors. *JM* Section 9-13.420I. As far as collecting the documents, the Filter Team agents must be on site during the execution of the search to ensure that prosecution team agents do not access any privileged information. *Id.* This policy is routinely violated because federal agencies typically send in dozens of agents to execute a search warrant at a corporation—meaning that agents from the squad investigating the matter will often lead the search and, therefore, be exposed to privileged material.

In regard to reviewing the documents, the DOJ's policy expressly mentions the possibility of using either (a) a judicial officer, (b) a special master, or (c) a Filter Team to conduct the review. This is significant because, in our experience, the DOJ always selects the Filter Team option and never opts for a special master. But given that the DOJ's policy also endorses the use of a judicial neutral, the DOJ cannot argue to a court that it is somehow improper or inappropriate to use a judicial neutral or special master in opposition to your motion challenging the use of their Filter Team. *JM* Section 9-13.420(F).

In addition, the lead prosecutor and case agent should also present the Magistrate Judge with the proposed Filter Team protocol that the Filter Team intends to use to both collect and review the seized materials. Doing so allows the court to either reject or modify aspects of the DOJ's proposed protocol before authorizing the search. The prosecutor should present the protocol to the court with the search warrant package—the warrant, the search warrant affidavit, and any motion to seal. That protocol should lay out exactly how the Filter Team will prevent the prosecution team from being polluted by exposure to privileged material. Notably, Section 9-13.420I merely suggests that the prosecutor "*may* attach written instructions or, at a minimum, should generally state the government's intention to employ procedures designed to ensure that attorney–client privileges are not violated." This is weak. No magistrate judge should allow the government to walk off with reams of attorney–client privileged information without understanding exactly what the government intends to do with it. If the prosecutor does not provide the court with the entire Filter Team protocol, it suggests that the prosecutor either (a) has little or no experience with Filter Teams or (b) wants to prevent any judicial oversight of their review of the privileged material. Both reasons are problematic. Thus, this may be a very ripe area for attack.

2.2 CHALLENGING FILTER TEAMS: HELPFUL CASES

As a practical matter, cost may be a prohibitive issue for some targets because the court may decide that the target has to bear the brunt of the cost of any privilege review by a special master—and judges are too busy to conduct the review on their own. However, if your client has the resources to mount a challenge, the law underlying the attorney–client privilege demonstrates that DOJ's Filter Team process constitutes a *per se* invasion of the privilege and, therefore, the Filter Team should be deemed presumptively illegal—a view endorsed by the leading cases from the Fourth and Sixth Circuits and an increasing number of district courts.

The attorney–client privilege is, perhaps, the most sacred of all legally recognized privileges, and its preservation is essential to the just and orderly operation of our legal system. *United States v. Bauer*, 132 F.3d 504, 510 (9th Cir. 1997), citing *Upjohn Co. v. United States*, 449 U.S. 383, 389 (1981). The privilege protects against more than just the *use* of privileged materials as evidence at trial; it protects against "*disclosure itself.*" *In re Lott*, 424 F.3d 446, 451 (6th Cir. 2005) (emphasis added); *In re Itron*, 883 F.3d 553, 561–62 (5th Cir. 2018); *Admiral Ins. Co. v. U.S. Dist. Court for Dist. of Arizona*, 881 F.2d 1486, 1491 (9th Cir. 1989) ("compliance with [a] discovery order against claim of privilege destroys [the] right sought to be protected"). As *Lott* states, "Mandatory disclosure of the communications is the exact harm the privilege is meant to guard against, and this disclosure is not remedied merely because a disclosed confidence is not used against the holder in a particular case." *In re Lott*, 424 F.3d at 451.

Thus, the Supreme Court has held that the *privilege protects against the disclosure of information to government investigators*, without considering whether the government would use the information as evidence in some future proceeding. *Upjohn*, 449 U.S. at 389 (privilege prevented disclosure to IRS investigators) (emphasis added). Courts also entertain motions for mandamus relief *before disclosure* of privileged materials—because *disclosure "destroys the right sought to be protected."* *Bogosian v. Gulf Oil Corp.*, 738 F.2d 587, 591 (3d Cir. 1984) (emphasis added); *In re Itron, Inc.*, 883 F.3d at 567 ("[A]ppeal after final judgment will come too late because the privileged communications will already have been disclosed"); *In re Lott*, 424 F.3d at 449–52 (same); *Chase Manhattan Bank, N.A. v. Turner & Newall, PLC*, 964 F.2d 159, 164 (2d Cir. 1992) (mandamus is appropriate because the privilege "prohibits disclosure to adversaries as well as the use of confidential communications as evidence at trial").

The leading cases rejecting the use of Filter Teams come from the Fourth and Sixth Circuits. In *United States v. Under Seal (In re Search Warrant Issued June 13, 2019,* 942 F.3d 159 (4th Cir. 2019)), the Fourth Circuit reversed a district court order denying a law firm's application for an injunction to stop a Filter Team from beginning its review of materials seized from the law firm. In finding that injunctive relief was warranted to stop any Filter Team review, the Fourth Circuit focused on separation of powers principles, emphasizing that the DOJ's Filter Team protocol improperly authorized the Executive Branch to make decisions on attorney–client privilege that the judicial branch must decide. *Id.* at 177; *see also In re Search of Elec. Commc'ns,* 802 F.3d 516, 530 & n.54 (3d Cir. 2015). The Fourth Circuit also emphasized that the Filter Team could make errors in its privilege analysis that would result in privileged material improperly being leaked to the prosecution team. *Id.*

In addition, the Sixth Circuit aptly described the most significant problem plaguing the DOJ's self-created Filter Team process by pointing out that "the government's fox is left in charge of [the target's] henhouse and may err by neglect or malice, as well by honest differences of opinion." *In re Grand Jury Subpoenas*, 454 F.3d 511, 523 (6th Cir. 2006).

District courts have increasingly begun to view the Filter Team process as a *per se* illegal intrusion on the target's attorney–client privilege. As stated in *United States v. Neill*, "while the parties dispute whether courts have sanctioned the Department of Justice's 'taint team' procedures, it is clear that the government's affirmative decision to invoke these procedures constitutes a *per se* intentional intrusion [into the privilege]." 952 F. Supp. 834, 840–41 (D.D.C. 1997); *see also United States v. Pedersen*, 2014 WL 3871197, at *29–30 (D. Or. Aug. 6, 2014) (Filter Team procedure is a *per se* intrusion into the attorney–client privilege); *United States v. Gallego*, No. CR-18-01537-001-TUC-RM (BPV), 2018 WL 4257967, at *1 (D. Ariz. Sept. 6, 2018) (granting temporary restraining order to stop Filter Team review and install a special master to review materials seized from law office search); *United States v. SDI Future Health, Inc.*, 464 F. Supp. 2d 1027, 1037–38 (D. Nev. 2006) (finding "it is doubtful that the court would have approved the Government taint procedures if SDI had challenged them," but holding an objection three years later was untimely); *United States v. Castro*, 2020 WL 241112, *2 (E.D. Mich. Jan. 16, 2020) (court rejects government's Filter Team and appoints special master to review Defendant's prison calls).

Why did the DOJ invent this Filter Team concept? Filter Teams help prosecutors in several critical ways but do nothing to help the targets of their investigations. First, as a practical matter, using a Filter Team allows agents executing search warrants to simply grab everything, including terabytes of the electronic data, during the execution of the search. The DOJ will argue that the Filter Team can parse through their overbroad haul of data later to protect against the prosecution team reviewing both privileged material and material that is outside the scope of the warrant. Basically, a "no harm, no foul" approach. The DOJ's approach, however, directly contradicts well-established common law privilege case law, as described above, because the law focuses on the *disclosure* of privileged information. Moreover, if courts forced the DOJ to fund the entire cost for a special master to review all that excessive data, prosecutors and agents would be much more likely to use subpoenas and would be far more selective regarding the volume of documents and electronic data they seized at target locations—both of which, ironically, are required pursuant to the DOJ policies summarized above.

Second, using a Filter Team allows the DOJ to control all the data without having a judicial neutral providing legitimate oversight over what the DOJ does with the data, which often results in leaks of privilege material to the prosecution team, either intentional or inadvertent.

Third, the DOJ affirmatively deploys Filter Teams to pierce privilege permanently for all documents seized because the DOJ uses its Filter Teams to build crime-fraud arguments against targets. Doing so is improper. As Judge Ancer Haggerty eloquently articulated in *Pedersen*, "[A] filter team is not entitled to review privileged materials, even under the auspices of a search for crime-fraud. . . . Only a court of competent jurisdiction can determine the applicability of the crime-fraud exception. If the government is concerned that there is crime fraud, . . . the government can request that the court conduct an in-camera review of privileged materials. Such a request must be supported with "a factual basis adequate to support a good faith belief by a reasonable person. . . . The government may not intentionally review privileged communications in order to develop the factual basis supporting an in-camera review." *Pedersen*, 2014 WL 3871197 at *30.

When challenged by a pre-indictment motion, the DOJ may respond by asserting that the court lacks jurisdiction to review this grand jury matter before indictment. Courts have routinely rejected the government's position based on the court's anomalous jurisdiction. The grand jury "may not itself violate a valid privilege, whether established by the Constitution, statutes, or the common law" and "[j]udicial supervision is properly exercised in such cases to prevent the wrong before it occurs." *United States v. Calandra*, 414 U.S. 338, 346 (1974); *In re Grand Jury Investigation of Hugle*, 754 F.2d 863, 864–65 (9th Cir. 1985); *United States v. Chapman*, 559 F.2d 402 (9th Cir. 1977). More importantly, most district judges have little patience for prosecutors who press this jurisdictional argument because the substantive issue relates to a separation of powers argument—whether the Judicial or Executive Branch should conduct the privilege review—and the whole focus of privilege law centers around disclosure. Thus, timing is a critical issue so a target should not have to wait until post-indictment to challenge the government's abuse of power if the target elects to move pre-indictment.

2.3 POTENTIAL REMEDIES WHEN FILTER TEAMS MISBEHAVE

In recent matters we have worked that involved Filter Teams, prosecutors and their case agents have committed a wide variety of glaring violations. For example, we have seen the following errors in investigations conducted by experienced federal prosecutors:

- The DOJ disclosed one target's entire set of privileged documents to counsel for another target.
- The DOJ failed to provide a Magistrate Judge with any description of any Filter Team protocol when they presented their search warrant affidavit.
- The FBI sent the lead case agent on their prosecution team—not a Filter Team agent—into a general counsel's office at the target company to select what documents to seize, and the FBI agent ended up seizing a host of documents clearly labeled attorney–client privileged.
- The FBI failed to send any Filter Team agents to a search location to identify what information needed to be shielded from the members of the prosecution team before the review process started—the only agents on site executing the search warrant were all members of the prosecution team.
- A USAO failed to replace its Filter Team attorney when the attorney left the office, thereby making the lead prosecutor on the prosecution team the *de facto* Filter Team attorney.

- The DOJ failed to actually conduct the Filter Team review that it told the court it was going to conduct.
- Case agents on the prosecution team routinely accessed the location where the Filter Team had stored paper copy documents clearly marked as attorney–client privileged material.
- The Filter Team passed material to the prosecution team that the Filter Team deemed to be not privileged without first consulting with either the court or the target's counsel so defense counsel could challenge the Filter Team's decisions before the prosecution team received the material—and, not surprisingly, the documents at issue included privileged material.
- The Filter Team refused to return materials to the target that the Filter Team had reviewed and concluded were privileged—the government simply intended to hold onto the target's privileged materials throughout its investigation even though the government has no legal basis to hold onto privileged material.

These gaffes are hard to explain given the DOJ's policies and are included here to illustrate a simple point: do not trust prosecutors to get it right when they ask that you consent to their Filter Team protocol and simultaneously demand that you provide them with a list of all of the attorneys who have provided legal work to your client. We have also encountered situations where the prosecutors were not satisfied with receiving a list of attorneys from defense counsel—the prosecutors expected defense counsel to provide detailed descriptions of the matters that the various outside counsel worked on for the target company. The prosecutors were surprised when we refused to provide the information they requested—even though that information was, yes, clearly privileged.

When confronted with these opportunities, your potential remedies will vary depending on the underlying facts and your objectives. Potential remedies include: (a) recusing the prosecutors and agents who have been exposed to the privileged material; (b) enjoining any further review by the Filter Team and inserting a judicial neutral to conduct the review at government expense; (c) suppression and return of the material seized; and (d) dismissal of the case for outrageous government misconduct.

For example, the Tenth Circuit has held that the government's intentional use of privileged material to support its indictment warranted dismissal of the indictment, disqualification of the guilty prosecution team, and the commencement of an entirely new investigation. *See United States* *v. Lin Lyn Trading, Ltd.*, 149 F.3d 1112, 1118 (10th Cir. 1998). In addition, a district court in Hawaii granted the defendant's request to suppress certain privileged material that had been seized by the Filter Team and shared with the prosecution—although the court rejected the defense attorney's request for dismissal. *United States v. Sullivan*, No. 17-00104 JMS-KJM, 2020 WL 1815220, at *10 (D. Haw. Apr. 9, 2020).

While the courts in *Lin Lyn Trading* and *Sullivan* did grant significant relief, courts typically reserve dismissal of the indictment or disqualification of the prosecution team for the most egregious cases where the prejudice to the defendant cannot be cured. *See United States v. Chapman*, 524 F.3d 1073, 1085–87 (9th Cir. 2008) (holding that dismissal of the indictment is warranted only in cases involving flagrant prosecutorial misconduct); *United States v. Walker*, 243 F. App'x 621, 622–24 (2d Cir. 2007) (affirming the district court's denial of a motion to disqualify a prosecutor who had limited exposure to several privileged documents); *United States v. Stewart*, 294 F. Supp. 2d 490, 494 (S.D.N.Y. 2003) (holding that disqualification of a prosecutor who had inadvertently reviewed privileged material was inappropriate).

Like many other aspects of criminal defense work, the government will often press the courts to conclude that their "mistakes" were harmless. Courts can be sympathetic to that argument. As a result, obtaining a truly equitable remedy can be difficult. In addition, some courts have refused to grant any relief where the Filter Team seized potentially privileged materials during the execution of a search warrant simply because the Filter Team's protocol allowed the corporation to challenge privilege determinations in court before the Filter Team passed any documents to the prosecution team. *See In re Search of 5444 Westheimer Road Suite 1570*, No. H-06-238, 2006 WL 1881370, at *1–2 (S.D. Tex. July 6, 2006); *see also In re Search of Law Office, Residence, and Storage Unit Alan Brown*, 341 F.3d 404, 414 (5th Cir. 2003) (holding that because the Filter Team gave the Plaintiff unfettered access to all of the seized records, the Plaintiff could not sufficiently show an irreparable injury).

However, in cases where the Filter Team did not give the target an opportunity to challenge privilege determinations or review seized materials, courts are more likely to afford relief. *See Heebe v. United States*, No. 10-3452, 2011 WL 2610946, at *6 (E.D. La. July 1, 2011) (noting that the government had not given the Plaintiffs any access to the seized material until after the evidentiary hearing, which disrupted their legitimate business operations, and thus warranted a return of *copies* of all seized material).

2.4 HOW TO OPPOSE A FILTER TEAM

When the DOJ approaches you to consent to their use of a Filter Team, consider the following approach:

1. Request that the DOJ provide you a copy of their Filter Team Protocol—to establish a baseline to show how they may have violated their own protocol.
2. Confirm whether the prosecutor provided the Filter Team Protocol to the magistrate judge when the government presented the warrant affidavit to the court—to understand whether the court reviewed the protocol before approving the search.
3. Request that the DOJ provide you with the investigative report identifying the agents who executed the search—to test whether prosecution team agents were on site (they likely were) to help build a case to recuse them from the investigation.
4. Request a copy of the search warrant and supporting affidavit—to assess whether the agents exceeded the scope of the warrant by seizing potentially privileged materials that fall outside the scope of the warrant.
5. If the DOJ refuses to provide any of this information, file a motion with the court seeking this information and an appropriate remedy for your case. Options include: (a) seeking recusal of any prosecution team member who has been exposed to privileged material; (b) appointing a Special Master to review the material at government expense; (c) obtaining the return of any material already identified as privileged; and (d) obtaining an order that the Filter Team cannot elevate any material to the prosecution team without advance notice to defense counsel so that defense counsel can raise objections to the court and/or seek to dismiss due to outrageous government conduct.

CHAPTER 3

Suppressing Wiretap Evidence

3.1 GOVERNING STATUTE FOR TITLE III WIRETAP INTERCEPTS

Wiretaps are an incredibly powerful tool for law enforcement. If a prosecutor can play tape recordings at trial of your client, the jury will nearly always convict. My experience as an Assistant U.S. Attorney (AUSA) in Miami repeatedly demonstrated that jurors trusted what they heard on wiretaps because they literally heard the crime happen. By contrast, juries in Miami were much more likely to acquit a defendant in a historical conspiracy where the government had to rely on testimony from a cooperating defendant, a jailhouse snitch, or a confidential informant. As a result, when confronted with a wiretap, the first order of business is to try to develop persuasive arguments to suppress the recordings. Unlike a motion to suppress the fruits of a traditional search warrant, which will be grounded solely in Fourth Amendment principles, a motion to suppress electronic surveillance is also governed by statutory requirements that the government must satisfy.

The applicable statute is Title III of The Omnibus Crime Control and Safe Streets Act of 1968, which Congress enacted to prosecute sophisticated criminal organizations such as organized crime families and international narcotics trafficking organizations. *See* Title 18 U.S.C. § 2510 *et seq.* Courts have recognized this statute reflects a "congressional intention to limit the use of intercept procedures to those situations clearly calling for the employment of this extraordinary investigative device." *United States v. Giordano*, 416 U.S. 505, 527 (1974). Most states model their wiretap statute on the federal statute so the issues you will confront in any challenge to a state wiretap will likely be very similar to how you would attack a federal wiretap.

Under the federal statute, "the Attorney General, Deputy Attorney General, Associate Attorney General, or any Assistant Attorney General . . . specially designated by the Attorney General may authorize a [wiretap] application to a Federal judge . . . and such judge may grant . . . an order authorizing or approving the interception of wire or oral communications." 18 U.S.C. § 2516(1). In addition, wiretaps are only appropriate for statutorily specified offenses—the statute contains a long list of covered offenses, but it is still worth confirming whether the government used wiretap evidence to charge a crime that falls outside the statute. *See United States v. Ward*, 808 F. Supp. 803, 821 (S.D. Ga. 1992).

Applications for wiretaps must also include the following information: (1) "the identity of the . . . officer making the application and the officer authorizing the application"; (2) "a full and complete statement of the facts and circumstances relied upon by the applicant, to justify [their] belief that an order should be issued . . ." (i.e., the alleged probable cause); (3) "a full and complete statement as to whether or not other investigative procedures have been tried and failed or why they reasonably appear to be unlikely to succeed if tried or to be too dangerous" (i.e., to demonstrate the "necessity" of the wiretap); (4) "a statement of the period of time for which the interception is to be maintained"; (5) "a full and complete statements of the facts concerning all previous applications to the individual authorizing and making the application." 18 U.S.C. § 2518(1)(a)-I.

The statute also includes procedural safeguards to prevent potential abuses. For example, wiretaps can only be approved for a maximum length of thirty days, although extensions may be granted. 18 U.S.C. § 2518(5). The issuing judge typically requires law enforcement to submit periodic reports to demonstrate what progress is being made in the investigation and to justify why any wiretaps should be continued beyond the initial thirty-day period. 18 U.S.C. § 2518(6); *see also United States v. Hamilton*, No. CR11-415-JCC, 2012 WL 5834886, at *18–20 (W.D. Wash. Nov. 16, 2012). The intercepted communications, applications, and orders granting the wiretap must also be sealed by the issuing judge to prevent alterations or tampering. 18 U.S.C. § 2518(8)(a). Furthermore, not "later than ninety days" after an application is denied or terminated, "the issuing or denying judge shall cause to be served, on the persons named in the order or the application . . . an inventory which shall include notice" of the order or application and the fact that communications were or were not intercepted. *Id.* at § 2518(8)(d). All these statutory requirements provide opportunities for law enforcement to make mistakes that might lead to the suppression of the wiretap evidence.

Section 2518(10)(a) expressly provides for suppression of evidence obtained in violation of the requirements of Section 2510 *et seq.*:

> [a]ny aggrieved person in any trial, hearing, or proceedings in or before any court . . . may move to suppress the contents of any wire or oral communication intercepted . . . or evidence derived therefrom, on the grounds that (i) the communication was unlawfully intercepted; (ii) the order of the authorization or approval under which it was intercepted is insufficient on its face; or (iii) the interception was not made in conformity with the order of authorization or approval.

See also Dahda v. United States, 138 S. Ct. 1491, 1497 (2018).

Many defense attorneys think it is impossible to suppress a wiretap because the DOJ uses such a detailed internal approval process through its Office of Enforcement Operations (OEO) at Main Justice. The typical approval process for a wiretap application includes internal review and approval of the affidavit at the field level of both the investigating agency and USAO. At the agency level, the line agent, Group Supervisor, and Assistant Special Agent in Charge should review and approve the affidavit before sending it to agency headquarters in Washington, D.C., for additional review. At the prosecutor level, the line AUSA, Deputy and/or Unit Chief, and Criminal Chief should conduct the same review. The USAO will then send the affidavit to OEO at Main Justice for approval. If the affidavit survives those levels of review, it gets presented to a Deputy Assistant Attorney General (DAAG) for signature. If DAAG signs off, the line agent and line AUSA present the wiretap affidavit to a federal district court judge for final authorization.

This level of scrutiny should eliminate any error or false statement in the affidavit, but recent history confirms that the DOJ still makes glaring mistakes in wiretap applications. In 2020, an FBI attorney in the FBI's Office of General Counsel in Washington, D.C., pleaded guilty to a false statement offense because he altered the contents of an email in a wiretap affidavit he submitted to the Foreign Intelligence Surveillance Act court regarding the Crossfire Hurricane investigation of the Donald J. Trump for President Campaign. https://www.justice.gov/usao-ct/pr/fbi-attorney-admits-altering-email-used-fisa-application-during-crossfire-hurricane. If a false statement in a wiretap affidavit could escape FBI/DOJ's review protocol in such a high profile investigation, a similar error can happen in any other wiretap affidavit under review at OEO at the DOJ.

As another example, the statue restricts wiretap orders to a specific list of federal crimes—not every federal crime is enumerated in the wiretap statute. Confirming that the crime alleged in the wiretap application is actually enumerated in the wiretap statute certainly seems like something that seven levels of review at the FBI and the DOJ would be able to accurately verify. But the government does not always get it right. In *United States v. Ward*, the court granted a motion to suppress where the order allowed evidence to be gathered for violations of 18 U.S.C. Section 1953 and 26 U.S.C. Section 7201, which are not specified offenses listed in Section 2516. 808 F. Supp. 803 (S.D. Ga. 1992).

In addition, I never had a district judge ask a single probing question to me or my lead agent in any of the over one hundred wiretap affidavits I presented to the court for approval during my tenure as a federal prosecutor. The district judges rely on the DOJ's purportedly rigorous approval process and assume that probable cause is a given by the time the affidavit hits their desk.

Moreover, the basis to suppress the wiretap evidence can arise *after* the initial wiretap has been approved by the court. No attorney at OEO or Main Justice continues to supervise what the line prosecutor and lead agent are doing after the court signs the initial interception order. For example, the agents may fail to minimize privileged calls between attorneys and their clients (the targets of the wire). Or the line AUSA fails to seal the intercepted calls or fails to send out a notice of interception to individuals who were intercepted on the wire. None of these actions are monitored by the leadership in the USAO or the DOJ. The line AUSA handles those tasks solo. Why would a line AUSA make such basic mistakes? The reality—often overlooked by defense counsel—is that very few AUSAs have any meaningful experience with wiretaps, and many AUSAs will do only one or two wiretap investigations in their career. So, an "experienced" prosecutor is likely a rookie in regard to how to navigate the unique statutory requirements presented in a wiretap investigation. That lack of experience with the wiretap statute can result in the AUSA overlooking some technical requirement in the statute—regarding sealing, minimization, notification, or presenting the entire authorization package to the issuing judge, for example. As a result, defense counsel should aggressively probe for a legitimate basis to suppress because the government commits far more errors on wiretap applications than judges realize.

3.2 THE SUPREME COURT ON WIRETAPS

The Supreme Court has issued very few decisions interpreting the wiretap statute. Several of these decisions occurred shortly after the enactment of the statute to address technical issues that DOJ has long since fixed. *See United States v. Giordano*, 416 U.S. 505 (1974) and *United States v. Chavez*, 416 U.S. 562 (1974) (analyzing who is an improper party to authorize a wiretap).

The most recent opinion from the Supreme Court is *Dahda v. United States*, 138 S. Ct. 1491, 1497 (2018). In *Dahda*, two Defendants in a drug conspiracy argued that the authorizing order was invalid on its face because it contained language that allowed the investigators to intercept calls from a location outside the district judge's jurisdiction. *Id.* at 1494. The judge signed the order in the District of Kansas, but the agents intercepted at least one call at a listening post in Missouri—that is, outside the jurisdictional territory of the district judge. *Id.* at 1495. The location of an intercept happens either where (a) the government's listening post is located (typically a "wire room" at the investigating agency inside the relevant judicial district) or (b) the target telephone is located. *Id.*

The Defendants argued that *any* defect that appears within the four corners of the order requires suppression of all the evidence generated by the wiretap. *Id.* at 1498. The government countered that suppression could only apply where the error impacted two "core concerns" underlying the statute: (1) protecting the privacy of wire and oral communications, and (2) delineating on a uniform basis the circumstances and conditions under which the interception may be authorized. *Id.* The Court rejected both positions and found a middle ground that was not as broad as the defense position nor as narrow as the government's argument.

The Court held that when an order lacks information that the wiretap statute requires it to include, an aggrieved person may suppress the fruits of the order. *Id.* at 1499–1500. In this case, the wiretap statute did not require the statement at issue, which authorized interception outside of Kansas. *Id.* at 1499. In addition, every intercepted call introduced at trial by the government was intercepted within the jurisdiction of the issuing judge; the government did not introduce the challenged call that was intercepted in Missouri. *Id.* at 1499. As a result, the Court viewed the technical error as an irrelevant glitch that did not make the affidavit "deficient" in any meaningful respect. *Id.*

However, the Court did not restrict the scope of its ruling to only situations where a "core concern" was implicated: if a wiretap order lacks information that the statute requires, that defect constitutes a separate and independent basis to suppress the wiretap. As a result, defense counsel should be hunting for evidence to show that the wiretap order/affidavit either (a) violates Congress' two core concerns, or (b) lacks information the wiretap statutes require it to include (making it "insufficient on its face"). Examples include agents using a wiretap before attempting to exhaust alternative methods to investigate the crime at issue, failing to minimize privileged communications, failing to seal the recordings immediately at the conclusion of the relevant period, and failing to present the district court with proper authorization from Main Justice.

3.3 CHALLENGING NECESSITY

To establish the "necessity" for using an invasive wiretap, the affidavit needs to demonstrate that alternative means of investigation would not detect the crime under investigation. Title 18 Section 2518(1)(c) requires "a full and complete statement as to whether or not other investigative procedures have been tried and failed or why they reasonably appear to be unlikely to succeed if tried or to be too dangerous." In other words, the affidavit should demonstrate that the agents exhausted these alternative methods of investigation before trying to initiate an intrusive wiretap investigation. While courts do not "require law enforcement to exhaust every possible technique before resorting to wiretapping," they are to "ensure that in the usual case wiretapping is not used as the first meaningful step in an investigation." *United States v. Gonzalez, Inc.*, 412 F.3d 1102, 1113 (9th Cir. 2005).

The description of "necessity" is often included in a section of the affidavit called "alternative means" or "alternative investigative procedures." Examples of common alternative procedures include physical surveillance, less invasive pen register or cell phone tracing technologies, confidential sources/undercover agents, the use of a grand jury that can subpoena documents and witnesses, traditional search warrants, ISP search warrants, and interviews of associates of the targets of the investigation.

There are two common errors that law enforcement makes with respect to demonstrating necessity: (1) including material misstatements or omitting facts in a wiretap application that mislead the issuing judge about the necessity element (*see, e.g.*, *United States v. Rice*, 478 F.3d 704 (6th Cir. 2007)), and (2) relying on generic statements that could apply to crimes in general instead of alleging facts specific to the case at hand to demonstrate how alternative investigation techniques are unlikely to succeed (*see, e.g.*, *United States v. Kalustian*, 529 F.2d 585 (9th Cir. 1975)).

Necessity is the most fertile area to challenge wiretap orders for three reasons. First, the agents may have an informant or undercover officer who could penetrate the targeted criminal organization without using a wiretap. However, agents and detectives are often too concerned about protecting the identity of their informants. As a result, they fail to fully disclose how involved their source is with the target. Instead, the agent provides a very general description that lacks specific facts known to the agent that prove that law enforcement could have used other legitimate investigative techniques to detect the crime at issue (like introducing an undercover officer or tape-recording controlled calls between the informant and target). While trying to protect the identity of an informant is a legitimate law enforcement concern, it does not eliminate the obligation to satisfy the necessity element. In the wiretap affidavits I have presented for approval, this was the most vulnerable aspect of nearly every affidavit. If an informant is close enough to the target to record a phone call discussing the crime at issue, defense counsel has a starting point to demonstrate that the informant could have introduced an undercover to the target, set up a meeting that agents could surveil to identify and follow the target, and so on. When you challenge necessity, courts will be sympathetic to the government's argument that the defendant is simply seeking to identify the snitch to pursue retribution. So, frame your questions around the informant's ability to advance the investigation in a way where law enforcement could have pursued another less intrusive investigative method—surveillance, undercover buys, etc.—to make their case against the target.

Law enforcement will try to shift the argument by claiming that the purpose of the wire was to identify and prosecute the target's entire organization. But that argument can still be defeated. For example, if law enforcement could have used their source to introduce an undercover officer to the target, the agents could have arrested the target following a meeting with an undercover officer. At that point, the agents could flip the target and run a historical investigation against the other members of the conspiracy—for example, the importers, distributors, and money launderers in a narcotics conspiracy. The FBI, DEA, and every local police department make historical cases in this fashion on a daily basis. Thus, this scenario demonstrates that the agents did not need the wiretap to investigate their case—and certainly did not exhaust all reasonable alternative investigative procedures before seeking the wiretap affidavit.

Second, the necessity section in the affidavit might be deficient because the agents failed to perform a sufficient amount of physical surveillance, or the affidavit inaccurately describes whatever surveillance they have done to date. When the agents are conducting this surveillance, they may have already decided to push for a wiretap so the surveillance may have simply been a "check the box" exercise. Push to understand when the agents first decided to pursue a wiretap because that might help you establish that the agents simply mailed in their attempt at physical surveillance. Their claims that they could not possibly follow the target might be subject to attack on cross-examination.

Third, some agents are lazy. Wiretap affidavits need to be drafted quickly because the approval process through OEO at the DOJ can take weeks. Probable cause can go stale, and targets can leave the country. How do lazy or inexperienced agents draft warrant affidavits in this scenario? The agent finds a recent sample from a prior investigation and simply copies the language related to necessity—particularly since the agent's chain of command is pushing the agent to get up on the phone as soon as possible. As a result, many wiretap affidavits contain boilerplate descriptions on necessity that agents poached from prior wiretap applications without customizing that section to fit the facts of their current investigation.

Based on all three of these reasons, a thoughtful and thorough cross-examination of the lead case agent at a motion to suppress hearing will likely yield helpful information to advance a necessity challenge. Topics to consider for cross-examination of the case agent include:

- Did the informant engage in any criminal activity with the target? If so, how and when?
- Does the informant or agent know where the target lives or works? If so, this makes physical surveillance much easier.
- Did the informant seek to introduce an undercover to the target? If not, hasn't the case agent had other situations where the introduction of an undercover led to a successful prosecution of the target?
- Did the agents have any information that the target would not flip and cooperate against other members of the criminal organization? The answer is likely "no," meaning that the introduction of an undercover could have led to the arrest of the target and the successful prosecution of the larger organization without the use of a wiretap.

- How many times did the agents attempt to conduct surveillance on the target?
- Was the first attempt at surveillance conducted after the agents began considering the use of a wiretap?

It is nearly guaranteed that the authorizing judge did not ask the agent and prosecutor any of these questions regarding necessity before approving the affidavit. A thoughtful cross-examination can prove to the court that law enforcement withheld relevant and material information from the necessity component of the affidavit.

Here is a summary of helpful cases on necessity challenges:

> *United States v. Rice*, 478 F.3d 704, 709–11 (6th Cir. 2007) (court grants necessity challenge where the affidavit implied that investigators had actually attempted physical surveillance when they had not and—if the misleading statements were removed—the affidavit only included generalized and uncorroborated information for why other less invasive investigative techniques would not work).
>
> *United States v. Gonzalez, Inc.*, 412 F.3d 1102, 1113 (9th Cir. 2005) (court grants necessity challenge, in part, because pen registers alone and a single incident of failed physical surveillance are insufficient to demonstrate necessity).
>
> *United States v. Blackmon*, 273 F.3d 1204, 1208–09 (9th Cir. 2001) (court grants necessity challenge where the affidavit against the Defendant was a "carbon copy" of an affidavit used against another target and therefore misstated prior surveillance and an informant's access to the Defendant).
>
> *United States v. Mondragon*, 52 F.3d 291, 293 (10th Cir. 1995) (court grants necessity challenge where the affidavit for a second supplemental application failed to outline alternative investigative procedures that were attempted or considered or specify any facts to explain why alternatives were unlikely to succeed or were likely to be too dangerous).
>
> *United States v. Carneiro*, 861 F.2d 1171, 1180–81 (9th Cir. 1988) (court grants necessity challenge where the affidavit failed to disclose that (1) the DEA did not conduct a traditional investigation prior to applying for the wiretap;

(2) no attempt at physical surveillance was made until after the wiretap had been issued; and (3) the DEA had not tried searching for informants, despite alleging in the application that "there [were] no known informants who have purchased illegal drugs from [the Defendant].").

United States v. Simpson, 813 F.2d 1462, 1471–72 (9th Cir. 1987) (court grants necessity challenge where agent understated confidential informant's ability to get close enough to the targets that she was able to introduce two undercover agents to the targets to purchase narcotics).

United States v. Ippolito, 774 F.2d 1482, 1485–87 (9th Cir. 1985) (court grants necessity challenge where FBI agent presented false information in affidavit by failing to disclose that the agent instructed his confidential informant to refuse to testify so the agent could get wiretap approved).

United States v. Spagnuolo, 549 F.2d 705, 711 (9th Cir. 1977) (court grants necessity challenge in gambling case where the affidavit for Wiretap A failed to describe any investigatory efforts by any officer using any alternative means and also held that evidence collected through subsequent Wiretaps C and D must also be suppressed because the probable cause described in the affidavits in support was tainted with the evidence collected through Wiretap A).

United States v. Kalustian, 529 F.2d 585, 589–90 (9th Cir. 1975) (court grants necessity challenge in gambling investigation because affiant merely alleged that his experience in prior gambling cases demonstrated that traditional investigative methods would not work in the current case—"[m]ere conclusions by the affiant are insufficient to justify . . . a wiretap order.").

3.4 CHALLENGING MINIMIZATION

Section 2518(5) of the statute notes that every wiretap order explicitly states that "the authorization to intercept . . . shall be conducted in such a way as to minimize the interception of communications not otherwise subject to interception." The interception of communications between attorney/client, husband/wife, priest/penitent, and doctor/patient could trigger a basis to file a motion to suppress.

The agents are obligated to "minimize" those calls—that is, the agents should shut down the recording and not monitor potentially privileged conversations. If a privileged call gets intercepted, that call should be suppressed. However, courts are reluctant to suppress every intercepted call based on this error. In addition, consider challenging any "re-up" extension order on the same phone or any additional wiretap of a new phone if any privileged call is used to support probable cause for a subsequent wiretap order. If you raise this challenge, expect the government to try to invoke the crime-fraud exception and argue that the call(s) at issue advanced the conspiracy under investigation.

In *United States v. Charles*, the Defendants, charged with violating federal narcotics and firearm laws, moved to suppress evidence obtained via wiretap. No. Crim. 97-10107-PBS, 1998 WL 204696 (D. Mass. Jan. 13, 1998). The court granted Defendants motion to suppress evidence "of the conversation protected by attorney–client privilege and subject to a minimization order, but denie[d] the motion with respect to all other evidence derived from wiretapped conversations." *Id.* at *1. The court determined that the interception of the privileged call was "inadvertent and unintentional, albeit negligent." *Id.* However, it was still a "literal violation of the minimization order." *Id.* at *12. The court would not suppress all intercepted calls, in part, because the officers duly minimized sixty-two other calls properly. *Id.* at *15.

3.5 CHALLENGING FACIAL INSUFFICIENCY

Section 2518 of the wiretap statute lists a series of technical requirements regarding the contents of the paperwork that law enforcement presents to the court and follow-on steps that law enforcement should take when executing the wiretap order. Examples of successful challenges on motions to suppress involve situations where the government failed to present the court with the appropriate paperwork, failed to seal the wiretap recordings after the conclusion of the wiretap, or failed to accurately describe the matter under investigation.

Here is a summary of helpful cases on challenging facial insufficiency:

> *United States v. Romero*, 2018 WL 6981231 (E.D. Tex. Nov. 2, 2018) (district court granted Defendant's motion to suppress because the wiretap order did not identify the specific Justice Department official who approved the application, thereby rendering the order facially insufficient under Section 2518(4)(d)).

United States v. Lomeli, 676 F.3d 734 (8th Cir. 2012) (motion to suppress affirmed where the AUSA failed to include the authorization order signed by the attorney general in the materials presented to the district judge).

United States v. Hill, 2012 WL 1161577 (W.D.N.Y. Apr. 6, 2012) (magistrate judge recommends granting motion to suppress where the government waited two days from the termination of the Title III Order to seal the record pursuant to Section 2518(8)(a), rejecting the government's claim that the district judge was unavailable because the judge "did not have a calendar" on those two days).

United States v. Royster, 2007 WL 4336321 (S.D. Ga. 2007) (district court grants motion to suppress evidence due to a six-day delay in sealing the intercepted recordings without a viable explanation for the delay but the court did not suppress other recordings or evidence subsequently obtained).

United States v. Staffeldt, 451 F.3d 578, 583 (9th Cir. 2006) (court suppresses evidence because the wiretap application's accompanying memorandum of authorization from the DOJ-OEO pertained to a different wiretap application for different targets using different cell phones in an unrelated case).

3.6 CHECKLIST FOR SUPPRESSING WIRETAP EVIDENCE

When confronted with wiretap evidence, work through the following checklist to see if you can identify a basis to suppress the evidence:

1. Does the affidavit identify a crime that is covered in the statute?
2. Was the affidavit authorized by the appropriate official at Main Justice per the requirements of the statute?
3. Did the prosecutor present the court with the authorization order signed by the official at Main Justice who authorized the interception?
4. Did the authorization order from Main Justice match what the prosecutor submitted to the judge—that is, same phone, same targets, same investigation?

5. Does the affidavit establish necessity, or could the investigators have used undercover cops, informants, or less intrusive methods of electronic surveillance to detect the crime at issue?
6. Does the affidavit disclose sufficient information about the informants who placed the "dirty" call to the target phone to justify the search?
7. Did the prosecution team submit a progress report to the district court midway through the thirty-day period of interception?
8. Did the prosecution team immediately seal the intercepted recordings at the end of the thirty-day period?
9. Did the agents in the wire room minimize potentially privileged calls, including lawyer/client, doctor/patient, priest/penitent, husband/wife?

CHAPTER 4

Grand Jury Issues

4.1 GRAND JURY BASICS

Successfully litigating prosecutorial misconduct related to the grand jury is unique for several reasons. First, defense attorneys and judges are not present in the grand jury with the prosecutors. As a result, obtaining a complete record of how the prosecutors behaved is not an easy task. Second, the grand jury operates in secrecy, so many defense attorneys have never seen a grand jury presentation. Thus, many of us do not know all the potential issues to raise to challenge a prosecutor's conduct with the grand jury. Third, the case law makes it exceptionally difficult to dismiss an indictment based on misconduct before the grand jury.

However, grand jury issues are ripe for misconduct for the very same reasons: rogue prosecutors who operate in a closed proceeding and believe that they will never be required to disclose the transcripts of those proceedings will commit errors that you can use to chip away at the credibility of the government's case. This chapter will show you how to obtain evidence of misconduct that can be used to advance the defense of your case. The Holy Grail of grand jury misconduct evidence is the colloquy portion of the transcript—the transcript section of the grand jury proceedings where there is no witness in the grand jury room and the prosecutor is either giving introductory or closing comments regarding the proposed indictment or answering questions grand jury members have asked about the evidence. This is where some prosecutors can't help themselves—it is the most likely place during the entire prosecution where a rogue prosecutor will make misleading statements about the facts or law because prosecutors are convinced that the colloquy transcript will never see the light of day.

To understand how to obtain the colloquy transcript and pursue other grand jury related challenges, we begin by describing the various rules and policies that govern a prosecutor's presentation of evidence to the grand jury. The Supreme Court has addressed many of these issues, so we will start with a high-level summary of key Supreme Court jurisprudence before providing an overview of Rule 6 of the *Federal Rules of Criminal Procedure* and the DOJ's policies on grand jury practice. After that description of the governing law and policies, we will provide you with the tools to successfully identify and litigate prosecutorial misconduct in grand jury practice.

4.2 THE SUPREME COURT ON GRAND JURY MISCONDUCT

In *United States v. Williams*, Justice Scalia provided a detailed description of the history of grand jury practice at common law and how that practice developed under our Constitution. 504 U.S. 36 (1992). Justice Scalia's opinion illustrates why courts view misconduct before the grand jury differently than misconduct before the trial court.

The grand jury is not mentioned in the body of the Constitution; the framers only referenced the grand jury in the Bill of Rights. *Id.* at 47. The Fifth Amendment states that "no person shall be held to answer a capital, or otherwise infamous crime, unless on a presentment or indictment of a Grand Jury." As a result, the Supreme Court views the grand jury as a "constitutional fixture in its own right"—a body that falls outside the first three Articles of the Constitution. The grand jury is not attached to the judicial, executive, or legislative branches of our government. It is a unique body that serves as "kind of a buffer or referee between the Government and the people." *Id.* Unlike a court whose jurisdiction is predicated on a specific "case or controversy," the grand jury can investigate merely based on suspicion that the law has been violated. *Id.* at 48. In addition, the grand jury is not an adjudicatory body like a court, it is simply an accusatory body: the grand jury sits merely to assess whether there is an adequate basis for bringing a criminal charge, not to determine guilt or innocence. *Id.*

Given the grand jury's unique placement in our system, trial judges do not possess the same power to punish prosecutors who misbehave in the grand jury as they do when a prosecutor misbehaves in their courtrooms. For example, in *Williams*, the Court held that prosecutors are not required to present exculpatory evidence to the grand jury when seeking an indictment. *Id.* at 55. Justice Scalia emphasized that "the courts have no authority to prescribe such a duty [to require *Brady* disclosures to the grand jury] pursuant to their inherent supervisory authority over their own proceedings." *Id.* By contrast, trial courts do possess the power to dismiss an indictment with prejudice for prosecutorial misconduct for *Brady* violations that occur before the court during pre-trial and trial proceedings—based on the Court's supervisory authority over their own proceedings. *United States v. Chapman*, 524 F.3d 1073, 1084 (9th Cir. 2004).

In *United States v. Mechanik*, decided a few years before *Williams*, the Court confirmed it is not likely to reverse convictions related to misconduct in the grand jury. 475 U.S. 66 (1986). The Court emphasized two points: (a) Rule 52(a) of the *Federal Rules of Criminal Procedure*, which provides that errors not affecting "substantial rights" shall be disregarded; and (b) the trial jury's decision to convict demonstrates that the grand jury had probable cause to charge so any error in the grand jury was harmless. *Id.* at 71–3. As a result, criminal defense attorneys must identify any grand jury misconduct before trial and consider moving on it immediately because a conviction at trial erases the misconduct. Notably, the facts in *Mechanik* related to a technical violation of grand jury procedure: allowing an unauthorized person into the grand jury session, which is not a constitutional violation, like a Fifth Amendment due process violation would be when the prosecutor presented false evidence to secure the indictment. *Id.* at 67–8. Nevertheless, very few convictions have been reversed due to prosecutorial misconduct involving the grand jury.

In *Bank of Nova Scotia v. United States*, in a poorly reasoned decision that prosecutors are quick to cite when challenged about grand jury abuse, the Court refused to dismiss an indictment where there was overwhelming evidence of flagrant grand jury misconduct. 487 U.S. 250 (1988). After ten days of hearings regarding the misconduct, Judge Kane from the District of Colorado dismissed a twenty-seven-count tax fraud indictment. Judge Kane invoked his supervisory power after finding that the prosecutors: (1) sponsored false testimony from IRS agents; (2) improperly argued with an expert witness during a recess after the witness gave testimony that was adverse to the government; (3) disclosed secret grand jury materials to unauthorized individuals at the IRS; (4) failed to notify the Court about those improper disclosures; (5) improperly disclosed the names of the targets of the investigation to witnesses; (6) instructed witnesses that they could not disclose their testimony to others; (7) allowed unauthorized individuals to appear before the grand jury; (8) violated the witness immunity statute by granting "pocket immunity" to numerous witnesses without judicial authorization; and (9) called a series of witnesses knowing that they intended to invoke their Fifth Amendment rights to make them look bad before the grand jury. *Id.* at 257–58. Confronted with this enormous amount of brazen prosecutorial misconduct, the Supreme Court still refused to dismiss the indictment. *Id.* at 263.

Justice Kennedy minimized the severity of the misconduct by stating that "these incidents occurred as isolated episodes in the course of a twenty-month investigation, an investigation involving dozens of witnesses and thousands of documents." *Id.* That observation ignores reality—nearly every white collar investigation and many other criminal prosecutions will include a twenty-month investigation, dozens of witnesses, and thousands of documents. Similar investigations exist in every prosecutor's office in the country. But very few criminal cases will include the amount and severity of prosecutorial misconduct that was present during the grand jury proceedings in *Bank of Nova Scotia.* This was a rare case of glaring prosecutorial misconduct. To make it worse, Justice Kennedy also emphasized that "we are not faced with a history of prosecutorial misconduct, spanning several cases, that is so systemic and pervasive as to raise a substantial and serious question about the fundamental fairness of the process which resulted in the indictment." *Id.* That observation suggests that defense counsel needs to meet a standard that exists nowhere else in criminal litigation. How are defense attorneys supposed to identify prosecutorial misconduct in other cases where they did not represent the defendants in those prior matters? And where else is defense counsel required to show violations of due process in unrelated cases to prove a violation of a client's due process in the client's case?

Given how high the Supreme Court set the bar for criminal defense attorneys in *Bank of Novia Scotia*, you may ask whether it is worth the time and resources to pursue misconduct before the grand jury. That is a fair question, but there are several reasons to still aggressively pursue grand jury misconduct. First, prosecutors understandably feel immune to any penalty for misbehaving in the grand jury so the likelihood for serious misconduct is much higher than during other phases of the prosecution. Second, many inexperienced prosecutors do not fully understand either Rule 6 or DOJ policies regarding grand jury practice so the error rate in grand jury proceedings is unusually high. Third, every interaction in the grand jury is transcribed by a court reporter, regardless of whether there is a witness in the room. Fourth, and most importantly, exposing prosecutorial misconduct in the grand jury to skilled trial judges like Judge Kane erodes the prosecutor's credibility on other battles you are likely to confront with the prosecutor regarding other issues at trial—for example, *Brady/Giglio* disclosures, Jencks Act disclosures, *Napue* issues, and making false statements during opening statement and closing argument. Trial judges are much more likely to consider using their supervisory powers to dismiss when they see that the entire prosecution process has been infected with misconduct—from grand jury to pre-trial discovery and through the trial. As a result, consider focusing on potential misconduct that relates to substantive issues that will anger an experienced trial judge and may reoccur during pre-trial motions and at trial: presenting false evidence, coercing witnesses to support the prosecutors' misguided narrative, misrepresenting the law in an opening/closing statement to the grand jury, and providing inaccurate information in response to questions from a grand jurors. Exposing those types of errors before the grand jury will help you gain traction with the trial judge when the prosecutors commit the same type of misconduct during trial.

4.3 GOVERNING STANDARDS

Rule 6 of the *Federal Rules of Criminal Procedure* and Section 9-11.000 of the *Justice Manual* describe how prosecutors should conduct themselves before the grand jury. Rule 6 focuses on some of the technical rules while the *Justice Manual* focuses a bit more on the ethical issues a prosecutor faces in grand jury practice.

For our purposes, the key aspects of Rule 6 include the following:

- The grand jury must be composed of sixteen to twenty-three persons. Rule 6(a)(1). To proceed before the grand jury and to have a proper vote on the indictment, the prosecutor needs a quorum of twelve or more grand jurors present.
- Only authorized persons may be present in the grand jury room while the grand jury is in session. Authorized persons include attorneys for the government, the witness being questioned, interpreters when needed, and the court reporter/audio recorder. Rule 6(d)(1).
- Only grand jurors may be present during deliberations and voting. The prosecutors and agents cannot be in the room. Rule 6(d)(2).

- All discussions between the prosecutors and grand jury must be recorded, even when a witness is outside the room. Rule 6(e)(1).
- Grand jury proceedings must be kept secret by the following individuals: prosecutors, interpreters, and court reporters. Rule 6(e)(2). Note that grand jury witnesses are not bound by this rule of secrecy. Witnesses are free to disclose their testimony publicly. There are also a few exceptions when other law enforcement officials can receive Rule 6(e) material from the assigned prosecutors, but they also have to abide by the secrecy rules.

DOJ's *Justice Manual* begins its discussion of grand jury procedures by emphasizing that "the prosecutor must be scrupulously fair to all witnesses and must do nothing to inflame or otherwise improperly influence the grand jurors." Section 9-11.010. In other words, the prosecutor should not present false or misleading testimony and should not make emotional appeals to indict.

Prosecutors must also use the grand jury only for the limited function it serves—assessing whether the evidence collected and presented demonstrates probable cause to indict. Prosecutors should not use the grand jury to obtain additional evidence against a defendant who has already been indicted, nor should they use the grand jury for pre-trial discovery or trial preparation. Section 9-11.120.

Prosecutors should not subpoena targets to the grand jury without first attempting to secure the target's appearance voluntarily and seeking approval from either the U.S. Attorney or responsible Assistant Attorney General. Section 9-11.150. The prosecutor should also attach an Advice of Rights form to any subpoena sent to a target or subject to make sure that witnesses are advised of their Fifth Amendment rights before responding to any questions under oath. Section 9-11.151. Unless the grand jury and U.S. Attorney insist on the target's appearance, the prosecutor should not present a target to the grand jury when both counsel for the target and the target confirm in writing that the target will invoke his or her Fifth Amendment rights. Section 9-11.154. The prosecutor should, however, allow a target to testify to the grand jury if the target requests to do so and that testimony will not burden or delay the proceedings. Section 9-11.152.

Prosecutors should not present evidence to the grand jury against a target that was obtained in violation of the target's constitutional rights. Section 9-11.231. This policy demonstrates why it is worth seeking to obtain a copy of a search warrant affidavit pre-indictment. If the search warrant affidavit clearly lacks probable cause and thereby violates the

Fourth Amendment, you have a basis to press the prosecutor to not present that illegally obtained evidence to the grand jury. If you win a suppression motion, consider seeking the grand jury transcripts to establish that the grand jury considered the suppressed evidence before indicting—and then move to dismiss the indictment.

Prosecutors are allowed to present hearsay evidence—typically through a case agent—but the DOJ requires that prosecutors inform the grand jury that the evidence is hearsay so that grand jurors are not misled into believing that the agent is giving his or her personal account of the evidence. Section 9-11.232: *see also United States v. Estepa*, 471 F.2d 1132 (2nd Cir. 1972) (conviction reversed with instructions to dismiss indictment where grand jury was misled into thinking it was getting eyewitness testimony from the agent whereas it was actually given an account whose hearsay nature was concealed); *United States v. Leibowitz*, 420 F.2d 39 (2nd Cir. 1969). Less experienced prosecutors often fail to warn the grand jury that the evidence is based on hearsay. Many prosecutors prefer to use hearsay testimony from agents who they do not intend to call as trial witnesses. Prosecutors do this to avoid having to turn over any witness transcripts because the hearsay agent is not a trial witness and, therefore, the Jencks Act does not compel the disclosure of that grand jury testimony. *See* 18 U.S.C. § 3500; *United States v. Kamerud*, 326 F.3d 1008, 1015 (8th Cir. 2003) (the Jencks Act only requires disclosure of the grand jury transcript by the trial witness related to that witness's grand jury testimony, not a hearsay summary from another case agent). In that scenario, the prosecutor would not have to provide defense counsel with any transcript of anything that occurred before the grand jury. As a result, the prosecutor will often neglect to give an appropriate warning to the grand jury about the hearsay nature of the presentation. This is another reason why you should seek all grand jury transcripts during pre-trial discovery: a hearsay witness may say something that is false or misleading, there might be unauthorized individuals present before the grand jury, and the prosecutor may not have provided an adequate warning to the grand jury.

As to *Brady* evidence, the DOJ requires that its prosecutors present evidence of actual innocence. Section 9-11.233 states that "when a prosecutor conducting a grand jury inquiry is personally aware of *substantial evidence that directly negates the guilt* of a subject of the investigation, the prosecutor *must* present or otherwise disclose such evidence to the grand jury before seeking an indictment against such a person" (emphasis added). The DOJ's policy requires more from prosecutors than the Supreme Court, which held that a prosecutor does not have an obligation to disclose exculpatory evidence. *United States v. Williams*, 504 U.S. 36 (1992).

While you should expect that the prosecutors will argue that certain evidence is not "substantial" or only impacts credibility (*Giglio*), and not actual innocence (*Brady*), this policy is a significant concession by the DOJ and one that is routinely violated by prosecutors. Thus, if you know that the prosecution team possesses *Brady* evidence pre-indictment, consider sending a letter to the prosecutor to make a record that you expect that the prosecutor will present all exculpatory evidence to the grand jury pursuant to Section 9-11.233. The DOJ's policy also states that "appellate courts may refer violations of the policy to the Office of Professional Responsibility for review." Section 9-11.233. As a result, prosecutors risk an OPR investigation for violating this policy. For example, if the government executed a search warrant and seized computers or a large cache of paper files, the prosecutors should do a full *Brady* review of all that material to comply with the DOJ's policy because the prosecutors are deemed to have actual knowledge of the contents of the seized material. *See United States v. Bryan*, 868 F.2d 1032, 1036 (9th Cir. 1989) (the prosecutor is deemed to have knowledge of and access to anything in the possession, custody, or control of any federal agency participating in the same investigation of the defendant). If the prosecutors refuse to do an appropriate *Brady* review of all seized evidence before indicting the case, you are in a position to challenge their conduct. As soon as you locate *Brady* evidence in the materials the government provides to you during pre-trial discovery, you have a basis to seek all the grand jury transcripts from all the witnesses as well as the colloquy transcript to see whether the prosecutor complied with DOJ policy and disclosed that *Brady* evidence to the grand jury. The prosecutors likely failed to do so, which gives you a basis to consider reporting the prosecutors to OPR and seeking their recusal from the case.

Like Rule 6(d)(1), DOJ policy prohibits the presence of unauthorized persons before the grand jury. Section 9-11.241. While this may be perceived as a technical violation, prosecutors violate this rule more often than defense attorneys realize. For example, if an attorney from a federal agency (e.g., the SEC), a local district attorney's (DA's) office in a joint investigation, or even an AUSA from another district appears before a grand jury, those attorneys need to (a) have obtained appropriate written authorization and (b) taken the oath of office as a Special Assistant U.S. Attorney. Sections 9-11.241 and 9-11.242. The reality is that prosecutors often fail to realize that they need to take these steps when they are joined by an out-of-district prosecutor. Given the various ways that a witness might be considered an "unauthorized person," violations do happen. *See, e.g., United States v. Pignatiello*, 582 F. Supp. 251, 255 (D. Colo. 1984) (indictment dismissed where SEC lawyer failed to take oath of office before appearing before the grand jury). If this is the only error in the grand jury presentation, it will not lead to dismissal of the indictment given the Supreme Court's subsequent decisions in *Bank of Nova Scotia, Mechanik,* and *Williams.* But if you have a series of other errors in grand jury or elsewhere, consider checking the government's compliance with this requirement because a violation will chip away at the prosecutor's credibility and help build your cumulative effect argument.

Another frequently violated policy relates to how and where the prosecutors store grand jury materials. Section 9-11.254(5) states that "prosecutors should take whatever precautions are necessary to protect grand jury materials, including, generally, keeping them in a locked file cabinet in a locked room." The same provision requires that prosecutors keep electronic data secure. *Id.* This policy is routinely violated by many U.S. attorney's offices across the country. Each district will be inspected every few years by experienced AUSAs from other districts. These inspectors assess a certain district's compliance with various DOJ policies. Maintaining the security of grand jury materials is a frequently failed metric because many AUSAs fail to maintain documents obtained via grand jury subpoenas and grand jury transcripts/exhibits in a secure, locked location. Again, standing on its own, keeping materials secure is a fairly technical violation. But if you have a case agent on the stand at a pre-trial hearing, this can be a fairly easy admission to obtain and might be worth pursuing if you know you can establish other misconduct in the grand jury proceeding.

4.4 GRAND JURY SECRECY: RULE 6(E) VIOLATIONS

As noted above, Rule 6(e) prohibits the prosecution team from leaking information about proceedings before the grand jury. Not surprisingly, this happens more than it should—particularly in high profile white collar and public corruption investigations. The leaks tend to come from the senior leadership at the investigating agency or the prosecuting office, not the line prosecutor and line agents. In a recent tax prosecution, a journalist sent me a copy of the *sealed* indictment and asked for my reaction to the charges *before* the DOJ arrested my client and *before* we appeared at my client's arraignment. Because the arraignment is where the prosecutor will unseal a previously sealed indictment, the only way the reporter could have received a copy of the sealed indictment was from someone on the prosecution team who leaked it to him—a clear violation of Rule 6(e).

If you see news articles pre-indictment where the press quotes "sources close to the investigation" who are disclosing negative information about your client, consider filing a miscellaneous motion to show cause with the duty judge to force the government to respond. If you can make a *prima facie* case that Rule 6(e) has been violated based simply on the contents of media reporting, the burden shifts to the government to come forward with evidence to negate your *prima facie* proof. *United States v. Eisenberg*, 711 F.2d 959, 963–64 (11th Cir. 1983); *In Re Sealed Case*, 151 F. 3d 1059, 1067–68 (D.C. Cir. 1998). At that point, the court should enter an order preventing the government from any further leaks of Rule 6(e) information. More importantly, the court should also require the government to submit information in camera to the court regarding who was responsible for leaking the grand jury information. *Eisenberg*, 711 at 963–64. If the case has not yet been indicted, defense counsel will be on the sidelines for most of this process because the government may have legitimate concerns about providing defense counsel the identity of witnesses and case agents who could have been involved in leaking the information. *Id.* at 965. However, if the court identifies who improperly leaked the information, the court should provide defense counsel with the names of the violators so that defense counsel may then play a role in hearings involving the imposition of contempt sanctions. *Id.* If you are concerned that the trial judge does not have the time to adequately investigate the matter, suggest that the court appoint a special master—at government expense—to assist the court.

The penalty for violating Rule 6(e) will not include either dismissal of the case or a criminal referral of the violators because this is a contempt proceeding. However, like other aspects of grand jury practice, litigating these issues will expose the government's misconduct and may lead the district court to be much more skeptical about the government's motives and integrity moving forward.

4.5 PRESENTING FALSE EVIDENCE TO THE GRAND JURY

In some pre-*Mechanik* cases, there have been a few instances where courts reversed convictions when the government presented false statements about the facts or law to the grand jury. In *United States v. Basurto*, the

Ninth Circuit reversed a conviction based on perjured testimony in the grand jury. 497 F.2d 781, 787 (9th Cir. 1974). The court based its ruling on the Fifth Amendment right to due process, not the court's supervisory power. In *Basurto,* an unnamed co-conspirator testified before a grand jury about the Defendant. *Id.* at 784. Following the indictment, the grand jury witness told the prosecutor that his grand jury testimony was false. *Id.* Before trial, the prosecutor disclosed the issue to defense counsel, but did not inform the grand jury or the court and also did not seek to re-indict the case without using the perjured testimony. *Id.* The Ninth Circuit emphasized that a prosecutor cannot "permit a person to stand trial when he knows that perjury permeates the indictment." *Id.* at 785. As a result, the Ninth Circuit reversed the conviction holding that "the Due Process Clause of the Fifth Amendment is violated when a defendant has to stand trial on an indictment which the government knows is based on partially perjured testimony, when the perjured testimony is material, and when jeopardy has not attached." *Id.*

In *United States v. Samango*, the Ninth Circuit affirmed the dismissal of an indictment for grand jury misconduct even when the prosecutor did not submit any false evidence to the grand jury. 607 F.2d 877, 884 (9th Cir. 1979). The court based its ruling on the district court's supervisory power to prevent having a defendant face trial based on an indictment returned by a biased grand jury. *Id.* at 881. In *Samango*, the prosecutor attempted to correct an indictment in front of a new grand jury by simply dropping off one thousand pages of transcripts and presenting the testimony of only one witness, a case agent who provided a hearsay account of the allegations covering ten years of alleged criminal conduct. *Id.* at 879. The court criticized the prosecutor for not covering the information in the one thousand pages of transcripts in more detail with the grand jury, for including a transcript that included a tense exchange with the target that was unnecessary to establish probable cause but made the target look bad, and failing to clarify that the agent was providing a hearsay account of the evidence. *Id.* at 883. The court emphasized that "the *cumulative effect* of the above errors and indiscretions, none of which alone might have been enough to tip the scales, operated to the defendants' prejudice by producing a biased grand jury." *Id.* at 884 (emphasis added).

In *United States v. Hogan*, the Second Circuit dismissed an indictment based on grand jury misconduct while recognizing that a court's power to dismiss an indictment following a conviction due to grand jury abuse is rarely granted. 712 F.2d 757 (2nd Cir. 1983). The target in *Hogan* was a retired police lieutenant who had served as a supervisor for a regional narcotics crime squad. *Id.* at 758. The authorities suspected that the retired officer was involved in narcotics distribution with members of organized crime. *Id.* As a result, law enforcement had an informant borrow money from the retired officer and then tried to set him up by having the informant insist on repaying the debt with heroin, not money. *Id.* The retired officer refused to accept the heroin and told an undercover officer in a recorded conversation that "it was against everything he ever believed in." *Id.* at 759. The prosecutor still pushed ahead with an indictment.

During grand jury proceedings, the prosecutor committed several acts of misconduct. The prosecutor responded to a juror who asked whether there was probable cause to indict by impugning the target's character—calling the retired officer a "real hoodlum" and stating that an indictment was appropriate as "a matter of equity." *Id.* at 760. The prosecutor also presented hearsay testimony where agents suggested that the retired officer was a suspect in two unrelated murders. *Id.* The prosecutor also suggested to the grand jurors that the retired officer had received bribes from gamblers—another accusation that was unrelated to the charges before the grand jury. *Id.* The prosecutor also had an agent testify that the agent had heard that the retired officer refused to accept narcotics as payment for the debt because an informant had tipped off the retired officer about the investigation. *Id.* The court stressed that the grand jury proceedings reveal what happens when a prosecutor is too determined to obtain an indictment: "the temptations to cut corners, to ignore the rights of an accused, and to toss fair play to the winds gain ascendancy." *Id.* at 757–58. As a result, the court found that the incidents were "flagrant and unconscionable" and thereby impaired the grand jury's integrity as an independent body. *Id.* at 762. The court based its ruling on its supervisory power to prevent prosecutorial impairment of the grand jury's independent role. *Id.* at 761.

4.6 PURSUING THE HOLY GRAIL: THE COLLOQUY TRANSCRIPT

There are two separate transcripts on grand jury matters: witness transcripts and the colloquy transcript. The witness transcripts contain everything that a witness says in the grand jury room under questioning from the prosecutor. By contrast, the colloquy transcript captures everything the prosecutors tell the grand jury when there is no witness in the room.

This includes (a) the prosecutor's opening statement, which should briefly summarize the evidence and the proposed charges; (b) the prosecutor's closing statement, which will summarize the evidence presented and how it ties to the various counts in the indictment; and (c) responses to any questions raised by any member of the grand jury when no witness was in the grand jury room. Experienced prosecutors typically excuse the witness from the room before asking if the grand jurors have any questions about the witness's testimony. Doing so puts that back and forth with the grand jury on the colloquy transcript—which the prosecutor is convinced will never be produced—and takes that conversation off the witness's transcript—which the prosecutor will have to produce to defense counsel as Jencks material if the witness will testify at trial. With the witness out of the room, the prosecutor will screen the questions and determine whether the prosecutor will themselves answer it on the spot, tell the grand jury that no answer is needed, or bring the witness back into the room to answer the question.

While the saying may be true that many grand juries will indict a ham sandwich, some grand jurors ask very probing and insightful questions. I had a grand juror ask me a question related to tricky venue issue on a case where a ship with several tons of cocaine had been interdicted on the high seas by the navy of a foreign country. Attorney General Janet Reno had asked us the exact same question before we presented the matter to the grand jury. Do not underestimate how savvy some grand jurors become as they serve their eighteen-month assignment on the grand jury. Some grand jurors pick up on problematic issues in cases very quickly. I also appeared before several grand juries that had a specific grand juror who would ask probing questions in every case brought before his or her grand jury. You knew walking into that grand jury that you were about to be cross-examined on the minutiae of your case. Inquisitive grand jurors are clearly in the minority, but the only way to find out if you were blessed with such an inquisitive grand juror on your case is by seeking to obtain the colloquy transcript.

The exchanges in these question and answer sessions on the colloquy transcript are a treasure trove for potential misconduct: prosecutors will get the law wrong, may mislead the grand jury about the facts, or will withhold *Brady* evidence even when the grand jury spotted the problem and asked a specific question that should have drawn out that helpful *Brady* information. Some prosecutors will actually refuse to answer relevant questions raised by grand jurors by telling them that the information is unnecessary to their analysis of the indictment.

Since prosecutors never produce the colloquy transcript, many courts and defense attorneys (and probably some prosecutors) do not even know it exists, and courts are very reluctant to order prosecutors to produce the colloquy. As a result, overly aggressive prosecutors may cross the line into prosecutorial misconduct on the colloquy transcript because they do not think it will ever be produced. That is exactly why you should pursue it in every criminal case.

Here are the background standards you will need to navigate to obtain the colloquy transcript.

- Rule 6(e)(3)(E)(ii) allows a court to order disclosure of transcripts of grand jury proceedings "at the request of a defendant who shows that a ground may exist to dismiss the indictment because of a matter that occurred before the grand jury."
- A trial judge should order disclosure of grand jury transcripts where the party seeking the transcripts demonstrates a "particularized need exists [for the transcripts], which outweighs the policy of secrecy." *United States v. Walczak*, 783 F.2d 852, 857 (9th Cir. 1986), quoting *Pittsburgh Plate Glass Co. v. United States*, 360 U.S. 395, 400 (1959).
- "Need" to receive the colloquy transcript can be established by showing that the defense has become aware of specific facts (e.g., eliciting false testimony from a witness), suggesting that severe misconduct jeopardized the independence of the grand jury. *United States v. Isgro*, 974 F.2d 1091, 1094 (9th Cir. 2011); *United States v. Way*, 2015 WL 8780540 at *3 (E.D. Cal. Dec. 15, 2015).
- "Need" can also be shown by demonstrating that the law was in flux at the time of the grand jury presentation, such that the prosecutor might have given inaccurate instructions about the legal elements of the crime before the grand jury voted on the indictment. *United States v. Islam*, 2021 WL 312681 at *3 (E.D. Pa. Jan. 29, 2021); *United States v. Patel*, 2022 WL 12358443 at *9 (D. Conn. Oct. 21, 2022).
- The prosecutors will argue that there is a continuing need for secrecy and you will need to satisfy a four-factor test described in *Douglas Oil Co. of California v. Petrol Stops Northwest* (441 U.S. 211, 219 (1979)) to show that there is no need for continued secrecy:
  (1) Whether the release of the transcripts would result in prospective witnesses becoming reluctant to testify;
  (2) Whether witnesses would be less likely to testify frankly because they might be open to retribution or inducement;

(3) Whether there is a risk that those about to be indicted will flee or try to influence grand jurors not to indict; and
(4) Whether persons who are accused by the prosecutors but exonerated by the grand jurors will be held up to public ridicule.

Here is one approach to consider when attempting to obtain the colloquy transcript.

First, at an initial status conference, request that the prosecutors provide the transcripts from their grand jury witnesses and argue that the trial will proceed more efficiently if you have the Jencks material before the pre-trial conference. Under *United States v. W. R. Grace*, district courts have the authority to enter pretrial case management and discovery orders to ensure that the parties are adequately prepared so the trial will proceed efficiently. 526 F.3d 499, 508–09 (9th Cir. 2008). In addition, check your local rules because they may suggest that the parties resolve Jencks issues before trial. *See, e.g.*, Northern District of California Local Rule 17.1-1. Most prosecutors will produce witness transcripts before trial because trial judges do not want to wait for defense counsel to review Jencks material while a trial witness is on the stand. Thus, you should be able to get the witness transcripts from the grand jury before the pre-trial conference. Some prosecutors will also produce the hearsay testimony of their lead case agent with the other witnesses' transcripts. If the prosecutor refuses to provide the hearsay transcript, file a motion to obtain it.

Second, scour the grand jury transcripts you receive in pre-trial discovery for any suggestion that a grand jury witness misstated a material fact. Also, identify any misstatement of the applicable law by the prosecutors at any pre-trial hearing. If either of these happened, you now have a basis to file a motion for the colloquy transcript. It is a rare win, but courts have granted defense requests for the colloquy transcript. *See United States v. Kilpatrick*, 575 F. Supp. 325, 326 (D. Colo. 1983) (Judge Kane orders disclosure of the entire grand jury transcript after reviewing evidence of certain potential misconduct in the grand jury proceeding); *United States v. Jacobsen*, 691 F.2d 110, 111 (2d Cir. 1982) (contradiction between government statements and evidence in transcripts previously produced led the court to order the disclosure of all grand jury transcripts); *United States v. Rogers*, 2018 WL 10809607 *1-2 (S.D. Ind. Jan. 24, 2018) (court grants request for colloquy transcript and grand jury materials where Defendant needed to assess whether grand jury was adequately instructed on eligibility factors in a death penalty case); *United States v. Benjamin*, 1986 WL 15567 at *1

(E.D. Cal. May 1, 1986) (court grants request for colloquy transcript where the prosecutor seemingly commingled civil and criminal investigations to gain an advantage and that misconduct would only be apparent from reviewing the transcripts); *United States v. Etienne*, 2019 WL 2548790 at *2 (N.D. Cal. June 20, 2019) (court grants request for transcript related to the legal instructions provided to the grand jury because the government misstated the legal standard for a RICO conspiracy at a pre-trial hearing); *United States v. Booth*, 2012 WL 2782598 at *1 (same).

CHAPTER 5

Charging Decisions

If severe prosecutorial misconduct surfaces during the investigative phase of a case, defense counsel should consider pressing for a declination before the government files charges. In corporate fraud investigations, we have represented many clients where the investigating agents and lead prosecutors were hell-bent on pursuing bank and accounting fraud charges when the conduct at issue clearly complied with the applicable Generally Accepted Accounting Principle (GAAP) standards. Many investigators and prosecutors simply do not understand GAAP, particularly where the investigation focuses on an emerging business practice or new technology—for example, how to price stock options or how the crypto currency market operates—and then take aggressive actions that violate various policies in the *Justice Manual* to try to make a cutting edge case. We have also represented clients who were targeted for improper reasons: their race or their political affiliation, to cover up misconduct by the prosecution team, or simply because the government did not understand their business model and resented that the company executives were making far more money than federal employees.

To get out in front of the charging decision in these types of investigations, defense counsel should consider seeking a meeting with the relevant supervisors at the prosecutor's office to request a declination. At those meetings, the supervisors typically expect defense counsel to focus their presentation on the governing standards related to how and when prosecutors should exercise their discretion to charge a crime. While discussing the misconduct is certainly an aspect of the presentation, the analysis should be delivered through the lens of the relevant charging standards that prosecutors are supposed to apply when considering an indictment. The supervisors—whether it is the U.S. Attorney, First Assistant, or the Office of the Deputy Attorney General at Main Justice (ODAG)—are likely to be more persuaded by legal analysis rather than a presentation that focuses on the facts. The reason for this approach is that line prosecutors will dispute your view of the facts and the supervisors won't intervene if the relevant facts are disputed. A pitch for declination then is much more likely to be successful if it focuses on legal analysis and recites only those facts that cannot be disputed by the line prosecutors.

If the matter is already indicted, defense counsel may consider filing a motion to dismiss based on either vindictive or selective prosecution. While these motions are very difficult to win, they should be considered in the right factual scenarios. At a minimum, these motions can force the government to answer publicly for misconduct that would otherwise remain buried and thereby potentially lay the groundwork for a subsequent motion to dismiss if the government continues to commit additional misconduct at trial.

5.1 GOVERNING STANDARDS

The DOJ, ABA, and National Association of District Attorney's all publish detailed criteria regarding the factors surrounding a prosecutor's charging decision. Referring to these standards can help frame the arguments you might want to pursue if you have an opportunity to advocate for a declination before the matter gets indicted.

Section 9-27.200 of the *Justice Manual* states that "the attorney for the government should commence or recommend federal prosecution if he/she believes that the person's conduct constitutes a federal offense, and that the admissible evidence will probably be sufficient to obtain and sustain a conviction, unless (1) the prosecution would serve no substantial federal interest; (2) the person is subject to effective prosecution in another jurisdiction; or (3) there exists an adequate non-criminal alternative to prosecution."

The factors considered regarding whether prosecution serves a substantial federal interest include: federal law enforcement priorities; the nature and seriousness of the offense; the deterrent effect of prosecution; the person's culpability; the person's criminal history; the person's willingness to cooperate with law enforcement; the person's personal circumstances; the interests of any victims; and the probable sentence or other consequences. *See JM* Section 9-27-230.

In considering a potential declination, the prosecutor should take into account the strength of another jurisdiction's interest in prosecution, the other jurisdiction's ability and willingness to prosecute effectively, and the probable sentence or other consequences if the target is convicted. *See JM* Section 9-27.240.

Improper factors to consider when looking at potential declination include: (1) the person's race, religion, gender, ethnicity, national origin, sexual orientation, or political association, activities, or beliefs; (2) the attorney's own personal feelings concerning the person, person's associates, or the victim; and (3) the possible effect of the decision on the prosecutor's own professional or personal circumstances. *See JM* Section 9-27.260.

For similar guidelines, *see* Standard 3-4.4, Discretion in Filing, Declining, Maintaining and Dismissing Criminal Charges in the *ABA's Criminal Justice Standards for the Prosecution Function* and Standards 4-2.1–2.4 of the *National Prosecution Standards* of the National DA's Association.

For corporate prosecutions, the *Justice Manual* contains a separate set of additional considerations that prosecutors should analyze before deciding to charge a corporation. *See JM* Sections 9-28.000–1740 of "Principles of Federal Prosecution of Business Organizations." In our experience, the DOJ will meet with defense counsel during the investigation to allow defense counsel to argue for a declination before seeking an indictment. Section 9-28.300 lists the factors that the prosecutors should consider in addition to the factors related to charging an individual. These additional factors include: the pervasiveness of wrongdoing within the corporation; the adequacy and effectiveness of the corporation's compliance program; the corporation's timely and voluntary self-disclosure; the corporation's remedial actions; collateral consequences to shareholders, pension holders, and employees; the adequacy of civil and regulatory enforcement; and the adequacy of prosecuting individuals (in lieu of charging the corporate entity).

5.2 VINDICTIVE PROSECUTION

Vindictive prosecution exists where a prosecutor seeks to penalize or punish a defendant for exercising a constitutional right. *Bordenkircher v. Hayes*, 434 U.S. 357, 363 (1978). To punish a person "because he or she has done what the law plainly allows is a due process violation of the most basic sort." *Id.* For an agent of the state to pursue a course of action whose objective is to penalize a person's reliance on his or her legal rights is "patently unconstitutional." *Id.*, citing *Chaffin v. Stynchombe*, 412 US. 17, 32–33, n. 20 (1973).

A defendant must prove prosecutorial vindictiveness by a preponderance of the evidence. *United States v. Dvorin*, 817 F.3d 438, 455 (5th Cir. 2016). The defendant must show either (a) actual animus or (b) sufficient facts to give rise to a presumption of vindictiveness. *Id.* Actual vindictiveness can be established by a statement made by a prosecutor, such as threats to up the ante if a defendant exercises a legal right. *Jackson v. Walker*, 585 F.2d 139, 142 n.3 (5th Cir. 1978) ("The unconstitutional motive may be simply the prosecutor's intent to discourage other criminal appeals in the future by 'upping the ante'"); *United States v. In Hyuk Kim*, No. CRIM. 07-00064, 2009 WL 5033934, at *5 (D. Guam Dec. 8, 2009) (finding actual vindictiveness where the prosecutor made improper statements, including "[y]ou file motions in this court, and we start looking for more charges to bring" and "we are punishing him for filing those motions"); *United States v. DeMarco*, 401 F. Supp. 505 (C.D. Cal. 1975), aff'd, 550 F.2d 1224 (9th Cir. 1977) (finding actual vindictiveness where during a phone call, the prosecutor informed defense counsel the government would consider bringing more counts against the Defendant if the Defendant successfully transferred his case to another state). This type of evidence is typically available "only in a rare case." *United States v. Johnson*, 221 F.3d 83, 94 (2d Cir. 2000) (declining to review district court's finding of no actual vindictiveness). As a result, defendants often attempt to show vindictiveness by proving a presumption of vindictiveness.

Federal circuits differ on what is required for a defendant to show a presumption of vindictiveness; however, a showing of an improper sequence in the government's decision making, the absence of any new factual development that could justify the government's retaliation against the defendant, and bringing more severe charges against the defendant may be sufficient to give rise to a presumption. *United States v. Tobin*, 598 F. Supp. 2d at 130 (finding a presumption of vindictiveness where after Defendant successfully appealed his conviction the government filed more severe charges without identifying any newly discovered evidence). In the Fifth Circuit, the court examines the prosecutor's actions in the context of the entire proceedings, and "if . . . the course of events provides no objective indication that would allay a reasonable apprehension by the defendant that the [additional] charge was vindictive, . . . a presumption of vindictiveness applies." *Id.*, quoting *United States v. Krezdorn*, 718 F.2d 1360, 1365 (5th Cir. 1983) (en banc).

If the defendant makes a sufficient showing to establish the presumption of vindictiveness, the burden shifts to the government to prove by a preponderance of the evidence "that events occurring since the original charge decision altered that initial exercise of the prosecutor's discretion." *Id.*; compare *Miracle v. Estelle*, 592 F.2d 1269, 1277 (5th Cir. 1979) (finding vindictiveness where a Defendant was granted a new trial, and without explanation, the prosecutor charged the Defendant with a more severe offense than the offense included in the original indictment) and *United States v. Phillips*, 664 F.2d 971, 1021 (5th Cir. 1981) (finding government rebutted presumption of vindictiveness where the prosecutor established that the basis for the superseding indictment was newly discovered evidence).

5.3 VINDICTIVE PROSECUTION: HELPFUL CASES

Here is a summary of helpful district and circuit level opinions on vindictive prosecution:

First Circuit

United States v. Tobin, 598 F. Supp. 2d 125 (D. Me. 2009) (defense motion to dismiss granted where government filed more severe charges against Defendant after Defendant successfully appealed his initial conviction on related but less severe charges, and government was unable to point to any newly discovered information regarding the new charges).

Second Circuit

United States v. Cady, 955 F. Supp. 164 (N.D.N.Y. 1997) (defense motion to dismiss granted where government filed a new indictment with more serious narcotics/firearms charges after the Defendant had appealed his sentence on a plea agreement involving lesser charges on the same conduct).

Third Circuit

United States v. Korey, 614 F. Supp. 2d 573 (W.D. Pa. 2009) (defense motion to dismiss granted where government filed a second indictment on same underlying conduct after Defendant was acquitted or pled guilty to counts in a prior indictment).

Fourth Circuit

United States v. Belcher, 762 F. Supp. 666 (W.D. Va. 1991) (defense motion to dismiss newly added charges granted after Defendant successfully appealed marijuana manufacturing charge—proceedings on remand limited to the charges in the initial indictment).

Fifth Circuit

Miracle v. Estell, 592 F.2d 1269 (5th Cir. 1979) (finding vindictiveness where a Defendant was granted a new trial and, without explanation, the prosecutor charged the Defendant with a more severe offense than the offense included in the original indictment).

Sixth Circuit

United States v. LaDeau, 734 F.3d 561 (6th Cir. 2013) (finding vindictiveness where government filed a superseding indictment charging Defendant with conspiracy to receive child pornography after Defendant had successfully defeated a one-count indictment of possessing child pornography with a successful motion to suppress).

United States v. McFadyen-Snider, 590 F.2d 654 (6th Cir. 1979) (Defendant wins vindictiveness challenge where government filed perjury charges against Defendant after Defendant successfully appealed a fraud conviction with court finding that government's perjury indictment improperly punished Defendant for pursuing her constitutional right to appeal).

Eighth Circuit

United States v. Terrell, 220 F. Supp. 3d 941 (N.D. Iowa 2016) (court strikes government's notice to seek enhanced penalties where government refused to allow Defendant to cooperate to decrease sentence exposure simply because Defendant had previously elected to proceed with a preliminary hearing following his arrest).

Ninth Circuit

United States v. Jenkins, 504 F.3d 694 (9th Cir. 2007) (court dismisses alien smuggling indictment where government belatedly charged Defendant for two prior alien smuggling incidents only after Defendant testified in a later drug smuggling case that she thought she was smuggling aliens, not narcotics, in this third smuggling incident).

United States v. Shaw, 655 F.2d 168 (9th Cir. 1981) (vindictiveness found where government moved to vacate plea agreement after Defendant raised subject matter jurisdiction to offense related to plea agreement).

Tenth Circuit

United States v. Wood, 36 F.3d 945 (10th Cir. 1994) (vindictiveness found and superseding indictment dismissed where Defendant beat initial indictment on appeal of a legal issue, and government reindicted with same charges and Defendant won on motion to dismiss and then government responded by filing a superseding indictment that contained new charges related to the same underlying facts).

D.C. Circuit

United States v. Meyer, 810 F.2d 1242 (D.C. Cir. 1987) (affirming District Court's order granting motion to dismiss a new count added to a superseding indictment where government increased the charges against protestors because they rejected proposed plea agreements and exercised their right to a jury trial).

5.4 SELECTIVE PROSECUTION

A selective prosecution claim is not a defense on the merits to the criminal charge itself but rather an independent assertion that the prosecutor has brought the charge for reasons forbidden by the Constitution. *United States v. Armstrong*, 517 U.S. 456, 463 (1996). Since a selective prosecution claim asks a court to exercise judicial power over a special province of the Executive Branch, "the showing necessary to obtain discovery should itself be a significant barrier to the litigation of insubstantial claims." *Id.* at 464. The claim is grounded in the equal protection component of the Due Process Clause of the Fifth Amendment—that is, the decision whether to prosecute may not be based on "'an unjustifiable standard such as race, religion, or other arbitrary classification.'" *Id.*, quoting *Oyler v. Boles*, 368 U.S. 448, 456 (1962).

To win on a selective prosecution claim, the defendant must show that the federal prosecutorial policy had both a *discriminatory effect* and was motivated by a *discriminatory purpose. Id.* at 465. To meet this standard, the defendant will need to provide the court with persuasive statistical evidence, which generally requires obtaining discovery from the government. To obtain discovery on these issues, the defense will need to show that similarly situated defendants could have been prosecuted but were not. *Id.* at 469. In *Armstrong*, the Supreme Court reversed because the Ninth Circuit did not require the defense to show that prosecutors had prosecuted African American defendants on crack cocaine offenses while refusing to prosecute caucasian defendants for the same crack cocaine offense. *Id.* at 470. By contrast, in *Yick Wo v. Hopkins* the Supreme Court held that the claimant successfully demonstrated that a municipality enforced a city ordinance only against Chinese nationals but not against other races. 118 U.S. 356, 374 (1886).

Defense counsel needs to tailor their supporting evidence so that the facts of their client's background directly oppose the designated pool of comparators who the authorities failed to prosecute. Furthermore, defense counsel should also try to show that the pool of comparators includes offenders of the same crime but with *more* evidence weighing against them than the defendant and who were *still* not prosecuted.

Using statistical evidence may be the only means of showing discriminatory effect. But given that courts hesitate to rely solely on general data, any statistical analyses must be substantially detailed. Courts rejected claims based on nationwide statistics in *United States v. Washington.* 869 F.3d 193, 214–15 (3d Cir. 2017). In addition, in *United States v. Venable* (666 F.3d 893, 901–03 (4th Cir. 2012)), the court held that statistical evidence of racial disparity is insufficient on its own to infer discriminatory purpose, as did *United States v. Jones* (287 F.3d 325, 333 (5th Cir. 2002)), with respect to the death penalty. These cases reinforce that the type, depth, and specificity of the statistical data, as well as the efficacy with which it captures comparable categories of people, determine its persuasiveness.

5.5 *SCRUSHY* ISSUES IN PARALLEL PROSECUTIONS

At times, the DOJ will use the civil enforcement arms of regulatory agencies—the SEC, IRS, or FDIC—to build its criminal case by using their civil discovery powers against the targets of the DOJ's criminal investigation. As an example, the SEC might send the target a document subpoena followed by a deposition notice. If the target mistakenly believes that the investigation is only an SEC civil matter, the target might fail to invoke his or her right against self-incrimination and then produce documents and provide testimony to the SEC—information that the DOJ could not discover on its own in its criminal investigation. Government misconduct in the coordination and execution of the civil and criminal investigations could potentially result in violations of your client's Fifth Amendment right to due process and Sixth Amendment right to a fair trial, and, in extreme cases, position defense counsel to seek a declination or dismissal.

There is a mountain of case law as well as several regulations that allow the DOJ and federal civil regulatory agencies to work parallel criminal and civil investigations against common targets involving the same underlying facts. *See, e.g., United States v. Posada Carriles*, 541 F.3d 344, 353 (5th Cir. 2008) (it is a well-settled rule that the government can conduct simultaneous civil and criminal investigations); *United States v. Teyibo*, 877 F. Supp. 846, 855 (S.D.N.Y. 1995), aff'd, 101 F.3d 681 (2d Cir. 1996) (criminal authorities may use evidence obtained in a prior civil proceeding); 15 U.S.C. §§ 77t(b), 78u(d) (permitting the SEC to transmit evidence to the attorney general to bring criminal actions); 12 C.F.R. § 308.503 (allowing the FDIC to refer allegations to the DOJ).

However, such "parallel proceedings" have been deemed improper where the government violates an individual's constitutional rights, "depart[s] from the proper administration of criminal justice," or otherwise acts in bad faith. *See United States v. Kordel*, 397 U.S. 1, 11–13 (1970); *United States v. Scrushy*, 366 F. Supp. 2d 1134, 1138, 1140 (N.D. Ala. 2005). For example, the government may violate a defendant's due process rights where: (1) the government brings "a civil action solely to obtain evidence for its criminal prosecution"; (2) the government fails to advise the defendant in the civil proceeding that it contemplates a criminal prosecution; (3) the defendant is without counsel; (4) the defendant "reasonably fears prejudice from adverse pretrial publicity or other unfair injury"; or (5) other special circumstances exist that suggest the criminal proceeding is unconstitutional or improper. *Kordel*, 397 U.S. at 11–12.

Essentially, the criminal and civil actions must truly be parallel, not intertwined or commingled. *Scrushy*, 366 F. Supp. 2d at 1139–40 ("To be parallel, by definition, the separate investigations should be like the side-by-side train tracks that never intersect."). Simultaneous proceedings may be considered impermissibly intertwined if the government manipulates the investigations for its own purposes. *Id.* at 1140. In *Scrushy*, the court found such manipulation where the SEC changed the location of a target's deposition at the DOJ's request so that "if he lies, he lies in our [the prosecutor's] district." DOJ personnel instructed the SEC to ask certain deposition questions (and withhold others), and the DOJ recruited the SEC to participate in later aspects of the criminal investigation. *Id.* at 1136–37, 1140.

Dual proceedings are more likely to be found improper where criminal authorities have both "notice and direct input" into the civil investigation, in contrast to situations where the SEC began its investigation several months (or years) before the DOJ initiated its criminal investigation. *Scrushy*, 366 F. Supp. 2d. at 1138; *United States v. Melvin*, No. 3:14-cr-00022-TCB, 2015 WL 7116737 at *18 (N.D. Ga. May 27, 2015) (report and recommendation adopted); 143 F. Supp. 3d 1354 (N.D. Ga. 2015), aff'd, 918 F.3d 1296 (11th Cir. 2017) (emphasizing that the indictment occurred more than two years after the SEC filed its civil complaint).

Another crucial factor is whether the government informed the defendants about a potential criminal prosecution. *Scrushy*, 366 F. Supp. 2d at 1139 ("When a defendant does not know about the criminal investigation, the danger of prejudice increases"). Although some courts have held that bad faith is not limited to "outright lies," many circuits require the government to have made some form of an affirmative misrepresentation for the proceedings to be considered improper. Compare *Scrushy*, 366 F. Supp. 2d at 1140 (rejecting the government's contention that it cannot be accused of bad faith simply because it did not outright lie) and *United States v. Rand*, 308 F. Supp. 1231, 1235 (N.D. Ohio 1970) (noting that courts have found unfairness where the government did not inform a civil defendant that a criminal prosecution was contemplated or recommended) with *United States v. Stringer*, 535 F.3d 929, 940 (9th Cir. 2008) (explaining that most circuits do not require government agents to "disclose the possibility or existence of a criminal investigation, so long as they made no affirmative misrepresentations").

However, the government has no obligation to conduct a criminal investigation openly. *Stringer*, 535 F.3d at 933. Simply disclosing the possibility that evidence in a civil action may be used in a criminal proceeding is often sufficient. *Id.* If the government advises a defendant represented by counsel of a pending criminal investigation and of his or her Fifth Amendment rights, the parallel proceedings will likely be found permissible. *Stringer*, 535 F.3d at 933, 940–41; *Melvin*, 2015 WL 7116737, at *18. For the SEC, this is often accomplished through their use of their Form 1662, which they typically present to a witness at the beginning of a deposition and that informs witnesses that there could be criminal actions brought against them.

If a court finds government misconduct, potential remedies include a stay of the civil proceeding, suppression of the evidence found in the civil action, or even a dismissal of the indictment altogether. Dismissal of an indictment is justified only in rare circumstances. *Posada Carriles*, 541 F.3d at 353. But it has happened. For example, in *Scrushy*, the court suppressed the SEC deposition testimony and dismissed the related perjury counts that relied on the suppressed SEC testimony. 366 F. Supp. 2d at 1135, 1140. In *United States v. Rand*, the court dismissed an indictment where the U.S. Attorney (falsely) assured the Defendant that he would be immune from prosecution for matters involved in the civil proceeding. 308 F. Supp. 1231, 1233 (N.D. Ohio 1970). And in *United States v. Parrott*, the court dismissed an indictment under Rule 48 of the *Federal Rules of Criminal Procedure* where the government used extensive civil discovery procedures and gave priority to the civil action, which contributed to an unjustified delay in prosecuting the criminal case. 248 F. Supp. 196, 202, 205–06 (D.D.C. 1965).

PART II

Prosecutorial Misconduct During Pre-Trial Discovery

CHAPTER 6

Brady/Giglio Challenges: Obtaining Exculpatory Information

6.1 *BRADY* BASICS

Prosecutors must provide defense counsel with any information that might exculpate the defendant, including any information that impacts the credibility of government witnesses. This includes exculpatory information in the possession of local police officers and federal agents acting on the prosecutor's behalf. *Brady* implicates constitutional obligations because withholding exculpatory evidence impacts a defendant's Fifth Amendment right to due process.

The four leading Supreme Court cases are *Brady v. Maryland*, 373 U.S. 83 (1963); *Giglio v. United States*, 405 U.S. 150 (1972); *United States v. Agurs*, 427 U.S. 97 (1976); and *Kyles v. Whitley*, 514 U.S. 419 (1995). In *Brady*, the Court found that due process requires that the government disclose all information to the defense showing that the defendant might be innocent. *Brady*, 373 U.S. at 85–86. The Court emphasized that (a) the evidence suppressed must be material to require a new trial, and (b) the good or bad faith of the prosecutor is irrelevant to the analysis. *Id.* at 87.

In *Giglio*, the Court extended *Brady*'s reach to evidence that negatively impacts the *credibility* of government witnesses, as opposed to evidence related to the defendant's innocence. 405 U.S. at 154. The Court held that when the reliability of a given witness may well be determinative of guilt or innocence, nondisclosure of evidence affecting credibility falls within *Brady*'s rule requiring disclosure. *Id.* Like *Brady*, *Giglio* contains a materiality requirement: a new trial is required only where the false testimony could in any reasonable likelihood have affected the judgment of the jury. *Id.*

In *Agurs*, the Court confirmed that the government's obligation to turn over material exculpatory evidence attaches even where the defendant either never requested the information or merely requested it in only a general way. 427 U.S. at 104–08.

In *Whitley*, the Court again extended *Brady*'s reach by holding that the individual prosecutor has a duty to learn of any exculpatory evidence known to others acting on the government's behalf in the case, including the police. 514 U.S. 438. As a result, the investigative files maintained by the police and federal agencies such as the FBI and DEA fall inside the scope of a prosecutor's *Brady* obligations.

Compliance with *Brady* and its progeny is not a technicality. *Brady* is a rule of fairness premised on the fact that the prosecutor's role is to search for the truth, not to obtain a conviction. As Justice Douglas stated in *Brady*, "[s]ociety wins not only when the guilty are convicted but when criminal trials are fair; our system of the administration of justice suffers when any accused is treated unfairly." 373 U.S. at 87. Courts analyze whether a prosecutor's conduct is consistent with the prosecutor's obligation to assist the defense in making its case or whether the prosecutor is acting strategically—for example, to limit the scope of disclosure or delay the timing of disclosure—which is antithetical to the prosecutors' duty to "transcend" their role as "an adversary." *United States v. Bagley*, 473 U.S. 667, 675 n.6 (1985); *Breakiron v. Horn*, 642 F.3d 126, 133 (3rd Cir. 2011) (expressing dismay that prosecutors still play games with justice by withholding exculpatory evidence from the defense long after the Supreme Court had decided *Brady*). As Justice Souter stated in *Whitley*, requiring prosecutors to disclose exculpatory evidence "will tend to preserve the criminal trial, as distinct from the prosecutor's private deliberations, as the chosen forum for ascertaining the truth about criminal accusations." 514 U.S. at 440.

Brady challenges continue to present a ripe area for either obtaining the evidence needed to win at trial or establishing a basis to obtain post-conviction relief on appeal. *Brady* issues are common in both reactive street cases and complex proactive white collar grand jury investigations. In reactive matters, the police might obtain statements from witnesses who provide a physical description of the perpetrator that does not match the defendant, or the witnesses might provide some other information that corroborates the defendant's alibi. In complex white collar matters, the investigating agency will often obtain a mountain of documents via subpoenas or search warrants that will contain some information that supports the defendant's theory of defense. For example, the government might possess information that shows that the defendant's accounting treatment was accurate or that the defendant had a good faith basis to make a certain disclosure to its investors related to its sales targets or ability to collect on a loan.

In addition, white collar investigations often involve parallel civil investigations conducted by the SEC, FDIC, IRS, and DEA. The regulatory agencies will litigate civil or administrative claims against the defendant and feed information through to the DOJ for use in the DOJ's criminal grand jury investigation. Then all the agencies involved issue press releases when the criminal charges are finally announced and congratulate themselves for all their hard work. You can use that press release against the DOJ because the press release identifies all the members of the "prosecution team" thereby broadening the scope of where the prosecutors must search for the exculpatory evidence that will help you defend the case. For example, the prosecutors may now need to review files at the SEC, FDIC, and/or IRS, along with files maintained at both the FBI and the DOJ. The files at the regulatory agency often provide information that is consistent with the defense theory of the case. The FDIC, for example, conducts a review of a failed bank that often identifies external factors (i.e., actions taken by individuals other than the bank's executives) that caused the bank to fail. That information will dovetail with a good faith defense by a bank executive.

Consider retaining a private investigator who previously worked at the relevant agency (FDIC, IRS, or SEC) because the investigator will be able to describe precisely what records and reports the agency will have in its files. That allows you to make very precise, detailed requests that will make even the most aggressive prosecutor concerned about the potential consequences of withholding this information. In addition, press for testimony from a representative from the agency if the prosecutor does not produce records that your investigator knows the agency should have in its files. The tardy and begrudging production of materials following motion practice will show the court that the prosecutor cannot be trusted, which will help you on subsequent *Brady/Giglio/Napue* battles as the case moves forward.

In large white collar cases, prosecutors will often dump ten to twenty million documents on the defense and claim that they have complied with their *Brady* obligations because they have *disclosed* everything to you.

You now have two problems. First, given the volume of documents in the production, you cannot possibly locate all the exculpatory needles of *Brady* information in the massive haystack of irrelevant documents that the DOJ just dumped on you. Second, you cannot confirm that the government actually gave you all the *Brady* information in its possession. Aggressive prosecutors may park your best *Brady* evidence at a regulatory agency—like the SEC or FDIC—to try to generate plausible deniability during discovery in the criminal case (i.e., the prosecutors had no idea that the SEC had documents that show that the company's board of directors exonerated your client of any wrongdoing on the facts at issue). It happens.

Moreover, in most criminal cases, the government uses confidential informants, cooperating defendants, and jailhouse snitches who are motivated to lie about the defendant—to obtain a monetary reward from the government, a reduced sentence, or some type of immigration or other benefit. Detectives and agents often withhold *Brady/Giglio* information about their informants/snitches from prosecutors and many prosecutors fail to press their detectives/agents for this information. So, push hard to force the prosecutor to obtain and disclose the information for *Brady/Giglio* purposes.

Despite repeated representations from prosecutors to trial judges in our matters stating that they had provided open file discovery to us, we have yet to have a case where the prosecutors actually produced all *Brady/Giglio* information in their possession. When confronted with prosecutors who tell the court that they have provided you with open file discovery, immediately demand that the prosecutor produce the following:

- The agency file related to any confidential informant, source of information, whistleblower, and cooperating defendant so you can identify all benefits the government has provided to them.
- The agent's raw notes of the interviews of all potential witnesses and informants so you can identify the discrepancies between the raw notes and the typed agent reports (FBI 302's, DEA-6's, etc.).
- All communications between any member of the prosecution team (agents and prosecutors) and any potential witness, informant, and alleged victim (and/or their respective attorneys) to identify all benefits provided to them and any admission by the prosecutors about the validity of the defense theory of the facts.
- All transcripts of all grand jury proceedings, including the colloquy transcript, to identify any false statements of fact/law as well as any other misconduct before the grand jury.

These requests take direct aim at the portions of the prosecutors' file that typically contain most helpful *Brady/Giglio* information. So, press for the production of this information to challenge the prosecutors to live up to their promise to you and the court about having provided you with open file discovery.

6.2 GOVERNING STANDARDS

6.2.1 The DOJ's *Justice Manual* on Disclosing Exculpatory Evidence

Sections 9-5.001 and 9-5.002 of the DOJ's *Justice Manual* describe how prosecutors should approach the disclosure of exculpatory information. In addition, in 2010, Deputy Attorney General David Ogden drafted a memo on *Brady* obligations that has been repeatedly cited by courts. Some prosecutors ignore these requirements, but courts will often cite the DOJ's internal standards in opinions involving *Brady* violations.

Here are some of the highlights from the *Justice Manual* and the Ogden memo:

- The DOJ prosecutors must disclose *Brady* and *Giglio* evidence regardless of whether defense counsel asks for it.
- Prosecutors should err on the side of disclosure.
- As to timing, prosecutors should disclose the information in sufficient time to permit the defendant to make effective use of the information, which typically means promptly after discovery.
- Prosecutors have an obligation to search for all exculpatory and impeachment evidence from all members of the prosecution team.
- Prosecutors should err on the side of inclusiveness in determining which agencies should be included on the "prosecution team," particularly in parallel prosecutions.
- Prosecutors should not delegate the disclosure determination to investigative case agents—the prosecutors should be actively involved in deciding what information is disclosed to defense counsel (this reduces the plausible deniability that certain prosecutors will try to build to protect themselves).

Section 9-5.002 of the *Justice Manual* provides a detailed list of the information the prosecutors must review to identify exculpatory information that they must disclose. This is important because prosecutors often try to narrow down where they will search and what information they will review. As a result, consider using their own policy to hold them accountable to search every area that might contain information that will help you defend your case. Section 9-5002 states that prosecutors should review:

- The investigative agencies' files, including emails and electronic documents.
- All files related to confidential informants, including all proffer/immunity agreements, payment information, and other potential witness impeachment information.
- All evidence gathered during the investigation, including via subpoena or search warrant.
- All substantive case related communications, including communications among prosecutors and/or agents and between the government and witnesses/victims (this should include all email communications, texts, and messages over social media platforms such as What'sApp, Facebook, and Signal as well as communications between the government and a witness's attorney).
- Potential *Giglio* information maintained by law enforcement regarding law enforcement witnesses, including findings of prior misconduct, past/pending criminal charges, and allegations of misconduct reflecting on the truthfulness or bias of the officer/agent.
- Potential *Giglio* information related to non–law-enforcement witnesses, including prior inconsistent statements, any benefits law enforcement provided to the witness, prior bad acts/convictions, and anything that could impact the witness's ability to perceive and recall events (e.g., drugs, mental health issues, etc.).
- Any information the prosecution team obtained in witness interviews and trial preparation with witnesses, including agents' draft and final memos, prosecutors/agents' notes of the witness interview, and notes taken by police officers.

6.2.2 Use the ABA Model Guidelines

Like the *Justice Manual*, the ABA has standards related to *Brady* issues that prosecutors should follow. Specifically, the *ABA Standards for Criminal Justice*, Section 3-3.11.1, provides three things.

First, a prosecutor should not intentionally fail to make timely disclosure to the defense at the earliest feasible opportunity of the existence of all evidence or information that tends to negate the guilt of the accused as to the offense charged or mitigate the offense charged or would tend to reduce the punishment of the accused.

Second, a prosecutor should not fail to make a reasonably diligent effort to comply with a legally proper discovery request.

Third, a prosecutor should not intentionally avoid pursuit of evidence because he or she believes it will damage the prosecution's case or aid the accused.

6.3 HOW TO PURSUE EXCULPATORY EVIDENCE

We typically have four core objectives related to our pursuit of exculpatory evidence. First, where it applies, we try to force the prosecutor to present evidence that negates the guilt of the target to the grand jury during the pre-indictment phase. Second, post-indictment, we push to obtain all exculpatory information as soon as possible. Third, in paper intensive cases, we try to force the prosecutors to specifically identify by Bates number every document in their possession that contains exculpatory information—the needles in the proverbial haystack. Fourth, we attempt to develop a foundation for either a motion to dismiss the indictment or an appeal of a conviction when the prosecutors fail to comply with their *Brady* obligations. *Brady* violations are a ripe area for obtaining the evidence needed to win both at trial and on appeal, so be aggressive in pursuing this evidence and litigating these issues pre-trial.

Here are some suggestions on how to fight to obtain *Brady* information.

6.3.1 Send a Pre-Indictment Letter to the Prosecutors Insisting They Present Exculpatory Evidence to the Grand Jury

If you represent a target in a grand jury investigation, consider sending a letter to the prosecutors insisting that they present all exculpatory information to the grand jury. The relevant case law does not require prosecutors to do so. *See In United States v. Williams,* 112 S. Ct. 1735 (1992) (a federal court's supervisory powers over the grand jury do not include dismissing an otherwise valid indictment where the prosecutor failed to introduce substantial exculpatory evidence to a grand jury). The *Justice Manual,* however, does require prosecutors to present evidence that negates the guilt of the target to the grand jury—that is, *Brady* but not *Giglio* evidence. *See Justice Manual,* Section 9.11-233. Sending the letter does two things. First, if there are serious issues with the evidence, it may cause the grand jury to reject the indictment. Second, and much more common, it establishes a record you can later use to try to obtain early discovery of the witness transcripts from the grand jury, including when the prosecutor uses a case agent who will not testify at trial. The prosecutor's failure to present *Brady* you identified to them, in violation of DOJ policy, may give you a basis to obtain a grand jury transcript that otherwise is not discoverable as *Jencks* material under 18 U.S.C. Section 3500. That witness transcript, which the prosecutors thought would never see the light of day, might contain false testimony that you can use to build a broader attack on the prosecutorial misconduct in the case, including a motion for terminating sanctions under *United States v. Chapman,* 524 F.3d 1073, 1084 (9th Cir. 2004). Prosecutorial misconduct is most likely to occur where the government is convinced there is no oversight of their conduct, as in when the prosecutors use a case agent to present hearsay testimony to the grand jury. Aggressively pursuing that type of evidence will advance your defense.

6.3.2 Make a Specific Demand for Exculpatory Information in Writing

While prosecutors have an obligation to disclose exculpatory information even when defense counsel does not request it, sending a written request to the government can help downstream because it may help establish the materiality of information the prosecutors ultimately do not turn over. In *United States v. Bagley*, the Supreme Court emphasized that "the more specifically the defense requests certain evidence, thus putting the prosecutor on notice of its value, the more reasonable it is for the defense to assume from the nondisclosure that the evidence does not exist and to make pretrial and trial decisions on the basis of this assumption." 473 U.S. 667, 682–83 (1985).

Here is a non-exhaustive list of favorable information to consider including in your written request:

- Any information that tends to cast doubt on the defendant's guilt on any element of any count.
- Any physical evidence, testing, or reports that make guilt less likely.
- Any evidence suggesting that percipient witnesses failed to accurately identify the defendant.
- Any evidence that potentially links someone other than the defendant to the crime.

- Any information that tends to support your theory of defense—lack of motive, mere presence, public authority, good faith business practice, ratification, coercion, entrapment, selective prosecution, advice of counsel, and so on.
- Any information that shows that the defendant's constitutional rights were violated.
- Any information related to inconsistent statements by government witnesses regarding the facts at issue.
- Any information related to the mental or physical impairment of a witness.
- Any information related to witness bias, including any involvement in any potentially criminal activity, benefits received from the government, animosity toward the defendant, officers/agents feeding information to the witness during questioning, and so on.
- Any information related to a witness' dishonesty or prior criminal record.

6.3.3 Establish the Largest Possible "Prosecution Team"

To obtain all the exculpatory evidence that you are entitled to, you should seek to establish who qualifies as a member of the "prosecution team." The prosecutor is deemed to have knowledge of and access to anything in the possession, custody, or control of any federal agency participating in the investigation of the defendant. *United States v. Bryan*, 868 F.2d 1032, 1036 (9th Cir. 1989). You want to put every possible local, state, and federal investigating agency on the prosecution team so the prosecutors will have to go to each of those agencies and hunt for exculpatory information to give to you—and their failure to do so generates a potential issue for a motion to terminating sanctions or post-conviction relief.

Many prosecutors, particularly those in parallel investigations with regulatory agencies, will try to define the prosecution team as narrowly as possible. They will attempt to leave the SEC, IRS, and FDIC off the prosecution team because those agencies will have reams of documents on the case, including information that will help the defense. For FDIC matters, the prosecutors will also try to carve out the FDIC-R (FDIC as Receiver) by suggesting that this segment of the FDIC did not participate in the criminal investigation. However, the FDIC-R takes over the records of a failed bank and those docs will contain exculpatory information. The prosecutors want to avoid the burden of searching through these materials and also may be concerned about statements documented by the SEC, FDIC, and/or IRS attorneys who often evaluate evidence more objectively in the early phases of their review (or they point to other executives/board members who the prosecutors decide not to charge so the prosecutors can turn those individuals against your client). The case law, however, is good for criminal defendants on this issue because courts typically prohibit prosecutors from parking exculpatory evidence at an investigating agency to keep it outside the scope of the prosecutor's *Brady* review. *See United States v. Blanco*, 392 F.3d 382, 388 (9th Cir. 2004) (the prosecutor cannot undermine *Brady* by keeping exculpatory evidence out of the hands of the defense by claiming that the prosecutor does not have the material when an investigating agency does).

Here's one way to approach it.

Have the prosecutors confirm in writing to you that every investigating agency/police department involved in the investigation is on the prosecution team, including any regulatory agency. If the prosecutor resists, take it to the judge and cite the inevitable DOJ press release where the DOJ announced the indictment. That press release will always list any federal agency and local police department who helped the DOJ during the investigation. Push for compliance pursuant to the *Justice Manual* standards and file a motion early in the discovery process if the prosecutors refuse to search and produce *Brady* material from everyone who should be on the prosecution team.

If you need to brief who qualifies as a member of the prosecution team, here are some helpful cases from various circuits. Ninth Circuit law is very good on this point.

Second Circuit

United States v. Avellino, 136 F.3d 249, 255 (2nd Cir. 1998) (for *Brady* purposes, the individual prosecutor has the duty to learn of evidence favorable to the Defendant that might be in possession of "others acting on the government's behalf in the case, including the police").

Third Circuit

United States v. Reyeros, 537 F.3d 270, 281 (3rd Cir. 2008) ("a federal prosecutor is charged with knowledge of information possessed by other agents of the federal government when those agents are part of a 'prosecution team,' which includes federal personnel involved in the investigation as well as the prosecution of a case.").

United States v. Risha, 445 F.3d 298, 304 (3rd Cir. 2006) ("cross-jurisdiction constructive knowledge [factors] include: (1) whether the party with knowledge of the information is acting on the government's 'behalf' or is under its 'control'; (2) the extent to which state and federal government are part of a 'team' are participating in a 'joint investigation' or are sharing resources; and (3) whether the entity charged with constructive possession has 'ready access' to the evidence").

Fifth Circuit

United States v. Antone, 603 F.2d 566, 569 (5th Cir. 1979) (stating that the "'prosecution team' . . . includes both [federal] investigative and prosecutorial personnel").

Seventh Circuit

United States v. Walker, 746 F.3d 300, 306 (7th Cir. 2014) ("The government's duty to disclose favorable evidence extends beyond evidence in its immediate possession to evidence in the possession of other actors assisting the government in its investigation").

United States v. Mota, 685 F.3d 644, 648 (7th Cir. 2012) ("Prosecutors may not claim ignorance of *Brady* material. . . . Instead, prosecutors have 'a duty to learn of any favorable evidence known to the others acting on the government's behalf in the case, including the police'").

Ninth Circuit

United States v. Cutting, 3:14-cr-139 (N.D. Cal. Jan. 12, 2017), ECF No. 339 (holding that the FDIC-R was on the prosecution team where the FDIC-R participated in the investigation and voluntarily provided documents to the prosecutors).

United States v. Blanco, 392 F.3d 382, 388 (9th Cir. 2004) (the prosecutor cannot undermine *Brady* by keeping exculpatory evidence out of the hands of the defense by claiming that they don't have the material when in fact an investigating agency does).

United States v. Wood, 57 F.3d 733, 737 (9th Cir. 1995) (the prosecutor cannot tell the court that there is nothing more to disclose while the agency interested in the prosecution holds information helpful to the Defendant in its files).

United States v. Bryan, 868 F.2d 1032, 1036 (9th Cir. 1989) (the prosecutor is deemed to have knowledge of and access to anything in the possession, custody, or control of any federal agency participating in the same investigation of the Defendant).

Tenth Circuit

United States v. Beers, 189 F.3d 1297, 1304 (10th Cir. 1999) ("Information possessed by other branches of the federal government, including investigating officers, is typically imputed to the prosecutors of the case," but the same cannot be said of state agencies who might have had peripheral involvement related to some part of the investigation).

Smith v. Secretary of N.M. Dep't of Corrections, 50 F.3d 801, 824 (10th Cir. 1995) (*Brady* encompasses not only the individual prosecutor handling the case, but also extends to the prosecutor's entire office as well as law enforcement personnel and other arms of the state involved in investigative aspects of a particular criminal venture).

Eleventh Circuit

United States v. Naranjo, 634 F.3d 1198, 1212 (11th Cir. 2011) (a prosecutor must disclose anything in his or her own possession or that of the people over whom he or she has direct control; the prosecutor need not make an effort to find impeaching evidence in other jurisdictions, and state agents are not imputed for *Brady* purposes).

D.C. Circuit

United States v. Safavian, 233 F.R.D. 12, 14 (D.C. Cir. 2005) (those people who, for the purposes of *Brady*, are part of the prosecution team include not only the prosecutors or the investigators, but also "other branches of government 'closely aligned with the prosecution'" or "working on the prosecution's behalf"; in addition, "[t]his personal responsibility cannot be evaded by claiming lack of control over the files . . . of other executive branch agencies").

6.3.4 File a *Cutting* Motion to Force the Prosecutors to Specifically Identify Documents with *Brady/Giglio* Material

At the initial status conference in white collar prosecutions, expect the prosecutors to proudly claim that they have complied with all their *Brady* obligations because they have disclosed millions of documents to you and have not held anything back. That is a trap. The prosecutors typically have no idea how their electronic documents were collected, searched, stored, and produced. They fear that you will press them about their ignorance on these topics because doing so will expose gaps in their compliance with their *Brady* obligations. As a result, they are often desperate to equate *disclosure* of the material with *compliance* of their *Brady* obligations—an argument that has been rejected by the courts.

In response, consider filing a motion that requires the prosecutors to specifically identify all *Brady/Giglio* material by Bates number in their production set, which basically forces the prosecutor to specifically identify the *Brady* needles in the massive haystack of irrelevant discovery they just dumped on you.

The prosecutors may respond by claiming (a) the mere act of disclosure satisfies their *Brady* obligations, and (b) they cannot know what you will consider to be *Brady* so it is unfair to require them to identify specific documents in their production. Basically, the prosecutors want to avoid doing a page-by-page review of documents that will identify the *Brady* material in the massive pile of documents they produced. However, even their internal guidelines state that they must do an actual review of the materials for *Brady*. Prosecutors should not be allowed to dump a huge stack of documents on you they have not reviewed for *Brady* and claim that the data dump satisfies the requirement to actually review documents for *Brady*.

One key consideration is whether your client has the resources to review every page produced. Forcing the prosecutors to identify *Brady* by Bates number means the government must go back and read every page they produced. That may help the prosecutors refine their own chronology and core theory of their case. If so, and you have the ability and resources to review everything, you may not want to press the issue further. However, in most cases you should consider filing this motion because the prosecutors may not be able to comply with the order in a timely manner, leading to a motion for terminating sanctions for non-compliance with a court order, a related Fifth Amendment due process, or Sixth Amendment speedy trial challenge. This order also places intense pressure on the government to constantly update and revise their *Brady* disclosures as they continue to meet with witnesses in the final pre-trial prep phase. Getting those updates will help you during the crush of trial when the prosecutors dump more documents on you. And winning this motion drops a ticking time bomb into the prosecution camp because they will likely fail to identify some obvious *Brady* information, thereby violating the court's prior order.

Here are some cases that will defeat the prosecutor's "mere disclosure is sufficient" argument:

> *United States v. Cutting*, Order Re: Motions for Discovery, 3:14-cr-139 (N.D. Cal. Jan. 12, 2017), ECF No. 339 (ordering the DOJ to identify *Brady/Giglio* information by Bates number where the government had produced millions of pages of material and their electronic production was marred with technical problems).
>
> *United States v. Salyer*, 271 F.R.D. 148, 155 (E.D. Cal. 2010) (there are times when the duty to disclose exculpatory evidence may be unfulfilled by disclosing too much; at some point, disclosure, to be meaningful, requires identification as well).
>
> *United States v. Hsia*, 24 F. Supp. 2d 14, 29 (D.D.C. 1998), reversed in part on other grounds, 176 F.3d 517 (D.C. Cir. 1999) (the government cannot meet its *Brady* obligations by providing the Defendant with access to 600,000 documents and then claim that she should have been able to find the exculpatory information in the haystack).

Here are two cases that counter the prosecutor's "we don't know *Brady*" argument.

> *United States v. Blankenship*, 2015 WL 3687864 at *7 (S.D. W.Va. June 12, 2015) (the United States, having determined the nature of the charges and having knowledge of the evidence and witnesses it intends to produce, is in a far better position than the Defendant to know what evidence might be exculpatory and/or impeachment under *Brady*).
>
> *United States v. Salyer*, 271 F.R.D. 148, 155 (E.D. Cal. 2010) (government personnel able to segregate evidence that might establish guilt can also segregate evidence that runs counter to the charges).

6.4 *BRADY/GIGLIO* PROGENY: HELPFUL CASES

Here is a list of cases where courts reversed convictions due to *Brady* violations.

> ### *Supreme Court*
>
> *Brady v. Maryland,* 373 U.S. 83 (1963) (government failed to disclose that a Co-defendant had admitted to performing the actual murder at issue in a death penalty case).
>
> *Giglio v. United States,* 405 U.S. 150 (1972) (trial prosecutor argued in closing that witness received no promises that he would not be indicted but grand jury prosecutor had promised witness that he would not be indicted if he testified to grand jury regarding the Defendant's actions).
>
> *United States v. Agurs,* 427 U.S. 97 (1976) (prosecutor failed to disclose that murder victim had a prior criminal record, including assault with a deadly weapon and carrying a deadly weapon (both knives) when Agurs' raised self-defense on the homicide charge after struggling with the victim over a knife).
>
> *United States v. Bagley*, 473 U.S. 667 (1985) (prosecutor failed to disclose that two witnesses had agreement to receive financial rewards for their cooperation from ATF and both witnesses testified to the contrary at trial).

Kyles v. Whitley, 514 U.S. 419 (1995) (prosecutors failed to disclose: eyewitness testimony from six witnesses that points at another suspect; records relating to the questioning of the other suspect, including his inconsistent statements about the murder; a computer printout showing that the Defendant's car was not at the crime scene; and evidence linking the other suspect to other crimes in the same area).

Strickler v. Greene, 527 U.S. 263 (1999) (overwhelming evidence of guilt but the government failed to disclose impeachment evidence related to the sole eyewitness, including correspondence with police and notes from interviews that showed that the eyewitness lacked confidence in her trial testimony).

First Circuit

Flores-Rivera v. United States, 16 F.4th 963 (1st Cir. 2021) (vacating conviction where the government failed to produce impeachment evidence that would have raised substantial questions about the credibility of three key government witnesses because the government relied on the uncorroborated testimony of impeachable witnesses to connect the appellant to a key piece of evidence in the criminal case).

United States v. Aviles-Colon, 536 F.3d 1 (1st Cir. 2008) (conviction reversed where government withheld DEA reports that contained evidence that could have been used by the defense to undermine and impeach the testimony of key witnesses).

Norton v. Spencer, 351 F.3d 1 (1st Cir. 2003) (*Brady* violated when prosecutor failed to disclose that witness, who ultimately did not testify, claimed that he and other witness made up their stories of molestation).

United States v. Udechukwu, 11 F.3d 1101, 1105 (1st Cir. 1993) (government withheld evidence favorable to Defendant's coercion defense by refusing to disclose that person who allegedly coerced Defendant was a known drug trafficker and government target).

Second Circuit

United States v. Triumph Capital Group, Inc., 544 F.3d 149, 165 (2d Cir. 2008) (conviction reversed where prosecution failed to disclose agent's notes from cooperating witness's proffer session containing information favorable to the Defendant).

Mendez v. Artuz, 303 F.3d 411, 412–13 (2d Cir. 2002) (prosecutors withheld evidence that contradicted their motive theory and established that someone else had a motive).

Third Circuit

Simon v. Government of the Virgin Islands, 929 F.3d 118 (3d Cir. 2019) (remanded for evidentiary hearing on materiality of *Brady* violation where the government failed to disclose a prior agreement with the key witness in the case).

Dennis v. Secretary, Pennsylvania DOC, 834 F. 3d 263 (3d Cir. 2016) (federal habeas relief granted for state suppression of a receipt corroborating Defendant's alibi, an inconsistent statement by the state's key eyewitness, and documents indicating that another individual committed the murder).

Breakiron v. Horn, 642 F.3d 126, 133 (3d Cir. 2011) (conviction reversed where prosecutor failed to disclose that government witness sought a deal from prosecutors to testify against the Defendant, was a suspect in another investigation at the time and ultimately was not charged, and had been convicted of another crime).

United States v. Perdomo, 929 F.2d. 967 (3d Cir. 1991) (vacated denial of motion for acquittal and new trial where prosecutor failed to provide Defendant with prior criminal record of prosecution's main witness).

Fourth Circuit

McDowell v. Dixon, 858 F.2d 945, 949 (4th Cir. 1988) (*Brady* violation where prosecutor failed to disclose that initial witness statement had indicated perpetrator was a different race than Defendant).

Fifth Circuit

Floyd v. Vannoy, 894 F.3d 143, 162 (5th Cir.), cert. denied, 139 S. Ct. 573 (2018) (*Brady* violation where the prosecution suppressed notes that revealed the Defendant's fingerprints did not match those found in the scene of the crime).

United States v. Fisher, 106 F.3d 622, 634–35 (5th Cir. 1997) (*Brady* violation where government failed to disclose interview with individual not called as a witness that undermined the credibility of a key government witness).

Lindsey v. King, 769 F.2d 1034, 1040 (5th Cir. 1985) (forceful condemnation of prosecutor's conduct for failing to disclose that witness initially told police that he did not see the assailant's face when witness later testifies at trial that he saw the Defendant's face).

Sixth Circuit

United States v. Paulus, 952 F.3d 717, 721–22 (6th Cir. 2020) (conviction reversed in a criminal medical malpractice trial where the government withheld evidence showing that the doctor's 7 percent error rate in all the surgeries he performed fell within a normal range for surgeons).

Thomas v. Westbrooks, 849 F.3d 659, 661 (6th Cir. 2017) (conviction reversed where key witness in a murder trial was paid $750 by the FBI but denied receiving any benefits during trial testimony).

Robinson v. Mills, 592 F.3d 730, 738 (6th Cir. 2010) (*Brady* violation where prosecution suppressed evidence that prosecution's lead witness was a confidential informant).

Schledwitz v. United States, 169 F.3d 1003, 1015–16 (6th Cir. 1999) (*Brady* violation where government presented witness as disinterested expert but witness had been actively involved in the criminal investigation).

Seventh Circuit

Sims v. Hyatte, 914 F.3d 1078, 1089 (7th Cir. 2019) (prosecution hid information that they hypnotized the victim to enhance the victim's recollection before the victim testified as the sole eyewitness in an attempted murder trial).

Eighth Circuit

White v. Helling, 194 F.3d 937 (8th Cir. 1999) (*Brady* violation when prosecutor failed to disclose that witness had initially identified another person as performing key actions during the robbery).

Ninth Circuit

Browing v. Baker, 875 F.3d 444, 464 (9th Cir. 2017) (finding a *Brady* violation where the prosecution hid evidence showing shoeprints that did not match the Defendant's were found at the crime scene).

United States v. Olsen, 737 F.3d 625, 626–32 (9th Cir. 2013) (in dissent, Judge Kozinski states that "there is an epidemic of *Brady* violations abroad in the land. Only judges can put a stop to it"; Judge Kozinski then identifies dozens of reported cases in other districts with *Brady* issues).

United States v. Kohring, 637 F.3d 895, 906 (9th Cir. 2011) (reversing conviction where prosecution suppressed notes showing that witness had difficulty remembering the details of key events).

United States v. Gamez-Orduno, 235 F.3d 453, 461 (9th Cir. 2000) (*Brady* violated in pre-trial context by suppression of report that would have demonstrated the Defendants had Fourth Amendment standing to challenge search).

Tenth Circuit

LeBere v. Trani, 746 F. App'x 727, 729 (10th Cir. 2018) (conviction reversed where prosecutor failed to disclose an offer to reduce the sentence of a jailhouse informant for his testimony against the Defendant).

Trammell v. McKune, 485 F.3d 546, 551–52 (10th Cir. 2007) (*Brady* violation where prosecution failed to disclose gas station receipts that supported Defendant's trial theory linking another person to the crime).

Nuckols v. Gibson, 233 F.3d 1261, 1266–67 (10th Cir. 2000) (*Brady* violation where government failed to disclose allegations of theft and sleeping on the job regarding police officer whose testimony was crucial to admissibility of confession).

Eleventh Circuit

United States v. Spagnoulo, 960 F.2d 990 (11th Cir. 1992) (government withheld psychiatric report demonstrating that Defendant may have a disorder, which could have made an insanity defense viable and otherwise changed defense strategy).

D.C. Circuit

United States v. Robinson, 68 F.4th 1340 (D.C. Cir. 2023) (conviction reversed where the government failed to disclose three reports that demonstrated that the appellant was attempting to alert the authorities of the illegal activity he was accused of participating in).

United States v. Pasha, 797 F.3d 1122 (D.C. Cir. 2015) (conviction reversed where government failed to reveal eyewitness to defense where government witnesses had had severe credibility problems: they were not forthcoming, were under the influence of drugs at the time of the criminal events, kept changing their story, and received favorable plea bargains in exchange for testimony).

United States v. Johnson, 592 F.3d 164 (D.C. Cir. 2010) (conviction reversed where the government withheld evidence obtained from a government informant that the appellant's cousin—not the appellant—possessed the narcotics seized by law enforcement; since the prosecution offered two evidentiary theories to the jury—the first of which was that the drugs belonged to the appellant—the withheld evidence directly contradicted the government's first theory).

In re Sealed Case No. 99-3096 (Brady Obligations), 185 F.3d 887 (D.C. Cir. 1999) (conviction vacated and remanded for evidentiary hearing where the government suppressed impeachment evidence about the witness's relationship with the government, and whether there were agreements between the witness and the government in place that could give the witness a personal stake in the appellant's conviction, which could have helped the appellant by serving as affirmative evidence of his own innocence because it provided insight into motive).

United States v. Cuffie, 80 F.3d 514 (D.C. Cir. 1996) (conviction reversed where the government withheld information that a key government witness had perjured himself in another proceeding).

United States v. Smith, 77 F.3d 511 (D.C. Cir. 1996) (conviction reversed where the government failed to disclose impeachment evidence relating to one of its witnesses: in exchange for the witness's testimony, the prosecutor agreed to dismiss two pending felony cases against him, and the government also failed to disclose information pertaining to the witness's psychiatric history).

CHAPTER 7

Disqualifying an Unethical Prosecutor

7.1 GOVERNING STANDARDS

Defense counsel can pursue recusal either directly with the DOJ or by filing a motion with the court. If the matter is pre-indictment, it might make sense to consider seeking recusal directly with the DOJ. The request to recuse will typically be decided by the General Counsel's Office at the Executive Offices for Unites States Attorneys (EOUSA) in Washington, D.C. If the matter is post-indictment, defense counsel can file an appropriate motion with the court.

The *Justice Manual* contains guidance regarding when a prosecutor or an entire U.S. attorney's office should be recused from a matter. Section 3-1.140 states that EOUSA should enforce recusal where "a conflict of interest exists or there is an appearance of a loss of impartiality." This should not be a high hurdle in cases with significant prosecutorial misconduct, but getting EOUSA to enforce its own standards in an objective fashion can be challenging.

As a matter of process, consider sending a letter summarizing the basis for recusal to the leadership of the relevant USAO before contacting EOUSA. Doing so provides the supervisors at the local office the ability to investigate the issue and potentially agree with your position. EOUSA will reach out to the local office immediately after you contact them, so it may help your application to EOUSA by demonstrating that you have already raised your concerns with the local leadership. Historically, EOUSA had earned a reputation for being an objective decision-maker on challenges related to ethics violations by federal prosecutors. My recent experience with EOUSA, however, indicates a shift in philosophy. EOUSA's approach to ethical challenges is now similar to the DOJ's OPR: both offices typically analyze the facts through an unreasonably biased pro-AUSA viewpoint. OPR clears prosecutors accused of misconduct on about 99 percent of the complaints it receives. While EOUSA does not release similar statistics regarding its decisions on recusals, you will likely need to make an overwhelming presentation to gain any traction with them. EOUSA will likely decide all disputed facts in the AUSA's favor, so you will need to prove the misconduct based on undisputed facts and controlling case law. The local USAO will not provide a copy of their response to EOUSA to you, which means the local AUSA may misrepresent the facts to EOUSA to get a favorable ruling and you probably will not be given the opportunity to file any meaningful reply to EOUSA. Going to EOUSA only makes sense then where (a) you have very persuasive evidence, and (b) winning on recusal through EOUSA might result in no charges being filed after you expose the problematic prosecutor.

Another option is to wait to file a motion with the court after the matter gets charged (a pre-indictment vindictiveness motion filed with the duty judge is a very difficult motion to win). Motions to disqualify are not subject to bright-line legal standards; rather, they are largely governed by the district court's interpretation of the relevant state and national ethical rules. *United States v. Beaulieu*, 2018 WL 6390524 at *8 (E.D. La. Dec. 5, 2018). Courts typically do not mechanically apply these rules when reviewing a motion for disqualification. Instead, district courts regularly consider the social interests at stake in the litigation. *F.D.I.C. v. U.S. Fire Ins. Co.*, 50 F.3d 1304, 1314 (5th Cir. 1995). These interests include (a) the defendant's right to a fair trial free from improper prosecutorial motives; (b) the government's interest in retaining its chosen counsel; and (c) the court's interest in protecting the integrity of the proceedings and maintaining public confidence in the judicial system. *United States v. Vega*, 317 F. Supp. 2d 599, 603 (D.V.I. 2004).

Disqualification motions are seen as a "drastic measure," which should only be imposed when absolutely necessary. *United States v. Bolden*, 353 F.3d 870, 878 (10th Cir. 2003). Consequently, "the party seeking disqualification bears a heavy burden of demonstrating that disqualification is necessary." *Id.* Despite the exacting level of scrutiny applied to these motions, "federal courts are obliged to take measures against unethical conduct occurring in connection with any proceeding before it." *Woods v. Covington County Bank*, 537 F.2d 804, 810 (5th Cir. 1976). In addition, "United

States Attorneys are expected to adhere to the highest standards of professional behavior and to be worthy of public trust and confidence." *United States v. Johnston*, 690 F.2d 638, 643 (7th Cir. 1982). As such, federal courts have the "duty and responsibility" to remove prosecutors whose unethical actions threaten the integrity of the judicial system. *Kevlik v. Goldstein*, 724 F.2d 844, 847 (1st Cir. 1984).

There are three common fact patterns that justify recusal: (1) the prosecutor is a witness in the action and should be recused under the advocate-witness rule, (2) the prosecutor suffers from a conflict of interest, and (3) the prosecutor has committed significant misconduct.

7.2 THE ADVOCATE-WITNESS RULE

The DOJ expressly warns its prosecutors to avoid situations that might trigger their recusal from a case. Section 9-5.0002(B)(8) of the *Justice Manual* states that "whenever possible, prosecutors should not conduct an interview without an agent being present to avoid the risk of making themselves a witness to a statement and being disqualified from handling the case if the statement becomes an issue." So, there is no excuse for prosecutors who put themselves in position to be recused under the advocate-witness rule.

Nevertheless, aggressive and inexperienced prosecutors can improperly inject themselves into an investigation in several ways that could trigger a viable recusal motion. First, some prosecutors like to ride along with their agents and be physically present during the execution of a search warrant, arrest warrant, or inspection of a crime scene. As a result, they might witness something that could become disputed at trial—a statement made by the defendant or the location of a piece of evidence at the crime scene, for example. There typically is no need for the prosecutor to be present during this aspect of an investigation—this is agent work.

Second, some prosecutors engage directly with confidential informants and snitches during the pre-trial phase of the case—for example, communicating directly over email, text, or WhatsApp with a whistleblower in a white collar case. Those communications can be highly relevant at trial. I had a matter where the informant sent emails to a federal prosecutor explaining how he was going to commit crimes against the target of the prosecutor's investigation. The prosecutor failed to stop the informant from committing the crimes, and then also refused to investigate and prosecute the informant after it happened. The emails between the prosecutor and informant were central to seeking to recuse the prosecutor from the investigation.

Third, the prosecutor might have a conversation with a witness, subject, or target of the investigation, and do so without having an agent present to witness the conversation. For example, a prosecutor might speak with a witness during pre-trial preparations where the witness changes a key aspect of their prior statement to law enforcement.

The advocate-witness rule exists to remedy these issues. The rule is reflected in the ABA's Code of Professional Responsibility, which states as an ethical consideration: "The roles of an advocate and of a witness are inconsistent; the function of an advocate is to advance or argue the cause of another, while that of a witness is to state facts objectively." *United States v. Johnston*, 690 F.2d at 642 (7th Cir. 1982). While the advocate-witness rule generally provides that an attorney who acts as a witness should withdraw from trial participation, the rule does not require *per se* disqualification. *See United States v. Perlmutter*, 637 F. Supp. 1134 (S.D.N.Y. 1986); *United States v Maloney*, 241 F. Supp. 49 (W.D. Pa 1965). Defense counsel must make a strong showing of necessity to justify disqualification. *Perlmutter*, 637 F. Supp. at 1137. Pursuant to the advocate-witness rule, disqualification of government counsel has been sought when prosecutors are called to the stand to testify for the state, or when they use independent personal information to testify indirectly.

Defense counsel must demonstrate that the evidence is vital to their case, and that their inability to present the same or similar facts from another source creates a "compelling need" for the testimony from the prosecutor. *United States v. Watson*, 952 F.2d 982, 986 (8th Cir. 1991); *United States v. Roberson*, 897 F.2d 1092 (11th Cir. 1990); *United States. v. Schwartzbaum*, 527 F.2d 249 (2nd Cir. 1975). Thus, some courts will state that the defense has an obligation to exhaust other available sources of evidence before the defense can call a participating prosecutor as a witness. *United States v. West*, 680 F.2d 652, 654 (9th Cir. 1982).

Notwithstanding the requirement to show compelling need, "an accused's right to call relevant witnesses and to present a complete defense may not be abrogated for the sake of trial convenience, or for the purpose of protecting a United States Attorney from possible embarrassment, where the prosecutor possesses information vital to the defense." *Gajewski v. United States*, 321 F.2d 261, 268–69 (8th Cir. 1963). Furthermore, both the quality and quantity of alternate sources of evidence are proper subjects for comparison with that sought directly from the participating prosecutor.

Importantly, one circuit has held that the prosecutor need not be the *sole* source of the necessary evidence. *United States v. Prantil*, 764 F.2d 548, 552 (9th Cir. 1985). In *Prantil*, the Defendant established his compelling need for the prosecutor's testimony when the prosecutor was a witness to and a participant in the factual events that lead to the criminal charge. *Id.* at 552. There, the Defendant was charged with harboring a fugitive, while actively negotiating the fugitive's surrender with the prosecutor in question. *Id.* The Ninth Circuit held that because the prosecutor was likely to have been called as a witness regardless of his status as an advocate in the case the Defendant had shown adequate need. *Id.*

Disqualification might also be justified to preclude the prosecutors from subtly imparting to the jury their firsthand knowledge of the events without having to swear an oath or be subject to cross examination. *United States v. Sanchez*, 2004 WL 315266 at *2 (S.D.N.Y. 2004). Thus, it would be improper for a government attorney who has independent personal knowledge about facts that will be contested at the trial to act as prosecutor if the prosecutor uses that inside information to testify indirectly by implying to the jury that he or she has special knowledge or insight. *United States v. Hosford*, 782 F.2d 936, 939 (11th Cir. 1986). This rule is intended to prevent prosecutors from taking advantage of the natural tendency of jurors to believe in the honesty of government attorneys and to preclude the blurring of the "fundamental distinctions" between advocates and witnesses. *Prantil*, 764 F.2d at 554.

The advocate-witness rule was the basis for a disqualification in *United States v. Edwards*, where the Ninth Circuit held that the prosecutor's continued performance as prosecutor in the case following his discovery of critical piece of evidence in the middle of trial constituted a form of improper vouching that affected the fundamental fairness of the defendant's trial. 154 F.3d 915 (1998). By contrast, the Second Circuit has held that simply witnessing the defendant's prior statements or even eliciting those prior statements does not warrant disqualification of the prosecutor. *United States v. Regan*, 103 F.3d 1072, 1083 (2d Cir. 1997) (holding that "the mere fact that a prosecutor took part in grand jury proceedings in which a defendant presented false testimony should not bar that prosecutor from participating in a subsequent trial for perjury").

In sum, the advocate-witness rule favors but does not require the disqualification of prosecutors who the defense needs to call as witnesses or who attempt to use their personal knowledge of some specific fact in the case to vouch for the government's evidence. Be prepared to show why it is necessary to call the prosecutor to testify to the relevant issue and why testimony from some other witness will not be sufficient.

7.3 CONFLICTS OF INTEREST

"A prosecutor has the responsibility of a minister of justice and not simply that of an advocate." ABA Model Rules of Professional Conduct, Rule 3.8 Cmt. 1. Prosecutors must represent not their own interest but "the interest of society as a whole." *Ferri v. Ackerman*, 444 U.S. 193, 202–03 (1979). For this reason, the DOJ claims that it will hold its prosecutors to ethical standards regarding actual and apparent conflicts of interest. *See, e.g.*, *Justice Manual* § 1-4.100 and 5 C.F.R. §§ 2635.401–403, 501–503 (prohibiting prosecutors from working on matters where they have financial and personal conflicts). Moreover, it is a violation of federal law for prosecutors to "participat[e] personally and substantially" in a "judicial or other proceeding" in which they have a personal or pecuniary interest. 18 U.S.C. § 208.

The absence of an impartial and disinterested prosecutor violates a criminal defendant's due process right to a fundamentally fair trial, and therefore serves as a justification for the disqualification of the prosecutor. *State of N.J. v. Imperiale*, 773 F. Supp. 747, 750 (D.N.J. 1991). Prosecutors do not need to be entirely "neutral and detached." *Marshall v. Jerrico, Inc.*, 446 U.S. 238, 248 (1980). In an adversarial system, prosecutors are permitted to be zealous in their enforcement of the law. *Id.* However, "[a] scheme injecting a personal interest, financial or otherwise, into the enforcement process may bring irrelevant or impermissible factors into the prosecutorial decision and in some contexts raise serious constitutional questions." *Jerrico*, 446 U.S. at 249–50.

These recusal issues were litigated recently in *State of Georgia v. Donald J. Trump, et al.* In that matter, former President Donald Trump and eight co-defendants sought to dismiss the indictment and disqualify the Fulton County District Attorney's Office by asserting that the DA (Fani Willis) obtained a personal stake in the prosecution by financially benefitting from her romantic relationship with Special Assistant District Attorney (SADA) Nathan Wade. Order on Defs.' Mots. to Dismiss and Disqualify the Fulton Cty. Dist. Att'y at 1, *Georgia v. Donald J. Trump, et al.*, No. 23SC188947 (Ga. Super. Ct. Mar. 15, 2024), Docket No. BL-148. After holding an evidentiary hearing, the court found that DA Willis hired SADA Wade to lead the prosecution team and agreed to pay him $250 per hour to prosecute the case. *Id.* at 5-6. The court further found that DA Willis and SADA Wade traveled together to Aruba, Belize, Miami, Napa Valley and numerous other cities in the United States. *Id.* at 6-7. The court further found that SADA Wade paid the initial expense for some of these trips. *Id.* DA Willis and SADA Wade testified that DA Willis reimbursed SADA Wade in cash and/or covered a comparable, related expense. *Id.* Neither DA Willis nor SADA Wade produced documentation corroborating any reimbursement, which the court felt was "unusual" and "understandably concerning." *Id.* at 7.

In Georgia, a finding of an actual conflict results in automatic disqualification whereas a finding of an appearance of impropriety does not automatically demand disqualification. *Id.* at 13. Here, the court found that the Defendants had not established an actual conflict because "the evidence did not establish the District Attorney's receipt of a material financial benefit as a result of her decision to hire and engage in a romantic relationship with Wade." *Id.* at 7-8. The court stated that "without sufficient evidence that the District Attorney acquired a personal stake in the prosecution, or that her financial arrangements had any impact on the case, the Defendants' claims of actual conflict must be denied." *Id.* at 9. The court, however, did find that the Defendants had demonstrated an "appearance of impropriety," which is defined in Georgia as "conduct or status that would lead a reasonable person to think that the actor is behaving or will be inclined to behave inappropriately or wrongfully." *Id.* at 9, 11, 15. Unlike an actual conflict, the finding of an appearance of impropriety does not automatically demand disqualification. *Id.* at 13. Here, the court concluded that the defendants had met the appearance of impropriety standard for three reasons: (1) DA Willis "chose to continue supervising and paying Wade while maintaining such a [romantic] relationship," (2) DA Willis "further allowed the regular and loose exchange of money between them without any exact or verifiable measure of reconciliation," and (3) DA Willis' relationship with Wade "has only 'cemented' after these motions and 'is stronger than ever.'" *Id.* at 15. As a result, the court ordered that the State had two options: either the DA had to choose to step aside or SADA Wade had to withdraw. *Id.* at 17. SADA Wade ultimately decided to withdraw from the prosecution team. *Id.*

As another example, in *Ganger v. Peyton*, the Fourth Circuit reversed the Defendant's conviction where the prosecutor represented the accused's wife in a divorce proceeding at the same time that the prosecutor handled the criminal matter. 379 F.2d 709 (4th Cir. 1967). Because the prosecutor had a financial interest in whether the Defendant was convicted of assault, the court ruled that disqualification was warranted. *Id.* In addition to financial interests, the existence of a personal interest on the part of the prosecutor has been held to violate a defendant's due process rights.

Prosecutors who have an emotional interest in seeking a conviction have been disqualified on the grounds of prosecutorial vindictiveness. To establish *actual* vindictiveness, the defendant must demonstrate: "(1) the prosecutor acted with genuine animus toward the defendant, and (2) the defendant would not have been prosecuted but for that animus." *United States v. Wilson*, 262 F.3d 305, 314 (4th Cir. 2001).

To establish a *presumption* of vindictiveness, the test is "whether, as a practical matter, there is a realistic or reasonable likelihood of prosecutorial conduct that would not have occurred but for hostility or punitive animus towards the defendant because he exercised his specific legal right." *United States v. Raymer*, 941 F.2d 1031, 1042 (10th Cir. 1991). If the defendant satisfies this burden, the prosecution must "justify its prosecutorial decision based on legitimate, articulable, objective reasons." *United States v. Sarracino*, 340 F.3d 1148, 1177 (10th Cir. 2003). However, if the defendant does not carry its burden of establishing either element, the court does not need to address the prosecution's justification for its actions. *Id.* In *United States v. Wood*, the Tenth Circuit upheld a finding of prosecutorial vindictiveness when the prosecutor's decision to indict the Defendant on a bribery charge was "not based on any new evidence or change in circumstances, and it was made soon after the defendant exercised a legal right to the government's advantage." 36 F.3d 945 (10th Cir. 1994).

7.4 PROSECUTORIAL MISCONDUCT

Misconduct may serve as the basis for a number of potential remedies—including recusal of the prosecutor—when the actions of the prosecutor "so infect the [prosecution] with unfairness as to make the resulting conviction a denial of due process." *Darden v. Wainwright*, 477 U.S. 168 (1986); *Bond v. McQuiggan*, 506 F. App'x 493 (6th Cir. 2012).

A motion to disqualify on the grounds of prosecutorial misconduct requires that the defendant prove both misconduct and prejudice. The court applies a two-part inquiry: (1) did the prosecutor engage in misconduct; and, if yes, (2) was the misconduct flagrant—that is, was it sufficiently prejudicial to deny the defendant a fair trial. *United States v. Samples*, 456 F.3d 875, 880 (8th Cir. 2006). Factors a court will consider in deciding flagrancy include whether the prosecutor's conduct actually misled the jury or prejudiced the accused; whether the misconduct was an isolated event or the result of a pattern of conduct; whether the misconduct was deliberate or accidental; and the strength of the government's evidence against the defendant.

In *United States v Omni International Corp.*, a prosecution on charges of tax evasion and related offenses, the court disqualified the prosecutor after finding "extensive and pervasive instances of false and incorrect testimony" given by the investigators and by the prosecutor himself. 634 F. Supp. 1414 (D. Md. 1986). The court also expressed its shock at the government investigators' deliberate attempt to circumvent the attorney-client privilege by interviewing the former secretary of the corporate defendant's lawyer. *Id.* However, in *United States v. Canino*, the Seventh Circuit held that similar improper conduct by the prosecutor, although inappropriate, did not deprive the defendants of a fair trial and had not required the granting of a subsequently filed motion to disqualify the prosecutor. 949 F.2d 928 (7th Cir. 1991). In this case, a prosecutor, angered at being called a liar in the presence of the jury by a defense attorney, verbally assaulted defense counsel. *Id.* While finding that the prosecutor's conduct was inappropriate, the court held that the defendant experienced no prejudice; thus, the court denied the defendant's motion to disqualify. *Id.*

7.5 RECUSING UNETHICAL PROSECUTORS: HELPFUL CASES

Here is a summary of helpful cases on recusing unethical prosecutors:

First Circuit

United States v. Candelario-Santana, 929 F. Supp. 2d 24 (D.P.R. 2013) (lead prosecutor in a capital murder prosecution was disqualified when she misused her subpoena power and improperly issued 107 Rule 17 subpoenas requiring witnesses to appear at the USAO for trial preparation).

United States v. Horn, 811 F. Supp. 739 (D.N.H. 1992), rev'd in part, 29 F.3d 754 (1st Cir. 1994) (lead prosecutor removed from a case involving conspiracy, bank fraud, and false statements when she reviewed, made copies of, and used documents for witness preparation that were pending a motion to seal and provided insight into defense tactics, strategy, and problems).

Fourth Circuit

United States v. Schell, 775 F.2d 559 (4th Cir. 1985) (convictions reversed and indictment dismissed where federal prosecutor had previously represented two of the Defendants in grand jury appearances on the same case).

Ganger v. Peyton, 379 F.2d 709 (4th Cir. 1967) (habeas corpus granted where prosecuting attorney's prosecution of Defendant in a criminal case while simultaneously representing Defendant's wife in a divorce proceeding rendered conviction constitutionally invalid for violating Due Process Clause).

Fifth Circuit

United States ex rel. S.E.C. v. Carter, 907 F.2d 484 (5th Cir. 1990) (circuit court, acting *sua sponte*, reversed appellants' contempt convictions finding plain error in the appointment of SEC attorneys as special prosecutors given their involvement in an underlying civil proceeding against the Defendants related to the same matter).

United States v. Treadway, 445 F. Supp. 959 (N.D. Tex. 1978) (district court quashes indictment where the prosecutor's continued presence in the grand jury room after also testifying as a witness was unauthorized under Rule 6(d) of the Federal Rules of Criminal Procedure).

Eighth Circuit

Wilkins v. Bowersox, 933 F. Supp. 1496 (W.D. Mo. 1996), aff'd, 145 F.3d 1006 (8th Cir. 1998) (habeas relief granted where Defendant facing the death penalty had previously been represented on another criminal matter by the prosecutor, who had gained insight into the Defendant's mental condition through the prior representation).

Ninth Circuit

United States v. Edwards, 154 F.3d 915 (9th Cir. 1998) (conviction reversed where prosecutor's discovery of key piece of evidence during trial constituted a form of improper vouching that affected the fundamental fairness of the Defendant's trial).

United States v. Mapelli, 971 F.2d 284 (9th Cir. 1992) (conviction reversed where prosecutors had been exposed to Defendant's immunized testimony in a previous proceeding).

United States v. Prantil, 764 F.2d 548 (9th Cir. 1985) (conviction reversed where trial court refused to recuse prosecutor who had direct interactions with the Defendant on the substance of the underlying charges in the indictment).

Eleventh Circuit

United States v. Spiker, 649 F. App'x 770 (11th Cir. 2016) (perjury conviction reversed on plain error review where prosecutor failed to recuse himself after Defendant attempted to kill the prosecutor and was separately charged for that conduct).

Walker v. Davis, 840 F.2d 834 (11th Cir. 1988) (conviction reversed where prosecutor testified at trial regarding a conversation with the Defendant in which the prosecutor contended that the Defendant confessed to him, and the prosecutor failed to recuse himself and have a colleague conduct the trial given his status as a witness).

CHAPTER 8

Speedy Trial

The Sixth Amendment states that "in all criminal prosecutions, the accused shall enjoy the right to a speedy and public trial." In our federal system, that means that the defendant can force the government to go to trial as soon as seventy days after indictment. 18 U.S.C. § 3161(c)(1).

Speedy trial issues arise in the prosecutorial misconduct context when the government delays bringing charges against your client to gain a tactical advantage at trial. This can happen when the government files a fairly vanilla indictment and then waits for years to spring a much more robust and wide-ranging superseding indictment—typically right on the eve of trial.

As an example, I had a case where the prosecutors waited three years to supersede a bank fraud indictment until the evening before the final pre-trial status conference, even though they possessed the underlying evidence related to the new charges for more than seven years. The prosecutors also intentionally waited to serve the superseding indictment until defense counsel were sitting in the courtroom with our clients the following morning. The prosecutors snickered at each other as they watched us looking at our cell phones struggling to read the greatly expanded indictment as the judge was taking the bench. Funny. But the prosecutors apparently had no idea that the Supreme Court frowns on this kind of thing and the remedy for violating the Speedy Trial Clause is dismissal *with prejudice.*

8.1 SIXTH AMENDMENT BASICS

The Sixth Amendment guarantees the accused in all criminal prosecutions the right to a speedy trial. *Doggett v. United States*, 505 U.S. 647, 651 (1992). The right is "fundamental" and exists not just to ensure "that all accused persons be treated according to decent and fair procedures" but also because "there is a societal interest in providing a speedy trial." *Barker v. Wingo*, 407 U.S. 515, 519 (1972) (citation omitted).

The Sixth Amendment speedy trial guarantee attaches upon formal indictment. *United States v. Marion*, 404 U.S. 307, 320 (1971). Like being arrested and held to answer, indictment is a constitutionally significant public act because it can disrupt liberty, drain financial resources, curtail associations, and create anxiety. *Id.* Along with prejudice to the accused's defense, these are some other "major evils" the constitution protects against. *Id.*

The Supreme Court has repeatedly confirmed that dismissal with prejudice is "the only possible remedy" for a Speedy Trial Clause violation. *Barker*, 407 U.S. at 522; *Strunk v. United States*, 412 U.S. 434, 438–40 (1973) (reversing an appellate court's attempt to impose a "less drastic" remedy it deemed more "appropriate" for the speedy trial violation in that case and confirming that dismissal with prejudice was "the only possible remedy").

8.2 *BARKER V. WINGO*: APPLYING THE SUPREME COURT'S FOUR-FACTOR TEST

The constitutional speedy trial analysis is governed by *Barker*'s four-factor balancing test. *Doggett v. United States*, 505 U.S. 647, 651 (1992). It evaluates: (1) the length of the delay; (2) whether the government or defendant is more to blame for that delay; (3) whether defendant asserted his speedy trial right in due course; and (4) prejudice to the defendant. *Id.* None of these factors is necessary or sufficient, individually, to establish a Sixth Amendment violation; they are considered together. *United States v. Mendoza*, 530 F.3d 758, 762 (9th Cir. 2008).

The first factor, length of delay, is measured from the time of indictment to the time of trial. *Mendoza*, 530 F.3d at 762. In cases involving superseding indictments, courts still tally speedy trial delay from the date of the first indictment, not the date of the superseding indictment. *United States v. Black*, 918 F.3d 243, 259–60 (2d Cir. 2019) (collecting cases); *United States v. Battis*, 589 F.3d 673, 679 & n.5 (3d Cir. 2009) (same). Importantly, when delay between the first indictment and trial exceeds one year, the delay is deemed "presumptively prejudicial" and triggers inquiry into *Barker*'s other three factors. *Black*, 918 F.3d at 254–55.

The second *Barker* factor—the reason for the delay—is "the focal inquiry" in the analysis. *United States v. Alexander*, 817 F.3d 1178, 1182. Winning on *Barker*'s second factor is "the 'flag all litigants seek to capture.'" *United States v. Velazquez*, 749 F.3d 161, 175 (3d Cir. 2014) (quoting *United States v. Loud Hawk*, 474 U.S. 302, 315 (1986)). Because the government has an affirmative duty to diligently bring a defendant to trial, the government bears the burden to justify pretrial delay. *McNeely v. Blanas*, 336 F.3d 822, 826–27 (9th Cir. 2003).

Notably, courts assign different weights to the various reasons for delay. *Barker*, 407 U.S. at 531. Courts "consider whether the delay was deliberate, neutral, or valid." *Black*, 918 F.3d at 260; *Alexander*, 817 F.3d at 1182; *United States v. Aguirre*, 994 F.2d 1454, 1456 (9th Cir. 1993). Defense counsel should press for a judicial finding of deliberate delay because an intentional delay to gain an advantage at trial provides the defendant "an overwhelming case for dismissal." *Doggett*, 505 U.S. at 656–57; *Aguirre*, 994 F.2d at 1456.

While not weighed as heavily as deliberate delay, a more neutral reason like negligence still amounts to an unacceptable reason for delay and weighs against the government. *Doggett*, 505 U.S. at 656–57.

Barker's third factor asks whether defendant asserted his rights "in due course." *Doggett*, 505 U.S at 651. This factor tends to be a push between the parties because a defendant's "prompt assertion of his speedy trial right weighs neither for nor against him." *United States v. Gregory*, 322 F.3d 1157, 1162 (9th Cir. 2003). In addition, agreeing to a continuance of the trial date does not foreclose a defendant from being able to assert a Sixth Amendment challenge. *United States v. Ramirez-Cortez*, 213 F.3d 1149, 1156 (9th Cir. 2000).

Barker's final factor measures the prejudice caused by the delay. Courts primarily focus on three harms caused by delay: "oppressive pretrial incarceration," the accused's "anxiety and concern," and "the possibility that the defense will be impaired." *Barker*, 407 U.S. at 532. The last is most serious "because the inability of a defendant to adequately to prepare his case skews the fairness of the entire system." *Id.* Furthermore, since "excessive delay presumptively compromises the reliability of a trial in ways that neither party can prove, or for that matter identify," prejudice is presumed when the delay is attributable to the government. *Doggett*, 505 U.S. at 655–56;

see Aguirre, 994 F.2d at 1456 ("[W]hether the defendant must show actual prejudice depends on whether . . . he or the government . . . is responsible for the delay"). This prejudice intensifies over time, and its weight depends on the length of delay and reason behind it (whether intentional or negligent delay). *Alexander*, 817 F.3d at 1182; *Mendoza*, 530 F.3d at 763. The government bears the burden to rebut presumptive prejudice—that is, affirmatively prove the delay "left the defendant's ability to defend himself unimpaired." *Mendoza*, 530 F.3d at 765 (citation omitted). This is a "difficult" task requiring proof of "a negative—the absence of any prejudice to a defense from the passage of years." *Velazquez*, 749 F.3d at 175.

8.3 *BARKER*'S PROGENY: HELPFUL CASES

Here is a summary of helpful cases regarding trial delays and the Sixth Amendment:

First Circuit

United States v. Handa, 892 F.3d 95 (1st Cir. 2018) (affirming dismissal of the added charge in the superseding indictment where the government waited six and a half years to bring an additional charge that could have been brought at the time of the initial charges).

Second Circuit

United States v. Black, 918 F.3d 243 (2d Cir. 2019) (affirming dismissal of the superseding indictment brought against three Defendants on the eve of their trial where Defendants had been held in pre-trial detention for over five years).

United States v. Pennick, 713 Fed. App'x 33 (2d Cir. 2017) (affirming dismissal of two counts of indictment due to extraordinary delay of over six years and government's failure to move the case to trial).

United States v. Velazquez, 749 F.3d 161 (2d Cir. 2014) (reversing conviction and ordering dismissal with prejudice where there was a nearly seven-year delay between the superseding indictment and scheduled trial date that was caused by the government's failure to diligently search for the Defendant).

Third Circuit

Kennedy v. Superintendent Dallas SCI, 50 F.4th 377 (3d Cir. 2022) (reversing denial of writ of habeas corpus where there was a delay of fifty months between date of arrest and commencement of jury selection where the defense was impaired by the delay based on inability to cross-examine a government witness and the police did not take a contemporaneous statement from a second witness such that her testimony was at risk of being "coached" by exposure to another witness's statement).

Fifth Circuit

United States v. Cardona, 302 F.3d 494 (5th Cir. 2002) (reversing conviction where government waited over five years to execute the arrest warrant where the Defendant had been openly living in New York and Connecticut and had multiple contacts with law enforcement during the five-year period without ever being informed of the warrant against him).

Sixth Circuit

United States v. Heshelman, 521 Fed. App'x 501 (6th Cir. 2013) (conviction reversed due to thirty-nine-month delay between indictment and trial violated the Defendants' Sixth Amendment speedy trial right by failing to pursue extradition of one of the Defendants).

United States v. Ferreira, 665 F.3d 701 (6th Cir. 2011) (conviction reversed where the government was solely responsible for a delay of thirty-five months and the Defendant properly and repeatedly asserted his right to a speedy trial).

Maples v. Stegall, 427 F.3d 1020 (6th Cir. 2005) (reversing denial of habeas corpus relief where there was a delay of twenty-five months, the Defendant was subjected to pretrial incarceration twice, suffered "anxiety and concern," and was prejudiced by the unavailability of a witness and of his Co-defendant).

Ninth Circuit

United States v. Myers, 930 F.3d 1113 (9th Cir. 2019) (finding speedy trial violation where federal prosecutors elected to allow a concurrent state matter to proceed first).

Tenth Circuit

United States v. Seltzer, 595 F.3d 1170 (10th Cir. 2010) (affirmed dismissal of indictment after a two-year delay where Defendant twice asserted his speedy trial rights, had been remanded into pre-trial detention, and federal prosecutors elected to allow a concurrent state matter to proceed first).

8.4 FIFTH AMENDMENT DUE PROCESS CHALLENGES RE PRE-TRIAL DELAY

Along with a Sixth Amendment objection, consider also raising a Fifth Amendment due process objection regarding any excessive pre-trial delay. The most significant difference is that a Fifth Amendment objection can include pre-indictment delay. Unlike the Sixth Amendment, which attaches when the defendant is arrested or charged, the Fifth Amendment attaches from the start of the government's investigation. *Compare Stoner v. Graddick*, 751 F.2d 1535 (11th Cir. 1985) ("[T]he Speedy Trial Clause is inapplicable where the delay concerns a period of time prior to indictment, information, or arrest") and *United States v. Marion*, 404 U.S. 307, 324 (1971) ("[T]he Due Process Clause of the Fifth Amendment would require dismissal of the indictment if it were shown at trial that the pre-indictment delay caused substantial prejudice to appellees' rights to a fair trial and that the delay was an intentional device to gain tactical advantage over the accused").

There are a few cases where courts have granted relief on due process grounds where the government has delayed the resolution of a criminal matter. *See United States v. Minkkinen*, No. 2:22-CR-00163, 2023 WL 4191261 (S.D.W. Va. Jun. 9, 2023) (court dismisses ten counts of a fourteen count indictment where six-year delay between the beginning of the investigation and the indictment violated Defendants' due process rights where two potential defense witnesses died and the government's case was based on circumstantial evidence); *United States v. Mills*, 704 F.2d 1553, 1557 (11th Cir. 1983) (death of key witness); *United States v. Lindstrom*, 698 F.2d 1154, 1158 (11th Cir. 1983) (death of two witnesses); *United States v. Shaw*, 555 F.2d 1295, 1298–99 (5th Cir.1977) (death of witness, failure of memory, and deteriorating health and financial condition of defendant). In state cases, this issue often arises in homicide investigations where the government holds off on filing charges hoping that it can identify additional evidence against a target but ultimately moves forward on the exact same evidentiary record—sometimes decades after the events at issue.

8.5 MLAT ABUSES TO IMPROPERLY EXTEND THE LIMITATIONS PERIOD

Another area of possible misconduct relates to prosecutors seeking to intentionally toll the statute of limitations because they need more time to complete their investigation. If prosecutors seek documentary evidence in a foreign country pursuant to a Mutual Legal Assistance Treaty (MLAT) request, the limitations period is typically tolled. *See* 18 U.S.C. § 3292(a)(1) (allowing the government to apply *ex parte* for suspension of the statute of limitations when it seeks evidence in a foreign country). However, prosecutors better have a good faith basis for issuing MLAT requests as the limitations are about to expire because courts have recognized the potential for abuse and will agree to dismiss the indictment for violating the limitations period. *See United States v. Trainor*, 376 F.3d 1325 (11th Cir. 2004) (dismissing indictment where the government failed to meet the minimum requirements under Section 3292 because it submitted an unsworn application accompanied only by a copy of an evidentiary request sent to Switzerland); *United States v. Meador*, 18 F.3d 986 (5th Cir. 1998) (affirming dismissal of indictment where government filed MLAT request with Germany only two months before the expiration of the limitations period and the German government took "final action" on the request shortly after receiving it).

CHAPTER 9

Plea Negotiations

Prosecutorial misconduct in plea negotiations occurs in three fact patterns: where the prosecutor (1) fails to disclose evidence of actual innocence to defense counsel, (2) insists on a coercive "release-dismissal" agreement where the government forces the defendant to waive a viable civil claim against the government, and (3) improperly imposes an appellate waiver on a defendant. Challenging plea agreements in all three scenarios typically hinges on an assessment of the coercive nature of the government's actions—tactics that would demonstrate that the defendant did not enter the plea agreement knowingly or voluntarily. The Supreme Court has stated that a plea can be unwound if it was not entered into knowingly or voluntarily. *Brady v. United States*, 397 U.S. 742, 748 (1970) (in holding that the defendant's plea was knowing and voluntary, the Court recognized that "waivers of constitutional rights not only must be voluntary but must be knowing, intelligent acts done with sufficient awareness of the relevant circumstances and likely consequences").

9.1 *BRADY* OBLIGATIONS IN PLEA NEGOTIATIONS

The issue involving the obligation to disclose exculpatory information during plea negotiations centers on the difference between evidence regarding actual innocence (*Brady* information) and evidence that merely relates to the credibility of government witnesses (*Giglio* information). The prosecutor is required to disclose the former during plea negotiations in some jurisdictions, but it is not required to disclose the latter in any jurisdiction. In *United States v. Ruiz*, the Supreme Court made clear that prosecutors do not need to disclose *Giglio* information during plea negotiations. 536 U.S. 622, 629 (2002) ("We must decide whether the Constitution requires that pre-guilty plea disclosure of impeachment information. We conclude that it does not."). The Supreme Court stated that impeachment information was not "critical information of which the defendant must always be aware prior to pleading guilty." *Id.* at 630. The Court, however, only resolved the question of whether the government must make pre-plea disclosure of impeachment evidence. It did not explicitly address whether the withholding of exculpatory evidence of actual innocence (*Brady* evidence) during the pretrial plea bargaining process would violate a defendant's constitutional rights. *See id.* at 630–33.

As to *Brady* information, there is a split in the circuits regarding whether a prosecutor must disclose evidence of actual innocence during plea negotiations. The Ninth Circuit continues to apply pre-*Ruiz* case law in finding that a defendant is entitled to exculpatory *Brady* material during plea negotiations. *Smith v. Baldwin*, 510 F.3d 1127, 1148 (9th Cir. 2007) ("When the accused enters a plea rather than proceeding to trial, however, materiality is determined by 'whether there is a reasonable probability that but for the failure to disclose the *Brady* material, the defendant would have refused to plead and would have gone to trial.'") (quoting *Sanchez v. United States*, 50 F.3d 1448, 1454 (9th Cir. 1995)).

The Seventh and Tenth Circuits have also recognized the distinction noted by the Supreme Court in *Ruiz* between impeachment and exculpatory evidence in the guilty plea context. *United States v. Ohiri*, 133 F. App'x 555, 556 (10th Cir. 2005) (explaining that the "government should have disclosed all known exculpatory information at least by that point in the proceedings" prior to the defendant's guilty plea entered on the first day of jury selection); *McCann v. Mangialardi*, 337 F.3d 782, 788 (7th Cir. 2003) ("*Ruiz* indicates a significant distinction between impeachment information and exculpatory evidence of actual innocence. Given this distinction, it is highly likely that the Supreme Court would find a violation of the Due Process Clause if prosecutors or other relevant government actors have knowledge of a criminal defendant's factual innocence but fail to disclose such information to a defendant before he enters into a guilty plea.").

By contrast, the First, Second, Fourth, and Fifth Circuits have all expressed doubts about a prosecutor's obligation to disclose exculpatory *Brady* material that the prosecution team possesses before the defendant enters a guilty plea. *See Alvarez v. City of Brownsville*, 904 F.3d 382, 394 (5th Cir. 2018), cert. denied sub nom. *Alvarez v. City of Brownsville, Tex.*, 139 S. Ct. 2690, 204 L. Ed. 2d 1103 (2019) ("The en banc court . . . abstains from expanding the *Brady* right to the pretrial plea bargaining context for Alvarez"); *United States v. Mathur*, 624 F.3d 498, 507 (1st Cir. 2010) ("*Ruiz* teaches that *Brady* does not protect against the possible prejudice that may ensure from the loss of an opportunity to plea-bargain with complete knowledge of all relevant facts . . . . [W]hen a defendant chooses to admit his guilt, *Brady* concerns subside"); *Friedman v. Rehal*, 618 F.3d 142, 154 (2d Cir. 2010) (stating that the "Supreme Court has consistently treated exculpatory and impeachment evidence in the same way for the purpose of defining the obligation of a prosecutor to provide *Brady* material prior to trial, and the reasoning underlying *Ruiz* could support a similar ruling for a prosecutor's obligations prior to a guilty plea"); *United States v. Moussaoui*, 591 F.3d 263, 285 (4th Cir. 2010) ("The *Brady* right . . . is a trial right" that "exists to preserve the fairness of a trial verdict and to minimize the chance that an innocent person would be found guilty").

Given the circuit court split, it makes sense to press prosecutors in all jurisdictions to disclose evidence of actual innocence before concluding any plea negotiations. Doing so will help preserve the issue for any collateral attack if the Supreme Court ultimately resolves the issue in favor of disclosure. If the prosecutors push back on your request, preserve your request on the record with the court to put your client in the best possible position on any potential future collateral attack.

In addition, point the prosecutors to Rule 5(f)(1) of the *Federal Rules of Criminal Procedure* and the *Justice Manual*. Both demonstrate that prosecutors should not sandbag defendants into pleading guilty by sitting on evidence of actual innocence. Enacted in 2020, Rule 5(f)(1) requires that the district court, at the defendant's initial appearance, issue an oral and written order that confirms the prosecutor's disclosure obligations under *Brady*—a clear signal that prosecutors should turn over any *Brady* in their possession immediately after the defendant's first appearance in court. Likewise, the *Justice Manual* requires that prosecutors disclose *Brady* information "promptly after discovery." *See* Section 9-5.001(D)(1) ("Exculpatory information must be disclosed reasonably promptly after it is discovered") and the David Ogden memo, CRM-165 "Guidance for Prosecutors Regarding Criminal Discovery" (Jan. 4, 2010) ("Providing broad and early discovery often promotes the truth-seeking mission of the Department and fosters a speedy resolution of many cases . . . . Prosecutors are encouraged to provide broad and early discovery consistent with any countervailing considerations . . . . Exculpatory information, regardless of whether the information is memorialized, must be disclosed to the defendant reasonably promptly after discovery."). Neither Rule 5(f)(1) nor the *Justice Manual* can be interpreted to suggest that prosecutors can withhold evidence of actual innocence during plea negotiations.

9.2 IMPROPER "RELEASE-DISMISSAL" PLEA AGREEMENTS

In response to situations involving severe misconduct by law enforcement, some prosecutors will insist that the defendant release the agents/detective/prosecutors from any civil claims regarding their misconduct against the target. For example, if the police use excessive force and break a defendant's arm when they arrest him for driving under the influence, some prosecutors will condition any plea agreement to the DUI charge on the defendant also agreeing to waive any civil claims the defendant might bring against the officers who broke his arm. The release of the civil claim in exchange for a potential benefit in the criminal case exerts a degree of coercion on the defendant to waive a right that might be very valuable.

This issue can arise at two stages of the case: during plea negotiations or later, when the defendant wants to pursue the civil claims waived in a previously executed release-dismissal agreement. In the first scenario, during actual plea negotiations, defense counsel can use the cases cited below to demonstrate that the government should offer the same plea deal in the criminal case but without the requirement that the defendant waive any civil claims. If the prosecutor pushes back, you may have obtained even more ammunition to take to the prosecutor's supervisor to request either recusal of the line prosecutor or some other relief because the prosecutor will likely have expressly confirmed to you that the government insists on enhancing the penalty extracted from the defendant unless the defendant waives his or her right to pursue civil claims against the government. In the second scenario, where the defendant pleads guilty but subsequently files a civil suit against the bad actors and seeks to void the release of the civil claim, the court will analyze whether the release of the civil claim was improperly coerced such that the defendant can still bring that civil claim.

The Supreme Court has held that the enforceability of a release-dismissal agreement is governed by a three-factor test. If the government wants to enforce a release-dismissal agreement, it must show that the agreement was (1) voluntary, (2) there was no evidence of prosecutorial misconduct, and (3) that enforcement of the agreement would not violate the public interest. *Town of Newton v. Rumery*, 480 U.S. 386, 398 (1987).

In *Rumery*, a New Hampshire grand jury indicted Rumery's friend, Champy, for sexual assault. Rumery learned about the charges and contacted a mutual friend to determine if the allegations were true. It turned out that the mutual friend was the alleged victim who reported Champy. Shortly after contacting the mutual friend, Rumery allegedly threatened her that if she went forward with the case, she might end up dead. The alleged threat led to Rumery being charged with witness tampering. The case against Rumery was eventually dismissed after Rumery's defense counsel proposed an agreement to have the charges dropped in exchange for Rumery foregoing any civil claims against the police, prosecutor, and witness. Ten months after the parties signed the agreement, Rumery had a change of heart and sued the town and the officers under 42 U.S.C. Section 1983. *Id.* at 389–91. The town and officers filed a motion to dismiss the Section 1983 claim because Rumery had executed the release-dismissal agreement. *Id.* at 391. The district court determined the agreement was valid and dismissed Rumery's suit. *Id.*

On appeal, the First Circuit reversed and adopted a *per se* rule invalidating all release-dismissal agreements. *Id.* The Supreme Court, in a plurality decision, rejected the First Circuit's *per se* rule, stating that not all release-dismissal agreements are *per se* invalid because they "may further legitimate prosecutorial and public interests." *Id.* at 397. But at the same time, the Supreme Court also recognized that "some release-dismissal agreements may not be the product of an informed and voluntary decision." *Id.* at 393. As a result, the Supreme Court enacted its three-factor test.

As to the first factor, voluntariness, the Supreme Court noted that "[w]e have no occasion in this case to determine whether an inquiry into voluntariness alone is sufficient to determine the enforceability of release-dismissal agreements." *Rumery*, 480 U.S. at 398 n.10. This point was amplified by an *en banc* panel in the Third Circuit in *Cain v. Darby Borough*, where the court stated "mere voluntariness is not enough to support enforcement of a release-dismissal agreement. The party seeking to enforce the agreement must show that upon balance the public interest favors enforcement." 7 F.3d 377, 381 (3rd Cir. 1993); *see also Coughlen v. Coots*, 5 F.3d 970 (6th Cir. 1993) (a voluntary agreement is not enough: there must also be no evidence of prosecutorial misconduct and that enforcement of the agreement would not adversely affect relevant public interests).

When determining voluntariness, a court will look to the following factors:

- Sophistication of the criminal defendant;
- Whether the defendant was in custody when he made the agreement;
- Whether the defendant was represented by counsel who drafted the agreement;
- Whether the defendant had ample time to consider the agreement before signing it;
- The nature of the criminal charges—the greater the charge, the greater the coercive effect; and
- Whether the agreement was formed under judicial supervision. *Patterson v. City of Akron, Ohio*, 619 Fed. App'x 462, 470 (6th Cir. 2015) (citing *Rumery*, 480 U.S. at 394, 401–02).

Regarding the second factor—the presence of prosecutorial misconduct—courts have recognized that prosecutorial overreach may occur when the prosecutor is influenced by pending civil claims to handle the criminal charges differently than otherwise. *Berry v. Peterson*, 887 F.2d 635, 640 (5th Cir. 1989). Specifically, courts will look at whether the prosecutor "inflated, mishandled, or trumped up" the charges pending against the accused to coerce the waiver of the civil claims. *Id.* In addition, a court must "consider whether 'the prosecutor had an independent, legitimate reason to make this [release-dismissal] agreement directly related to his prosecutorial responsibilities.'" *Patterson*, 619 Fed. App'x at 475 (quoting *Rumery*, 480 U.S. at 398). The purpose of having a legitimate reason is to ensure "that the prosecutor acts consistent with his [or her] duties to uniformly enforce the criminal law, rather than as the agent for the private interests of potential [civil] defendants." *Id.* (quotations omitted). The burden is on the government to show a legitimate criminal justice reason for conditioning the agreement on the release. *Id.* An example of a legitimate reason is described in *Rumery* where the court believed that protecting an alleged sexual assault victim from further trauma from testifying at both a civil and criminal trial was legitimate. *Rumery*, 480 U.S. at 398.

To prove that the prosecutor is acting improperly, invoke controlling ethical standards in your jurisdiction. In seeking the release of civil claims, the prosecutor is likely violating ethical rules against conflicts of interest by seeking to protect the misbehaving cops/agents. The prosecutor's client is the public, not the misbehaving cops/agents. *See ABA Standards for Criminal Justice,* 3-1.3 (the prosecutor does not represent law enforcement personnel who have worked on the matter and such law enforcement personnel are not the prosecutor's clients). If the prosecutor claims that he or she is not bound by the *ABA Standards*, point out that the *Justice Manual* expects all the DOJ prosecutors will comply with the ABA's ethical standards. *See Justice Manual* 9-2.101 ("The American Bar Association Standards for Criminal Justice have not been adopted as official policy by the Department; however, since the courts utilize the Standards in determining issues covered by them, it is recommended that all United States Attorneys familiarize themselves with them.").

The third factor for enforcing a release-dismissal agreement is whether the agreement would offend the relevant public interest claimed to be protected with the release. This factor tends to overlap somewhat with the prosecutorial misconduct factor. To enforce a release-dismissal agreement, the government must show there is a public interest supporting the release. "The public interest reason proffered by the prosecutor must be the prosecutor's actual reason for seeking the release." *Cain*, 7 F.3d at 381. The Third Circuit explained that a court must look at the actual public interest expressed by the prosecutor because considering only what might have been the prosecutor's reasons might excuse an improper motive. *Id.; see also Livingstone v. N. Belle Vernon Borough*, 12 F.3d 1205, 1215 (3d Cir. 1993) ("a general belief by prosecutors that release-dismissal agreements serve valid purposes is not sufficient to satisfy the public interest prong of the *Rumery* test").

Courts have recognized a fairly narrow set of public interests that justify a prosecutor's attempt to enforce a release-dismissal agreement. In *Cain*, the Third Circuit interpreted *Rumery* as limiting the public policy interests to two narrow categories: (1) "protecting officials from the burden of defending 'marginal' or 'frivolous'" claims, and (2) "expeditiously resolving minor criminal charges while allocating the scarce resources of the criminal justice system to the prosecution of more serious charges." *Id.* at 380 (citing *Rumery*, 480 U.S. at 395–96). The Third Circuit qualified the first interest, stating that there are "strong public interests against release-dismissal agreements that bar colorable [civil rights] claims. Litigants who bring meritorious [civil rights] claims advance societal interests because the vindication of their constitutional rights helps provide an important check on public officials and presumably deters a range of official misconduct." *Id.* at 380–81.

Similarly, Justice O'Connor stated that "[t]he coercive power of criminal process may be twisted to serve the end of suppressing complaints against official abuse, to the detriment not only of the victim of such abuse, but also of society as a whole." *Rumery*, 480 U.S. at 400; *see also MacDonald v. Musick*, 426 F.2d 373 (9th Cir. 1970) (coercing an accused into releasing potential civil claims against the government characterized as extortion under California law).

9.3 APPELLATE WAIVERS

Appellate waivers have become fairly routine in plea agreements in many jurisdictions. They are not *per se* illegal. But appellate waivers can be coercive when a defendant enters a plea and the government fails to abide by its obligations under the agreement, or where the government sandbagged the defendant into pleading guilty by withholding evidence of actual innocence. There are a few cases that have upheld a defendant's challenge to an appellate waiver where there was evidence of prosecutorial misconduct. *See, e.g., United States v. Irizarry-Rosario*, 903 F.3d 151, 154 (1st Cir. 2018) ("In short '[t]he government must keep its promises or the defendant must be released from the [plea] bargain'"); *United States v. Davis*, 923 F.3d 228, 235 (1st Cir. 2019) (citing *Irizarry-Rosario* to hold that defendant could appeal his guilty plea based on alleged prosecutorial misconduct, skirting the waiver of his right to appeal, but losing on the merits). Courts will also unwind a defendant's waiver of the right to appeal if the waiver was not made voluntarily and knowingly. *Brady v. United States*, 397 U.S. 742, 748 (1970); *United States v. Goodson*, 544 F.3d 529, 536 (3d Cir. 2008). Some courts, but not many, apply fairness concerns and unwind waivers of the right to appeal when enforcing the waiver would be a miscarriage of justice. *Goodson*, 544 F.3d at 536.

PART III

Prosecutorial Misconduct During Trial

CHAPTER 10

Jury Selection

Prosecutors commit reversible misconduct during jury selection in different ways: by making improper statements during their questioning of the panel in voir dire, by striking jurors for improper reasons, and by trying to drive pro-defense jurors off the panel for cause when no just cause exists. Obtaining meaningful relief for misconduct during voir dire is challenging, and in this chapter we will lay out factual scenarios where courts have intervened.

There are three primary reasons to object during voir dire. First, it sends an immediate signal to the prosecutors and trial judge that you know the law and will aggressively object throughout trial—during opening statement, witness exams, and summation. That typically leads good prosecutors to dial back their approach thereby eliminating some potentially prejudicial (and objectionable) statements during opening statement and closing argument. Second, with the few unreasonable prosecutors who intend to violate your client's rights throughout the trial, objecting during voir dire will add more examples to the bucket of misconduct that you will be collecting throughout the trial, helping you build and preserve a cumulative effect argument for dismissal at a later point in trial or on appeal. For example, if the prosecutor misstates the law in closing argument, you can remind the judge that the prosecutor did the same thing in voir dire, demonstrating that the prosecutor's actions are intentional and not an innocent mistake. With an objective trial judge, this will help you gain traction on your argument for dismissal or a mistrial. Third, in the typical federal criminal trial, the government receives only six peremptory challenges to the jury pool. *See Federal Rules of Criminal Procedure* 24(b)(2).

Raising *Batson* challenges and opposing bogus government arguments to strike jurors for cause will hopefully keep as many pro-defense jurors as possible in the venire panel, thereby increasing the odds that more pro-defense jurors will ultimately be selected to hear the case. The potential domineering and persuasive pro-defense juror may be among the jurors you save by raising objections based on the case law summarized below. This extra effort in voir dire can alter the outcome in a criminal trial.

10.1 THE JURY SELECTION AND SERVICE ACT: CHALLENGING STRIKES MADE BY THE COURT CLERK

The Jury Selection and Service Act of 1968 outlines the manner in which federal courts create jury pools. 28 U.S.C. § 1865. Under the law, the clerk of court may generally strike jurors for not being a citizen; being under eighteen years of age; not having resided in the district for one year; the inability to read, write, understand, or speak English; incapacity by way of physical infirmity; or a charge pending against them for the commission of a crime or for a crime that may incarcerate for longer than one year. *Id.* Furthermore, a juror may be:

> (1) excused by the court, or by the clerk under supervision of the court if the court's jury selection plan so authorizes, upon a showing of undue hardship or extreme inconvenience, . . . or (2) excluded by the court on the ground that such person may be unable to render impartial jury service or that his service as a juror would be likely to disrupt the proceedings, or (3) excluded upon peremptory challenge as provided by law, or (4) excluded pursuant to the procedure specified by law upon a challenge by any party for good cause shown, or (5) excluded upon determination by the court that his service as a juror would be likely to threaten the secrecy of the proceedings, or otherwise adversely affect the integrity of jury deliberations.

28 U.S.C. § 1866(c)

While the Act mirrors voir dire dismissals, its procedures are distinct from voir dire. *United States v. Price*, 573 F.2d 356, 361 (5th Cir. 1978); *United States v. Gallegos*, 108 F.3d 1272, 1279 (10th Cir. 1997); *see also*

Arbuckle Broadcasters, Inc. v. Rockwell Intern. Corp., 513 F. Supp. 407, 410 (N.D. Tex. 1980) (noting the case law and legislative history dictate that challenges under the Act must come before the start of voir dire).

As dismissals under the Act occur prior to voir dire, there are limited opportunities for defense counsel to object to a dismissal. However, if you are handling a matter in a district where you have due process concerns about the overall fairness of the trial, consider asking the trial judge to identify all potential jurors dismissed by the Clerk of Court prior to voir dire. Most experienced and objective trial judges provide this information without prompting, but other judges may not. In rare cases, you might see the clerk excusing jurors from the venire for potentially improper reasons—including race, gender, ethnicity, or political affiliation—to stack the venire pool in a way that favors the prosecution. Defense attorneys who have objected at this phase of jury selection have been able to win on appeal. *See, e.g.*, *United States v. Candelaria-Silva*, 166 F.3d 19, 31 (1st Cir. 1999) (finding the court abused its discretion by finding undue hardship for a juror who was working a night shift but who had not requested removal from the jury pool).

10.2 IMPROPER COMMENTS DURING VOIR DIRE

The Supreme Court standard for establishing prosecutorial misconduct is that (1) the prosecutor's remarks must be improper, and (2) the remarks must prejudicially affect the substantial rights of the defendant. *Darden v. Wainwright*, 477 U.S. 106 S. Ct. 2464 (1986). Once a court has determined that the prosecutor's voir dire question is improper, the court must then determine whether the defendant's substantive rights were violated by the prosecutor's remarks. *Id.* at 2466. The court should assess whether the prosecutor's comments "so infected the trial with unfairness as to make the resulting conviction a denial of due process." *Id.*

Circuit courts give a high level of deference to the trial court's rulings on objections during voir dire. However, circuit courts have also shown some appetite to criticize certain types of questions as improper, even though they rarely reverse a conviction solely based on misconduct during voir dire. Not surprisingly, the types of voir dire questions that appellate courts criticize are very similar to improper comments during a prosecutor's opening statement or closing argument that can trigger a reversal of a defendant's conviction. *See* Chapter 13.5.

Most objectionable comments in voir dire fall into six categories. Prosecutors should not: (1) create hypotheticals that mirror the case; (2) express their own personal beliefs; (3) misstate the law; (4) attack the credibility of defense counsel; (5) refer to inadmissible evidence; or (6) ask jurors to put themselves in the same position as the victim of the crime at issue.

10.2.1 Using Hypotheticals That Mirror the Charges

A prosecutor cannot use hypotheticals that mirror the allegations of the indictment. Doing so is improper because it implicates the defendant in the crime charged. In *United States v. Carter,* the Sixth Circuit reversed a conviction where the prosecutor described the events of the alleged crime and implied that the Defendant was involved in the crime. 236 F.3d 777, 789 (6th Cir. 2001). Other courts have criticized prosecutors for making similar comments, although they did not reverse the Defendant's conviction. *See United States v. Jefferson*, 432 F. App'x 382, 389 (5th Cir. 2011) (stating that it is "highly suspect" when a prosecutor asks the jury "how it would weigh evidence that it had not heard."); *United States v. Fambro*, 526 F.3d 836, 847 (5th Cir. 2008) (court states that it did not approve when the prosecutor created a hypothetical with certain facts and evidence, and then asked jurors about their willingness to convict based on that hypothetical).

10.2.2 Expressing Personal Opinion

Prosecutors should not express their personal opinion during their questioning of the jury. For example, it is improper for a prosecutor to "comment on what they think the victim was feeling or thinking." *Nields v. Bradshaw*, 482 F.3d 442, 451 (6th Cir. 2007). This line of questions is improper because the prosecutor is asking the jury to speculate on facts not in evidence and is doing so in a highly prejudicial manner. *Bennett v. Rewerts*, 2018 WL 8732861 (6th Cir. 2018) (criticizing a prosecutor for "emphasiz[ing] the traumatic nature of sexual assault during voir dire"); *United States v. Bartos*, 51 F. App'x 957 (6th Cir. 2002) (improper for prosecutor to inject his personal opinion by classifying evidence as "repulsive material" during voir dire); *James v. United States*, 622 F. App'x 689 (9th Cir. 2015) (improper for prosecutor to express his personal opinion that the Defendant was a "violent kingpin" and similar to Gambino family crime boss John Gotti).

10.2.3 Improper Misstatement of Law

Since jurors are predisposed to believe prosecutors and will rely on the prosecutor's description of the governing law, it is clearly improper for prosecutors to misstate the law to jurors during voir dire. In *Lang v. Gundy*, the prosecutor misstated the crime of aiding and abetting. 399 F. App'x 969, 975 (6th Cir. 2010). Doing so was improper, although the court immediately remedied the error by providing the jury with a correct statement of the law. *Id.; see also Byrne v. Butler*, 845 F. 2d 501, 505–06 (5th Cir. 1988) (improper for prosecutor to tell the jury that "there are only two choices, one is life imprisonment without parole or suspension of the [Defendant's] sentence" because those options belonged to the parole board, not to the jury).

10.2.4 Criticizing Defense Counsel

It is improper for a prosecutor to express negative generalizations about defense counsel. Juries are predisposed to believe prosecutors and be skeptical of defense counsel. *See United States v. LaPage*, 231 F.3d 488, 492 (9th Cir. 2000). Thus, this type of negative attack on defense counsel during voir dire potentially violates both the Due Process Clause of the Fifth Amendment and the Sixth Amendment right to an impartial jury. In *United States v. Steele*, the prosecutor asked the following question to a prospective juror who was a former public defender: "In the course of trying [felony robbery] cases, did you ever make a decision that your client was guilty and you've just got to do whatever you have got to do because that's your job?" 298 F.3d 906, 912 (9th Cir. 2002). The court stated that while the prosecutor may not have intended to make a generalization about all defense attorneys, the statement could still cause the jury to assume that all defense lawyers believed that their clients were guilty. *Id.; see also Wilson v. Sirmons*, 536 F.3d 1064, 1119 (10th Cir. 2008) (improper for a prosecutor to imply that defense counsel intended to lie to the jury by asking members of the jury "if they would let a smoke screen fool them").

10.2.5 Referencing Inadmissible Facts

A prosecutor should not describe facts that may not be admitted at trial because doing so is both irrelevant and unduly prejudicial under *Federal Rules of Evidence* (FRE) 401 and 403, and a potential violation of the defendant's Sixth Amendment right to a fair trial. In *United States v. Gill*, the court criticized a prosecutor who stated in voir dire, "Now, in this case, there was four coconspirators charged with this crime, three have pled guilty, we have one remaining." 42 F. App'x 323, 325 (5th Cir. 2016). The court said that referring to the Co-defendants' pleas was improper given that those pleas were inadmissible in the trial against the remaining Defendant. *Id.*

10.2.6 Violating the Golden Rule

Many trial judges have their own local rules where they warn trial lawyers to not have jurors place themselves in the shoes of the alleged victims—known in some circles as the "Golden Rule"—and applies to prosecutors who want jurors to imagine the pain the victim experienced as he or she suffered through the alleged crime. While doing so is highly improper, aggressive prosecutors pursue this tactic on a regular basis. The proper objection here is to invoke both the Fifth Amendment (due process) and Sixth Amendment (right to a fair trial/impartial jury). As an example, in *Roman v. Filion*, the prosecutor concocted an example in which he asked jury members to imagine themselves in the shoes of the victim, and then asked if the Defendant should be prosecuted. No. 04 CIV 2005 WL 1383167 (S.D.N.Y. June 10, 2005). The court held that the prosecutor's voir dire question was improper because the prosecutor "appealed to the fears and sympathies of the jury by improperly asking them to think of themselves as crime victims." *Id.*

10.3 *BATSON* CHALLENGES FOR IMPROPER PEREMPTORY STRIKES

In addition to making prejudicial comments during voir dire, prosecutors also commit misconduct when they exercise peremptory strikes for improper reasons. The seminal case in this area is *Batson v. Kentucky,* 476 U.S. 79, 79 (1986). In *Batson,* the Supreme Court held that the Equal Protection Clause forbids a prosecutor from challenging potential jurors solely on account of their race, or on the assumption that jurors as a racial group are unable to impartially consider the case at hand. The prosecutor used his peremptory challenges to strike all four African American persons on the venire, and a jury composed only of Caucasian persons was selected. *Id.* at 83. While a defendant has no right to a jury composed in whole or in part of his own race, a defendant does have a right to be tried by a jury whose members are selected pursuant to nondiscriminatory criteria. *Id.* at 86. The Court found that purposeful racial discrimination in selection of the jury violates a defendant's right to equal protection because it denies the defendant the protection that a trial by jury is intended to provide. *Id.*

10.3.1 The Reach of *Batson*

Over the years, the Supreme Court has expanded *Batson* in a few meaningful respects. For example, a defendant of *any* race may raise a *Batson* claim, and a defendant may raise a *Batson* claim even if the defendant and excluded juror are not the same race; in other words, *Batson* is not limited to only African American defendants and jurors. *Flowers v. Mississippi*, 139 S. Ct. 2228, 2243 (2019); *Powers v. Ohio*, 499 U.S. 399 (1991). *Batson* also applies to a criminal defendant's own peremptory strikes and civil cases. *Georgia v. McCollum*, 505 U.S. 42, 59 (1992); *Edmonson v. Leesville Concrete Company*, 500 U.S. 614 (1991). In addition, the Court extended *Batson* to apply to discrimination based on gender and ethnicity. *J.E.B. v. Alabama*, 511 U.S. 127 (1994); *Hernandez v. New York*, 500 U.S. 352, 354 (1991).

The Court, however, has not yet extended *Batson* to other protected groups that are recognized by other anti-discrimination laws or selective prosecution claims such as religious orientation, sexual orientation, and political affiliation. The circuits tend to split on these issues. Since the case law is evolving and progressing in this area, it makes sense to preserve all potential constitutional objections (i.e., due process, right to an impartial jury, and equal protection) if your client falls into these other groups because the Supreme Court should extend *Batson* protection to them at some point in the future.

For example, the Court has not extended *Batson* to cover religious orientation, declining to hear a case involving whether religious affiliation was a cognizable class. *Davis v. Minnesota*, 511 U.S. 1115 (1994). The Second Circuit, however, has expressly extended *Batson* to religious affiliation. *U.S. v. Brown*, 352 F.3d 654, 655 (2d Cir. 2003). The First Circuit assumed *Batson* extended to discrimination based on religion in examining a challenge but has not expressly extended this principle. *U.S. v. Girouard*, 521 F.3d 110 (1st Cir. 2008). By contrast, the Fifth and Ninth Circuits have declined to extend *Batson* to religious affiliation, in line with the Supreme Court's lack of extension on the same class. *Fisher v. Texas*, 169 F.3d 295, 303 (5th Cir. 1999); *Cash v. Barnes*, 532 F. App'x 768 (9th Cir. 2013).

Likewise, the Supreme Court has not yet extended *Batson* to sexual orientation. While the Ninth Circuit has expressly extended *Batson* to include this cognizable class in *Smithkline Beecham Cop. v. Abbott Laboratories* (740 F.3d 471 (9th Cir. 2014)), the Eighth Circuit has expressly declined to extend *Batson* to sexual orientation in *U.S. v. Blaylock* (421 F.3d 758, 769 (8th Cir. 2005)).

As to political affiliation, both the Second and Tenth Circuits have declined to extend *Batson* protection to groups based on their political beliefs. *U.S. v. Prince*, 647 F.3d 1257, 1261 (10th Cir. 2011); *Jaquith v. South Orangetown Cent. School Dist.*, 349 F. App'x 653, 654 (2d Cir. 2009). This issue will likely emerge in the courts in the near future given the recent flurry of prosecutions of political officials who will likely advance selective prosecution challenges.

10.3.2 The Three-Part *Batson* Test

To analyze a *Batson* objection, the trial court should deploy a three-part test that includes shifting burdens of proof. First, the defendant must establish a *prima facie* case of discrimination. *Batson*, 476 U.S. at 98. The defendant must show that he or she is a member of a cognizable group being singled out for differential treatment, and that the prosecutor has exercised peremptory challenges to remove members of the defendant's race from the jury. *Johnson v. California*, 545 U.S. 162, 167 (2005). A defendant must then show facts and any other relevant circumstances sufficient to raise an inference that the prosecutor used peremptory challenges to exclude potential jurors on account of their race. *Id.* at 171. A permissible inference of discrimination that the trial court can draw based on a wide variety of evidence is sufficient to establish a *prima facie* case of discrimination under *Batson*. *Id.* This first step is not intended to persuade the judge that this challenge was more likely than not the product of purposeful discrimination. *Id.* Instead, a defendant must merely produce evidence sufficient to permit the trial court to draw a permissible inference that discrimination occurred. *Id.* After this inference is drawn, defendant's *prima facie* case has been established.

Once the defendant makes this showing, the burden shifts to the prosecutors to demonstrate a race-neutral explanation for their peremptory challenge. *Batson*, 476 U.S. at 98. Prosecutors cannot meet this burden by simply asserting they did not discriminate. Instead, prosecutors must provide a specific example to show that they used race-neutral criteria as their basis to strike the juror. *Id.* This does not require an explanation that is persuasive or plausible. *Purkett v. Elem*, 514 U.S. 765, 769 (1995). The prosecutor's race-neutral explanation only needs to be valid on its face to be deemed acceptable, unless a discriminatory intent is inherent in the prosecutor's explanation. *Id.* For example, the prosecutor in *Purkett* struck a juror because he had long, unkempt hair, a mustache, and a beard. *Id.* The Court held that the prosecutor's justification was an acceptable race-neutral explanation and satisfied the prosecutor's burden of articulating a nondiscriminatory reason for the peremptory strike, as these characteristics are not unique to any race. *Id.*

The trial court must then determine if the race-neutral explanation stands, or if the prosecutor's stated reason was pretextual for purposeful discrimination. *Snyder v. Louisiana*, 552 U.S. 472, 484 (2008). The defendant has the burden to persuade the court that the prosecutor committed intentional discrimination. *Id.* At this stage, the court focuses on whether the prosecutor's race-neutral explanation for a peremptory challenge should be believed or was motivated in substantial part by discriminatory intent. *Id.* Implausible and fantastic justifications at this stage are likely pretexts for purposeful discrimination. *Id.* Ultimately, the court's assessment of whether purposeful discrimination occurred turns on the credibility of the prosecutor—another reason to keep chipping away at a prosecutor's credibility in earlier phases of the case by pursuing other instances of potential misconduct (*Brady* issues, grand jury challenges, or motions for *Franks* hearings, for example). When assessing pretext, credibility can be measured by the demeanor of the opposing party, by how reasonable or how improbable the race-neutral explanations are, and by whether the proffered rationale has some basis in accepted strategy. *Miller-El v. Cockrell*, 537 U.S. 322, 337 (2003) (*Miller-El I*).

The Supreme Court has identified a few categories of evidence that defense counsel should use to show discriminatory intent, including (a) statistical evidence about the prosecutor's use of peremptory strikes against African American prospective jurors when compared to Caucasian prospective jurors; (b) disparate questioning of different jurors based on race; and (c) side-by-side comparisons of African American and Caucasian prospective jurors who were struck and not struck are often informative of whether a prosecutor's peremptory strikes were made on the basis of race. *Miller-El I*, 537 U.S. at 341–345.

The Court has further recognized that a prosecutor's misrepresentation of the record when defending strikes during a *Batson* hearing can demonstrate pretext, as can any relevant history of the government's peremptory strikes in past cases. *Miller-El v. Dretke,* 545 U.S. 231, 241 (2005). This is a non-exhaustive list of factors, and all other relevant circumstances that bear on the discriminatory issue are used in the trial court's analysis as well. *Flowers v. Mississippi*, 139 S. Ct. 2228, 2243 (2019). In sum, as the third and final step in a *Batson* challenge, the trial court weighs all available evidence to determine if the prosecutor's use of a peremptory strike was motivated by discriminatory intent.

After the trial court has made this determination, a successful *Batson* challenge typically requires that the court seat the juror at issue. If the trial court decides the prosecutor's peremptory strike was not discriminatory, the juror is excused and the case moves forward. Upon appeal of the *Batson* challenge, the appellate court should use the clearly erroneous standard to review the trial court's conclusion. *Snyder*, 552 U.S. at 472. This high standard of review requires an explicit showing of error in applying the *Batson* test to overturn a conviction based on a subsequent *Batson* appeal, leading appellate courts to grant a high level of deference to the trial court's decision.

10.4 IMPROPER CHALLENGES FOR CAUSE

How the prosecutor executes strikes for cause represents a third area where prosecutors might improperly eliminate good defense jurors from the venire pool. The defense objection is based primarily on the Sixth Amendment, which guarantees an impartial jury. *Ross v. Oklahoma*, 487 U.S. 81, 85 (1988). To enforce this guarantee during voir dire, a court may dismiss a juror for partiality or prejudice. *Swain v. Alabama*, 380 U.S. 202, 220 (1965), overruled on other grounds, *Batson v. Kentucky*, 476 U.S. 79 (1986) ("[C]hallenges for cause permit rejection of jurors on a narrowly specified, provable and legally cognizable basis of partiality"). Jurors may be stricken for cause by the court on two grounds: actual bias and implied bias. *See, e.g.*, *Dennis v. United States*, 339 U.S. 162, 165–66 (1950); *United States v. Haynes*, 398 F.2d 980, 983 (2d Cir. 1968); *Casias v. United States*, 315 F.2d 614, 619 (10th Cir. 1963) (Murrah, J., concurring).

An overly aggressive prosecutor, however, may improperly attempt to push potential pro-defense jurors off the panel for cause where no just cause exists. For example, if you have a matter where you believe jurors with a particular political view are favorable to your defense, the prosecutors may press to have the court dismiss those jurors for cause without being able to show either actual or implied bias. *See, e.g., United States v. Salamone*, 800 F.2d 1216 (3d Cir. 1986) (holding that the trial court erred in summarily dismissing all members of the National Rifle Association (NRA) at the prosecution's request in a prosecution of a gun offense). In another example, in a narcotics prosecution the government may try to run off any juror who believes marijuana should be legalized. *United States v. Padilla-Mendoza*, 157 F.3d 730, 733 (9th Cir. 1998) (finding the district erred by implying bias and dismissing two jurors who believed marijuana should be legalized without first assessing for actual bias but ultimately finding the error was harmless).

A related defense attack is viable where the defense can show that a juror withheld relevant information from defense counsel during voir dire that could have led the defense to try to exclude the juror for cause. *United States v. Colombo*, 869 F.2d 149, 151 (2d Cir. 1989) (reversing conviction and remanding for a new trial in part because juror deliberately concealed that her brother-in-law was a government attorney such that bias could be presumed); *Sampson v. United States*, 724 F.3d 150 (1st Cir. 2013) (finding a juror was biased when they deliberately withheld information about past victimhood similar to the alleged crimes of the Defendant).

While this is an admittedly difficult area to win reversal on appeal, many trial judges and prosecutors confuse actual and implied bias thereby creating error in the trial record that can be exploited on appeal. As a result, understanding the differences between actual and implied bias can help you properly preserve an objection that may help on any subsequent appeal.

10.4.1 Actual Bias

Actual bias "is based upon express proof, e.g., by a voir dire admission by the prospective juror of a state of mind prejudicial to a party's interest." *United States v. Haynes*, 398 F.2d 980, 984 (2d Cir. 1968). A trial court has "a serious duty to determine the question of actual bias, and a broad discretion in its rulings on challenges therefor." *Dennis v. United States*, 339 U.S. 162, 168 (1950). Doubts concerning actual bias are normally "resolved against permitting the juror to serve." *United States v. Nelson*, 277 F.3d 164, 202 (2d Cir. 2002); *see also United States v. Sithithongtham*, 192 F.3d 1119, 1121 (8th Cir. 1999); *Bailey v. Bd. of County*

Comm'rs, 956 F.2d 1112, 1127 (11th Cir. 1992); *United States v. Nell*, 526 F.2d 1223, 1230 (5th Cir. 1976). "When a juror's impartiality is at issue, the relevant question is 'did a juror swear that he could set aside any opinion he might hold and decide the case on the evidence, and should the juror's protestation of impartiality have been believed.'" *Dennis v. Mitchell*, 354 F.3d 511, 520 (6th Cir. 2003) (quoting *Patton v. Yount*, 467 U.S. 1025, 1036 (1984)).

Trial court determinations of actual bias receive highly deferential abuse of discretion appellate review and are rarely, if ever, overturned. *See Patton v. Yount*, 467 U.S. 1025, 1038 (1984) (stating that trial court determinations of juror impartiality are due "special deference"); *United States v. Gordon*, 954 F.3d 315, 324 (1st Cir. 2020); *United States v. Tibesar*, 894 F.2d 317, 319 (8th Cir. 1990); *States v. Porth*, 426 F.2d 519, 523 (10th Cir. 1970) (collecting cases).

10.4.2 Implied Bias

Implied bias exists when the law presumes bias based on a juror's relations, mental state, or past experiences. *See Smith v. Phillips*, 455 U.S. 209, 222 (1982) (O'Connor, J., concurring). As a concept, its roots date back to Chief Justice John Marshall. *United States v. Burr*, 25 Fed. Cas. 49, 50 (C.C. Va. 1807) (discussing why the law disfavors allowing relatives of the accused to serve as jurors). Although the Supreme Court has never expressly recognized implied bias, Justice O'Connor endorsed the concept in her concurrence in *Smith v. Phillips*. 455 U.S. at 222. As a result, the circuit courts have different approaches to determining what constitutes implied bias. For example, some circuit courts have found implied bias "constitutes clearly established federal law as determined by the Supreme Court" such that state court errors concerning implied bias may be considered by federal courts on writ of habeas corpus. *See, e.g., Green v. Quaterman*, 213 Fed. App'x 279, 281 (5th Cir. 2007); *Conaway v. Polk*, 453 F.3d 567, 588 (4th Cir. 2006); *but see Sedillo v. Hatch*, 445 Fex. App'x 95, 103 (10th Cir. 2011) (assuming without deciding).

Voir dire responses are not relevant to implied bias itself. *See United States v. Haynes*, 398 F.2d 980, 984 (2d Cir. 1968). Thus, implied bias can exist even if the prospective juror swears they will be impartial. *Id.* But voir dire responses considered along with a bias prone relationship can equate to actual bias, leading to a valid for cause dismissal. *See, e.g., United States v. Caldwell*, 543 F.2d 1333, 1345–46 (D.C. Cir. 1974).

Situations that lead to a finding of implied bias are "extreme" and "extraordinary," and courts have carefully emphasized how narrow implied bias should remain. *Smith v. Phillips*, 455 U.S. 209, 222 (1982) (O'Connor, J., concurring); *see also Amirault v. Fair*, 968 F.2d 1404, 1405–06 (1st Cir. 1992). Implied bias arises in "situations in which the circumstances point so sharply to bias in a particular juror that even his own denials must be discounted." *United States v. Nell*, 526 F.2d 1223, 1229 n.8 (5th Cir. 1976). Classic examples include a juror related to one of the parties in the case, a close acquaintance to a party in the case, a juror who has a financial interest in the outcome, or a juror who was a victim of the crime being prosecuted. *See, e.g., Conaway v. Polk*, 453 F.3d 567, 586 (4th Cir. 2006); *Caterpillar Inc. v. Sturman Industries, Inc.*, 387 F.3d 1358, 1372 (Fed. Cir. 2004); *United States v. Polichemi*, 219 F.3d 698, 704 (7th Cir. 2000); *Hartzell v. United States*, 72 F.2d 569, 576 (8th Cir. 1934). Implied bias can also exist when a juror or a close relative has been "personally involved in a situation involving a similar fact pattern." *Tinsley v. Borg*, 895 F.2d 520, 527 (9th Cir. 1990). However, courts disfavor creating new categories of implied bias. *Id.*; *United States v. Brown*, 644 F.2d 101, 104–05 (2d Cir. 1981).

Broadly speaking, four distinct fact patterns have resulted in courts acknowledging that implied bias does *not* exist: (1) a prospective juror's general group or personal affiliations; (2) a prospective juror's generalized beliefs or knowledge; (3) a prospective juror or a family member having been a distant victim of a crime or other wrongful act; or (4) a prospective juror inadvertently misspeaks during voir dire with an inaccurate answer. As a result, be mindful when a prosecutor tries to run a juror off the panel for cause by making one of these arguments. *United States v. Calabrese*, 942 F.2d 218 (3d Cir. 1991) (holding that the trial court erred in summarily dismissing a juror based only on a passing acquaintance with the Defendant at the prosecution's request); *United States v. Salamone*, 800 F.2d 1216 (3d Cir. 1986) (holding that the trial court erred in summarily dismissing all members of the NRA at the prosecution's request in a prosecution of a gun offense).

A court should not find a prospective juror to have implied bias based solely on their group or personal affiliations. *Thiel v. Southern Pacific Co.*, 328 U.S. 217, 220 (1946) (jury competence is an individual rather than a group or class matter.) Merely belonging to a group that may have some distant or generalized interest in the litigation will not alone support a finding of implied bias. *Salamone*, 800 F.2d 1216, 1225 (3d Cir. 1986). Standing alone, most personal acquaintances, very distant relatives, and political and issue organization affiliations will not rise to implied bias. *See, e.g., Calabrese*, 942 F.2d at 224–25 (loose acquaintances, collecting cases); *United States v. Rhodes*, 177 F.3d 963, 966 (11th Cir. 1999) (cousin); *Salamone*, 800 F.2d at 1225 (NRA membership); *Connors v. United States*, 158 U.S. 408, 414 (1895) (political party); *but see Conaway v. Polk*, 453 F.3d 567, 585 (4th Cir. 2006) (finding first double cousin once removed had implied bias). Note that these relationships can easily become actual bias if compounded with other information. *See, e.g., United States v. Henderson*, 613 Fed. App'x 113, 115 (3d Cir. 2015); *United States v. Allsup*, 566 F.2d 68, 71–72 (9th Cir. 1977); *United States v. Nell*, 526 F.2d 1223, 1230 (5th Cir. 1976); *Sims v. United States*, 405 F.2d 1381, 1384 n.5 (D.C. Cir. 1968). When encountering these potentially bias-forming relationships, the court should question jurors about their relationships to ascertain actual bias. *See Patton v. Yount*, 467 U.S. 1025, 1036–37 (1984) (noting that voir dire aims to determine whether a juror "can lay aside his opinion and render a verdict based on the evidence presented in court").

The Third Circuit in *United States v. Salamone* succinctly laid out why personal affiliation cannot, standing alone, imply bias:

> To allow trial judges and prosecutors to determine juror eligibility based solely on their perceptions of the external associations of a juror threatens the heretofore guarded right of an accused to a fair trial by an impartial jury as well as the integrity of the judicial process as a whole. Taken to its illogical conclusion, the government's position would sanction, inter alia, the summary exclusion for cause of NAACP members from cases seeking the enforcement of civil rights statutes, Moral Majority activists from pornography cases, Catholics from cases involving abortion clinic protests, members of NOW from sex discrimination cases, and subscribers to *Consumer Reports* from cases involving products liability claims.

800 F.2d 1216, 1225 (3d Cir. 1986)

This concept finds some synergy with "fair cross section" Sixth Amendment challenges. *See Duren v. Missouri*, 439 U.S. 357, 367 (1978). If a jury pool has systemically excluded certain segments of society such as a race, gender, or other distinctive group, it unconstitutionally deprives the accused of a jury that represents a fair cross section of society. *Id.*

The circuits are divided on whether a mere passing acquaintance with one of the parties or attorneys in the case constitutes an implied bias sufficient to dismiss for cause. The Third, Eighth, and Tenth Circuits have held a passing acquaintance alone is not sufficient to find implied bias. *United States v. Calabrese*, 942 F.2d 218 (3d Cir. 1991); *United States v. Bradshaw*, 787 F.2d 1385, 1390 (10th Cir. 1986) (this ruling may have tacitly overturned *United States v. Redmond*, 546 F.2d 1386 (10th Cir. 1977), which upheld the dismissal of jurors acquainted with the attorneys); *United States v. Kelton*, 518 F.2d 531, 533 (8th Cir. 1975). But because the Fifth and Eleventh Circuits have held a passing acquaintance is alone sufficient to dismiss the juror. *United States v. Paradies*, 98 F.3d 1266, 1279–80 (11th Cir. 1996); *United States v. Bailey*, 468 F.2d 652, 658 (5th Cir. 1972); *but see United States v. Allred*, 867 F.2d 856, 870 (5th Cir. 1989) (stating that a mere acquaintance did not warrant dismissal for cause where there was no socializing during the trial and the two had no allegiances).

Membership in a political or issue organization that is only generally or loosely interested in the case (i.e., not a party) does not constitute implied bias. *Person v. Miller*, 854 F.2d 656, 665 (4th Cir. 1988); *United States v. Salamone*, 800 F.2d 1216, 1225 (3d Cir. 1986); *Connors v. United States*, 158 U.S. 408, 414 (1895). Likewise, employment with an institution with a nebulous interest in the case does not amount to implied bias. *Dennis v. United States*, 339 U.S. 162, 171–72 (1950); *United States v. Boyd*, 446 F.2d 1267, 1275 (5th Cir. 1971); *Williams v. United States*, 418 F.2d 372, 376–77 (10th Cir. 1969). Nor does being a certain race, even where the prosecution is for a race-based hate crime. *United States v. Greer*, 968 F.2d 433, 435 (5th Cir. 1992); *Person v. Miller*, 854 F.2d 656, 665 (4th Cir. 1988).

In addition, a juror's general views or knowledge should not trigger implied bias. *See United States v. Padilla-Mendoza*, 157 F.3d 730, 733 (9th Cir. 1998) ("To presume that personal beliefs automatically render one unable to act as a juror is improper."). Prospective juror belief is often litigated in capital murder cases. In capital cases, a juror cannot be dismissed solely for expressing "conscientious or religious scruples" against the death penalty unless the court determines through voir dire that the juror will never vote in favor of the death penalty. *Witherspoon v. Illinois*, 391 U.S. 510, 515 n. 9 (1968); *see, e.g., Rousan v. Roper*, 436 F.3d 951, 956 (8th Cir. 2006); *United States v. Chanthadara*, 230 F.3d 1237, 1269 (10th Cir. 2000); *Turberville v. United States*, 303 F.2d 411, 419 (D.C. Cir. 1962). The goal of the court on voir dire is to determine just how firmly held the prospective juror's preexisting beliefs are and whether they can set them aside on the instructions of the court. *Witherspoon*, 391 U.S. at 515.

This same logic has been applied to beliefs other than the death penalty. *See Padilla-Mendoza*, 157 F.3d at 733 (concerning beliefs about drug legalization). For example, a general belief that marijuana should be legalized does not alone imply bias in a prosecution for drug crimes. *Id.* However, some circuits have found these belief-based exclusions are indeed proper, particularly when combined with voir dire responses. *See, e.g., United States v. Henderson*, 613 F. App'x 113, 115 (3d Cir. 2015) (finding that a belief in legalized marijuana combined with voir dire questions that ascertained actual bias is cause to dismiss); *United States v. Brooks*, 175 F.3d 605, 607 (8th Cir. 1999) (Heaney, J., dissenting) (lamenting that the majority opinion agreed that supporters of legalization are presumed biased in drug prosecutions); *United States v. McCarthy*, 961 F.2d 972, 976 (1st Cir. 1992).

Some courts have suggested that a prospective juror's professional background alone cannot imply bias, even if it is relevant to the case. *See, e.g., Tinsley v. Borg*, 895 F.2d 520, 529 (9th Cir. 1990). However, courts appear to be wary of the potential of actual bias clouding the juror's impartiality. *See, e.g., id.* (noting that the circumstances of the juror's professional background reduced the chances of bias); *Verfes v. Newland*, 1998 WL 1148898, *8 (N.D. Cal. 1998).

Another common fact pattern is when a juror or someone close to the juror was a victim of the same crime at issue. The key factor here is timing: how recently was the juror victimized? If it was recent, courts imply bias. *See Amirault v. Fair*, 968 F.2d 1404, 1405–06 (1st Cir. 1992); *Hunley v. Godinez*, 975 F.2d 316, 319 (7th Cir. 1992) (collecting cases); *Burton v. Johnson*, 948 F.2d 1150, 1159 (10th Cir. 1991) (finding a juror was impliedly biased in a murder trial where the defense was battered-wife syndrome and the juror was a victim of domestic abuse); *United States v. Eubanks*, 591 F.2d 513, 517 (9th Cir. 1979). However, where the juror was victimized years earlier, a court should not presume the juror is unable to be impartial, even where the facts of the case resemble their own or a close relative's experience. *See Amirault*, 968 F.2d at 1405–06. Naturally, if the facts of the juror's victimhood do not resemble the crime being tried, a court will not imply bias. *See United States v. Medina*, 430 F.3d 869, 876–77 (7th Cir. 2005). In addition, this is rarely a fact pattern where the defense team wants to keep the juror but the prosecutor wants to use a cause strike to keep that juror off the panel.

A court should not find a prospective juror to have implied bias solely based on their making an inadvertently incorrect or incomplete statement during voir dire. *See United States v. Estey*, 595 F.3d 836, 841 (8th Cir. 2010); *United States v. Solorio*, 337 F.3d 580, 595–96 (6th Cir. 2003). An honest mistake that conceals relevant information by itself will not constitute implied bias, but it can be used as an indicator for bias that a judge can follow up on. *See Sampson v. United States*, 724 F.3d 150, 167 (1st Cir. 2013); *cf. McDonough Power Equipment, Inc. v. Greenwood*, 464 U.S. 548, 555 (1984) (juror's honest but mistaken response in voir dire did not warrant a new trial even though the Defendant would have used a preemptory challenge). However, if a juror's concealment or lying is deliberate or they repeatedly lie during voir dire, it can evidence a motive for actual or implied bias that will warrant dismissal. *See Sampson*, 724 F.3d at 167 (noting that the distinction between actual and implied bias is not essential to these inquiries); *United States v. Colombo*, 869 F.2d 149, 151 (2d Cir. 1989); *United States v. Perkins*, 748 F.2d 1519, 1531–33 (11th Cir. 1984).

10.5 IMPROPER CONTACT WITH JURORS

In rare circumstances, a prosecutor might have improper contact with a juror during the trial. This would trigger a jury interference claim for violating the defendant's Fifth Amendment right to due process, Sixth Amendment right to a fair trial by an impartial jury, and the "interest of justice" standard Rule 33 of the Federal Rules of Criminal Procedure. *United States v. Lawhorne*, 29 F. Supp. 2d 292, 311 (E.D. Va. 1998) (asserting a Sixth Amendment violation for jury bias in connection with communication between the prosecutor and a juror); *United States v. Blauvelt*, 2009 WL 1230264, at *1 (D. Md. May 1, 2009) (asserting a Fifth Amendment violation regarding improper contact between prosecutor and juror); *United States v. Smith*, 139 F. App'x 475, 476–77 (3d Cir. 2005) (seeking new trial under Rule 33).

When deciding to grant a new trial or to declare a mistrial, trial courts traditionally apply a multipart test focusing on whether the alleged communication between the prosecutor and juror had the possibility of influencing the jury's verdict. *Blauvelt*, 2009 WL 1230264 at *1 (applying a three-part test focusing on whether the communication was "innocuous" and whether it influenced the jury's decision-making process); *Lawhorne*, 29 F. Supp. 2d at 308 (similarly applying a two-part test focusing on whether the communication was "innocuous" and whether the jury's verdict was "influenced by the improper communication"); *see also United States v. O'Brien*, 972 F.2d 12, 14 (communication between a police officer and a jury member focusing on whether the communication was prejudicial to the defendant or harmless). The defendant has the burden of first showing that the prosecutor's communication with the jury was improper by either being private or dealing with the trial at hand. *Blauvelt*, 2009 WL 1230264 at *1. After that, the government has the burden of showing that the communication did not affect the disposition at trial. *Lawhorne*, 29 F. Supp. 2d at 308 (describing this burden as "heavy").

Defendants who win on a jury interference challenge need to: (1) show that someone (including a prosecutor) communicated with a jury member about the case at hand. *United States v. Remmer*, 347 U.S. 227, 229–30 (1954) ("In a criminal case, any private communication, contact, or tampering directly or indirectly, with a juror during a trial about the matter pending before the jury is, for obvious reasons, deemed presumptively prejudicial"); *Blauvelt*, 2009 WL 1230264 at *1 (citing *Remmer* in the context of alleged prosecutor communication with a juror). Or, (2) show that the communication between the prosecutor and jury member demonstrates jury bias (*Lawhorne*, 29 F. Supp. 2d at 317–18). Or, (3) show that the district court failed to seriously investigate the potential influence that a prosecutor's communication had on a jury member (*United States v. Betner*, 489 F.2d 116, 119 (5th Cir. 1974)).

CHAPTER 11

Presenting False Testimony At Trial: *Napue* Issues

11.1 *NAPUE* BASICS

A criminal defendant is denied due process when a prosecutor knowingly presents false evidence or fails to correct the record when unsolicited false evidence is introduced at trial. *Napue v. Illinois*, 360 U.S. 264, 269–71 (1959). When a prosecutor sees that false evidence has been presented—for example, when a prosecutor's witness lies—the ethical prosecutor interrupts the questioning and immediately fixes the problem by either questioning the witness or requesting a sidebar with the judge and defense counsel to notify them about the problem. *See United States v. LaPage*, 231 F.3d 488, 492 (9th Cir. 2000). Too often, however, prosecutors fail to correct the false evidence they introduce in criminal trials.

While most courts describe false evidence challenges as a *Napue* issue, the Supreme Court issued important decisions on this topic both before and after it decided *Napue* in 1959. We will summarize those decisions below. We will also provide detailed descriptions of this doctrine in the various circuits because there is tension within the circuits that may yield different results on the same set of facts. In addition, in some circuits, the applicable legal standard for a direct appeal of a *Napue* issue arising out of a federal conviction is different than a review of a state conviction via habeas review.

If a prosecutor elicits false evidence at trial, make your record by objecting and moving for a mistrial as soon as you become aware that the evidence is false. Failure to do so will often lead to the more stringent plain error review on appeal. *United States v. Alli*, 344 F.3d 1002, 1007 (9th Cir. 2003). Note that in some circuits failure to object at trial may waive the issue completely. *United States v. Mangual-Garcia*, 505 F.3d 1, 10–11 (1st Cir. 2007).

In addition, consider moving to dismiss the indictment with prejudice by arguing that the prosecutors invited the mistrial because they have now seen your defense and a mistrial would give the prosecutors the opportunity to restructure their case around your defense on a retrial. Prosecutors who invite a mistrial motion to try to save a floundering prosecution are likely violating the Double Jeopardy Clause in the Fifth Amendment. *See Oregon v. Kennedy*, 456 U.S. 667, 679 (1982) (double jeopardy bars re-prosecution if the government has engaged in conduct where it intended to provoke defense counsel to move for a mistrial); *United States v. Cornelius*, 623 F.3d 486, 497 (7th Cir. 2010) (prosecutors cannot engage in trial misconduct intending to precipitate a successful motion for mistrial and expect to prosecute the defendant in a subsequent trial on the same charges); *United States v. Rodriguez, 229* F. App'x 547 (9th Cir. 2007) (same).

11.2 LEADING SUPREME COURT CASES FROM *MOONEY* TO *NAPUE* TO *AGURS*

The Supreme Court has long recognized "the special role played by the American prosecutor in the search for the truth in criminal trials." *Strickler v. Greene*, 527 U.S. 263 (1999). The first key case in this area was decided in 1935. In *Mooney v. Holohan*, a state prisoner filed a habeas petition alleging that the prosecutor's presentation of false evidence violated his constitutional right to due process. 294 U.S. 103, 110 (1935). The government opposed by arguing that "the acts and omissions of the prosecutor" can never amount to a denial of due process. *Id.* at 111–112. The Supreme Court disagreed and rejected the government's narrow view of due process. *Id.* at 112. The Court held that a prosecutor's deliberate deception of the judge and jury was "inconsistent with the rudimentary demands of justice." *Id.*

Seven years later, the Supreme Court decided *Pyle v. Kansas*, 317 U.S. 213, 216 (1942). In *Pyle,* it extended this due process principle beyond perjured testimony to also include "the deliberate suppression by those same authorities of evidence favorable to [the criminal defendant]."

In 1957, the Supreme Court recognized that due process protection also extended to cases where a prosecutor knowingly allowed a witness to merely create a false impression to the jury. *Alcorta v. Texas,* 355 U.S. 28, 29–30 (1957). In *Alcorta*, the prosecutor instructed a witness not to volunteer damaging information and then sat mute while the witness committed perjury. *Id.* at 31. The Supreme Court granted the habeas petition due to the prosecutor's failure to correct that false impression, thereby setting the stage for *Napue.*

In *Napue,* the Defendant was convicted for murdering an off-duty officer during a shootout in a botched robbery of a cocktail lounge. 360 U.S. at 265. The principal government witness was one of Napue's co-conspirators, who had previously been convicted and was serving a 199-year sentence when he testified against Napue. *Id.* At trial, the prosecutor elicited testimony from the cooperating witness where he stated that the prosecutor had not promised him any consideration for testifying against Napue. *Id.* That testimony was false and the prosecutor knew it. After Napue was convicted, the prosecutor filed a petition seeking a sentence reduction for the witness where the prosecutor confirmed that he had promised the cooperating witness that he would seek a sentence reduction if the witness testified against Napue. *Id.* The Court reversed Napue's conviction because "the false testimony used by the State in securing the conviction of petitioner *may have had an effect on the outcome of the trial.*" *Id.* at 272 (emphasis added).

The *Napue* decision illustrated several key principles regarding false evidence challenges:

- False evidence from government witnesses implicates a defendant's due process rights: "a conviction obtained through use of false evidence, known to be such by representatives of the State, must fall under the Fourteenth Amendment." *Id.* at 269.
- The false evidence does not need to be elicited by the prosecutor; it is subject to attack even if the government witness lies on cross-examination: "the same result obtains when the State, although not soliciting false evidence, allows it to go uncorrected when it appears." *Id.*
- False evidence related to both actual innocence (like *Brady*) and the credibility of a government witness (like *Giglio*) is subject to attack: "the principle that a State may not knowingly use false evidence, including false testimony, to obtain a tainted conviction, implicit

in any concept of ordered liberty, does not cease to apply merely because the false testimony goes only to the credibility of the witness." *Id.*

- *Napue* and its progeny are not limited to false *testimony*—the opinion addresses false *evidence*, which is a broader concept. *Hayes v. Brown*, 399 F.3d 972, 980–81 (9th Cir. 2005).
- *Napue* does not require that the witness could be successfully prosecuted for perjury. *United States v. Freeman*, 650 F.3d 673, 680 (citing *United States v. Boyd*, 55 F.3d 239, 243 (7th Cir. 1995)). "Half-truths and vague statements that could be true in a limited, literal sense but give a false impression to the jury" qualify as false. *Id.*
- *Napue* did not create a *per se* rule of reversal. The constitutional error must be material, which *Napue* described as facts that "may have had an effect on the outcome of the trial." 360 U.S. at 272. That statement has evolved into the "reasonable likelihood" test used in most circuits, discussed below.

In *Giglio v. United States*, 405 U.S. 150 (1972), the Supreme Court extended the *Napue* doctrine to include situations where the government (writ large) but not the trial prosecutor knew or should have known the evidence was false. In *Giglio*, a government cooperator falsely testified on cross-examination that the government had not made any promises to him about any potential leniency. *Id.* at 150–51. The prosecutor who handled the case before the grand jury had promised the witness that he would not be prosecuted if he testified against the Defendant. *Id.* at 152–53. A different prosecutor handled the trial, but for the Supreme Court it did not matter. The Court stated that "a promise made by one attorney must be attributed, for these purposes, to the Government." *Id.*

In *United States v. Agurs*, a case that did not involve perjured testimony, the Supreme Court separated *Brady* violations into three separate categories. 427 U.S. 97, 103 (1976). Relevant for present purposes is that the first category included situations where the undisclosed evidence involved perjured trial testimony from government witnesses, where the prosecution team either knew or should have known of the perjury. *Id. Mooney, Napue,* and *Giglio* are all examples of this first category. For this fact pattern, the Supreme Court confirmed that it "has consistently held that a conviction obtained by the knowing use of perjured testimony is fundamentally unfair and must be set aside if there is any reasonable likelihood that the false testimony could have affected the judgment of the jury." *Id.*

The Supreme Court's pronouncement of this "reasonable likelihood" test in *Agurs* is often used to guide the *Napue* analysis related to false testimony challenges. Most courts use a three-factor test to analyze a *Napue* issue. To prevail, the defendant must show that (1) the testimony or evidence was actually false, (2) the prosecution knew or should have known that the testimony or evidence was actually false, and (3) the false evidence or testimony was material. *Hayes v. Brown*, 399 F.3d 972, 984 (9th Cir. 2005); *United States v. Freeman*, 650 F.3d 673, 678 (7th Cir. 2011). In deciding materiality, most courts determine whether there is any reasonable likelihood that the false evidence or testimony could have affected the judgment of the jury. *Hayes*, 399 F.3d at 984.

Finally, in *California v. Trombetta*, the Supreme Court confirmed that the prosecutor has a "constitutional obligation to report to the defendant and the trial court whenever government witnesses lie under oath." 467 U.S. 479, 485 (1984). In other words, prosecutors cannot remain silent when they realize (or should realize) that false evidence has been presented to the jury. Defense counsel should emphasize this failure when pressing a *Napue* issue because it may lead the trial judge to take a more defense friendly approach to the materiality analysis.

11.3 DIRECT APPEALS VS. STATE HABEAS PETITIONS

One other aspect that results in some confusing opinions in the circuits involves the difference between whether the claim is a direct appeal following a federal prosecution or a habeas claim following a state prosecution.

If it is a habeas matter, some circuits apply a pro-government heightened standard of review following the Supreme Court's decision in *Brecht v. Adamson,* 507 U.S. 619 (1993). The First, Sixth, Eighth, and Eleventh Circuits all require an additional harmless-error analysis before granting relief for a constitutional violation in a habeas petition. *See, e.g., Gilday v. Callahan*, 59 F.3d 257, 268 (1st Cir. 1995); *Rosencrantz v. Lafler*, 568 F.3d 577, 587–90 (6th Cir. 2009); *United States v. Clay*, 720 F.3d 1021, 1026–27 (8th Cir. 2013); *Trepal v. Sec'y, Florida Dep't of Corr.*, 684 F.3d 1088, 1111–13 (11th Cir. 2012). Under this test, the defendant also must show that the *Napue* error "had a substantial and injurious effect or influence in determining the jury's verdict." *Brecht*, 507 U.S. at 623. As a result, the appellate court can analyze the overall strength of the government's evidence as a basis to deny relief even after finding that the prosecutor knowingly sponsored false evidence to deceive the court and the jury.

By contrast, the Third and Ninth Circuits use a more defendant-friendly approach. *See, e.g.*, *Haskell v. Superintendent Greene SCI*, 866 F.3d 139, 150–51 (3d Cir. 2017); *Hayes v. Brown*, 399 F.3d 972, 984 (9th Cir. 2005). In *Hayes*, the court held *Brecht*'s harmless error analysis was not needed because "the required finding of materiality necessarily compels the conclusion that the error was not harmless." 399 F.3d at 984. The discussion by the Third Circuit in *Haskell* provides the best analysis of the circuit split on this issue, where they concluded that *Brecht* did not apply to false testimony claims because (a) the test for materiality in the reasonable likelihood analysis supplies the test for harmlessness, (b) the deliberate deception of the court and jury is inconsistent with the rudimentary demands of justice, and (c) excluding perjured testimony claims from the *Brecht* analysis would not degrade the prominence of the trial. *Id.* at 151.

Due to the circuits' use of different standards on habeas claims, the government routinely cites the wrong legal standard—selecting the higher bar for the defendant to clear—in *Napue* claims by attempting to apply the more onerous habeas standard in a direct federal prosecution. We have confronted this issue in several matters in different jurisdictions on cases handled by different prosecutors. The best approach is to drill down on the law in your circuit to identify the applicable standard of review and then cross-reference some other pro-defense rulings from other circuits to see if you can apply some of the favorable language in those cases to your matter. You should gain credibility in any appellate court—and the government should lose credibility—when you repeatedly correct the government when the prosecutor recites the wrong legal standard to the court.

11.4 KEY DEFENSE POINTS IN *NAPUE* CLAIMS

The best pro-defense analysis and/or quotes appear in the following cases. There will be some authority in other jurisdictions that may disagree with these points, but these key points will provide circuit level authority to counter likely government arguments on the core issues in a *Napue* challenge.

- If it is established that the government knowingly permitted the introduction of false testimony, reversal is virtually automatic. *United States v. Wallach*, 925 F.2d 445 (2d Cir. 1991).

- The defendant does not need to show actual perjury; instead, simple mistaken testimony is sufficient since it still misleads the jury. *United States v. Cargill*, 17 F. App'x 214, 224 (4th Cir. 2001); *United States v. Freeman*, 650 F.3d 673, 680 (7th Cir. 2011).
- *Napue* and its progeny are *not* limited to false *testimony*—the opinion addresses false *evidence*, which is a broader concept. *Hayes v. Brown*, 399 F.3d 972, 980–81 (9th Cir. 2005).
- The defendant does not need to show that the prosecutor actually knew the evidence was false; simply showing that the prosecutor should have known it was false is sufficient. *Cargill*, 17 F. App'x at 224.
- Providing pre-trial Rule 16 discovery that might help defense counsel cross-examine the witness on the topic at issue does not obviate the need for the prosecutor to correct false evidence during trial. *Id.*
- Defense counsel does not waive a *Napue* challenge where they were aware of and failed to correct a prosecutor's misrepresentation because the duty to correct false testimony lies with the prosecutor at all times. *United States v. Foster*, 874 F.2d 491, 495 (8th Cir. 1988)
- Defense counsel's cross-examination about the false testimony elicited on direct examination by the prosecutor does not preclude relief. Juries are often skeptical of criminal defense attorneys, who they view as advocates, and prosecutors possess a special duty to assure that every defendant receives a fair trial. *United States v. LaPage*, 231 F.3d 488, 492 (9th Cir. 2000)

11.5 *NAPUE*'S PROGENY: HELPFUL CASES

The following summary contains an analysis of the state of play in each federal circuit, with a focus on pro-defendant rulings.

First Circuit

The First Circuit does not have any significant decisions reversing a conviction for a *Napue* violation. The leading case is a pro-government opinion. *United States v. Mangual-Garcia*, 505 F.3d 1, 10–11 (1st Cir. 2007). In *Mangual-Garcia*, the government confirmed at sidebar that the government had no intention of prosecuting the cooperating witness. However, on cross-examination, the witness stated that he could be put in jail because of his testimony. The prosecution did not correct the witness's testimony.

Id. The First Circuit determined this was a *Napue* violation because the prosecution knew the testimony was false and let it go uncorrected. *Id.* at 10. However, the court held it was not a reversible error because defense counsel was aware of the false testimony and chose not to pursue it. The court recognized a split in the circuits on the issue but emphasized that "when the defendant knows about the false testimony and fails to bring it to the jury or the court's attention, the assumption is that he did so for strategic reasons, and the defendant will not be allowed to question his own strategic choices on appeal." *Id.* at 10–11.

Second Circuit

Decisions in the Second Circuit illustrate the schizophrenic approach that the circuits take on *Napue* issues. The Second Circuit applies two different standards on direct federal appeals on *Napue* claims. The court has expressly acknowledged the differences between its two standards but has not expressly rejected one approach over the other. *See United States v. Ferguson*, 676 F.3d 260, 282–83 (2d. Cir. 2011) (acknowledging the tension with having two separate tests for assessing false testimony claims but suggesting that the tests "are not necessarily incompatible").

The more favorable test appears in *United States v. Wallach*, 925 F.2d 445 (2d Cir. 1991). In *Wallach*, the Second Circuit reversed the Defendant's conviction on a false testimony claim. The court applied a two-factor test. The court considered "(1) whether the perjury was material to the jury's verdict; [and] (2) the extent to which the prosecution knew or should have known about the perjury." *Id.* at 456. Critical to success on this test is establishing that the government knew or should have known the testimony was false. The court stated that "*if it is established that the government knowingly permitted the introduction of false testimony reversal is virtually automatic.*" *Id.* (quotations omitted) (emphasis added). By contrast, if the government was unaware of the perjury, the defense must show that "but for the perjured testimony, the defendant would most likely not have been convicted." *Id.* In *Wallach,* the court reversed the convictions because it concluded that the government knew or should have known that their witness had perjured himself. *Id.* at 457.

The less favorable test is a four-factor test announced in *United States v. Zichettello*, 208 F.3d 72, 102 (2d. Cir. 2000). That test requires the defendant to prove (1) the witness actually committed perjury, (2) the alleged perjury was material, (3) the government knew or should have known of the alleged perjury at the time of trial, and (4) the perjured testimony remained undisclosed at trial. *Id.* This test is tougher for defendants to meet because the perjured testimony often is disclosed and hotly debated at trial. In *Wallach,* for example, defense counsel did a masterful job investigating and impeaching the false testimony during cross-examination. 925 F.2d at 455–56.

Zichettello is flawed because it potentially rewards the government for knowingly sponsoring false testimony simply because the defense challenged it during trial. This makes no sense because courts have recognized that juries view criminal defense attorneys with skepticism—cross-examination by defense counsel of a lying witness might not remove that taint. *See United States v. LaPage,* 231 F.3d 488, 492 (9th Cir. 2000). The Supreme Court has also recognized that jurors often place too much trust in statements from prosecutors because they represent the government. *United States v. Young,* 470 U.S. 1, 18 (1985) (a statement from a prosecutor in closing argument "carries with it the imprimatur of the Government and may induce the jury to trust the Government's judgment rather than its own view of the evidence.").

The confusion continues in the Second Circuit because some later cases apply the *Wallach* test (*United States v. Stewart,* 433 F.3d 273, 297 (2d. Cir. 2006)) while others apply the *Zichettello* test. *See United States v. Josephberg,* 562 F.3d 478, 494 (2d. Cir. 2009).

Third Circuit

The Third Circuit uses a four-factor test to make out a constitutional violation under *Napue. Lambert v. Blackwell,* 387 F.3d 210, 242–43 (3d Cir. 2004). In *Lambert,* the court granted a habeas appeal of a state homicide conviction. The *Lambert* test requires defendants to show that (1) the witness actually committed perjury, (2) the government knew or should have known of the witness's perjury, (3) the testimony went uncorrected, and (4) there is a reasonable likelihood that the false testimony could have affected the verdict. *Id.* Importantly, the "reasonable likelihood" element of the *Lambert* test—which represents the materiality element of a *Napue* claim—encompasses and forecloses any additional consideration harmless error analysis. *Haskell v. Superintendent Greene SCI,* 866 F.3d 139, 150–51 (3d Cir. 2017) (the test for materiality supplies the test for harmlessness and there is no need to look to *Brecht* to supply a harmless-error standard).

In *Haskell*, the court emphasized that a knowing presentation of perjured testimony "cuts to the core of a defendant's right to due process" and justifies a "lower, more favorable to the defendant, and hostile to the prosecution" standard. *Id.* at 152. As a result, a showing of materiality in the Third Circuit forecloses application of the actual prejudice standard of *Brecht* in habeas cases and demands reversal of a conviction. *Id.* (granting habeas relief for defendant where witness falsely testified that he had not received any consideration from the prosecution in exchange for his testimony about the identity of the assailant because such testimony implicated the witness's credibility and was thus material).

Fourth Circuit

The Fourth Circuit's opinion in *United States v. Cargill* contains one of the most reasoned applications of Supreme Court precedent. 17 F. App'x 214, 228–29 (4th Cir. 2001). The court persuasively rejected a series of arguments the government often raises to oppose false evidence claims. While the court ultimately found for the government on the final factor—the strength of the evidence at trial—the court was exceptionally critical of the AUSA's conduct at trial.

The case involved a federal drug conspiracy where the government's primary cooperating witness provided false testimony about his involvement in another drug conspiracy—a conspiracy the trial AUSA had prosecuted so the AUSA was very familiar with the cooperator's role in the other conspiracy. *Id* at 220. At trial, the AUSA failed to notify the court or defense counsel about the false testimony and instead bolstered the cooperator's credibility in both redirect and closing argument. *Id.* at 220–23.

The court reviewed four factors: (1) was the testimony false, (2) did the AUSA know the testimony was false, (3) did the AUSA disclose to defense counsel and the court that the testimony was false, and (4) was there any reasonable likelihood that the false testimony affected the judgment of the jury. *Id.* at 223. On the falsity prong, the government argued that the defendant needed to prove that the witness committed actual perjury, not merely that the testimony created a false impression of a material fact. *Id.* The court disagreed, citing *Giglio* for the proposition that the defendant need only show the testimony was false, which includes whether the witness was simply mistaken. *Id.* at 224. The court stated that "it matters not whether the witness giving false testimony was mistaken or intentionally lying. If the prosecution knows the witness's statement is untrue, it has a duty to correct it." *Id.*

As to the prosecutor's knowledge, the government argued that the defendant had to show that the prosecutor intentionally offered false testimony. *Id.* at 225. The court rejected the government's argument because prior cases only required that the prosecutor knew *or should have known* that the testimony was false. *Id.*

As to the disclosure requirement, the government argued that its pretrial disclosures about the criminal history of the cooperating witness absolved the prosecutor of needing to notify the defense counsel and court about the false trial testimony. *Id.* The court rejected the government's argument, citing *California v. Trombetta* (467 U.S. 479, 485 (1984)) for the proposition that "the government is always under a strict duty to inform a defendant of false testimony by one of its witnesses." *Id.* The Fourth Circuit emphasized that once the witness testified falsely at trial, "the AUSA was under a duty to inform the defendants of that fact." *Id.*

The court also analyzed the "reasonable likelihood" test in some detail. The court noted that the *Giglio* standard for assessing false testimony claims was more defense friendly than the *Brady* standard for assessing failure to disclose evidence because "the government's knowing use of false testimony is more serious than a *Brady* violation since it 'involves a corruption of the truth-seeking function of the trial process.'" *Id.* at 227–28 (quoting *United States v. Bagley*, 473 U.S. 667, 680 (1985)).

In another case, *Campbell v. Reed*, the Fourth Circuit reviewed whether a witness's inaccurate description of a plea bargain may present a due process problem because the presence of such an agreement affects a jury's assessment of the witness's credibility. 594 F.2d 4 (4th Cir. 1979). The court considered whether there was any reasonable likelihood that a witness's testimony claiming he had not been promised leniency from the government in return for his testimony would have affected the judgment of the jury. *Id.* at 8. Finding the witness's testimony "was extremely important since he was the only witness who could link Campbell to the burglary in question," the court reversed the district court's judgment because the "prosecution allowed a false impression to be created at trial when the truth would have directly impugned the veracity of its key witness." *Id.* (quoting *United States v. Sutton*, 542 F.2d 1239, 1243 (4th Cir. 1976)). However, the Fourth Circuit is more reluctant to reverse a conviction when false testimony affecting the credibility of a witness is exposed or corrected during cross-examination. *United States v. Chavez*, 894 F.3d 593, 601 (4th Cir. 2018).

Fifth Circuit

In *United States v. Barham*, the Fifth Circuit reiterated that it interpreted the "reasonable likelihood" standard from *Agurs* to mean that "[a] new trial is necessary when there is any reasonable likelihood that disclosure of the truth would have affected the judgment of the jury." 595 F.2d 231, 242 (5th Cir. 1979). In addition, the "reasonable likelihood" standard is a "low threshold" standard that is akin to "harmless beyond a reasonable doubt." *Id.* The court emphasized this point because false testimony corrupted the "truth-seeking function of the trial process." *Id.*

In *Barham*, despite defense counsel's cross-examination of the government witnesses on their false testimony, the court reversed the Defendant's conviction where the prosecutor elicited and failed to correct false testimony from three witnesses regarding whether they would receive favorable treatment from the government in exchange for their testimony. *Id.* 241–42. The court determined this case required reversal because "credibility weighed so heavily in the balance" and knowledge of favorable treatment would have given the jury a "concrete reason" to believe the witnesses might have fabricated their testimony. *Id.* at 243.

Sixth Circuit

Like the First Circuit, the Sixth Circuit does not have any key cases reversing a conviction for a *Napue* violation. Citing *Napue*, the Sixth Circuit applies a three-step test, known as the *Coe* test, requiring defendants to show (1) that the testimony was actually false, (2) the statement was material, and (3) the prosecution knew it was false. *Coe v. Bell*, 161 F.3d 320, 343 (6th Cir. 1998). Under the *Coe* test, the defendants bear the initial burden of showing that the testimony in question was actually perjured or "indisputably false." *Id.*; *see also Rosencrantz v. Lafler*, 568 F.3d 577, 584, 586 (6th Cir. 2009). Like the Fourth Circuit, mere inconsistencies do not constitute indisputable falsity. *Rosencrantz*, 568 F.3d at 585 (citing *Coe*, 161 F.3d at 343). Moreover, "[i]ndisputable falsehood is not established by a swearing contest." *Id.* at 586 (if a prosecutor presents potentially false testimony, defense counsel is responsible for exploring the veracity of the testimony on cross-examination).

Once testimony is established as indisputably false, the Sixth Circuit adopts a similar defendant-friendly "reasonable likelihood" materiality standard. *Id.* at 587 (acknowledging that the court "will only excuse perjury as immaterial if we can 'say that no reasonable jury could have been affected by the undisclosed information'" (quoting *Gilday*, 59 F.3d at 269)); *see also Smith v. Metrish*, 436 F. App'x 554, 566 (6th Cir. 2011) ("[F]alse testimony claim demands a lower showing of materiality than a *Brady* claim"). When determining whether any reasonable likelihood that the false testimony could have affected the jury's judgment existed, the Sixth Circuit considers whether the prosecution reinforced the allegedly false statement or merely allowed the statement to go uncorrected. *United States v. Lochmondy*, 890 F.2d 817, 823 (6th Cir. 1989). In *Lochmondy*, the Sixth Circuit distinguished *Barham* and found no reversible error because, unlike in *Barham*, the inconsistent testimony was not reinforced by additional misleading questions posed by the prosecution to other witnesses. *Id.* (citing *Barham*, 595 F.2d at 243 n.17).

In the context of habeas petitions, the Sixth Circuit requires an additional hurdle of proving actual prejudice to warrant reversal of a conviction for failure to correct otherwise material false testimony. *Rosencrantz*, 568 F.3d at 585 (affirming conviction where false testimony that otherwise satisfied the *Coe* test constituted harmless error). In *Rosencrantz*, the court assumed materiality of the allegedly false testimony—thus assuming constitutional error—but then analyzed the testimony under a harmless-error review guided by the Supreme Court's ruling in *Brecht*. *Id.* at 589–90 (citing *Brecht v. Abrahamson*, 507 U.S. 619, 637 (1993)). Under *Brecht*, "a knowing-presentation error harms the accused when the error had a 'substantial and injurious effect or influence in determining the jury's verdict.'" *Id.* at 590 (citing *Brecht*, 507 U.S. at 637). The court ultimately concluded that a witness's denial of a meeting with prosecution prior to trial, while material because the witness was key for the prosecution, constituted harmless error because exposure of the lie would not have substantially influenced the jury's deliberation in light of additional evidence supporting conviction. *Id.* at 591. In affirming the conviction, the court emphasized that "prosecutorial culpability cannot . . . outweigh *Brecht's* policy" interests in finality and sovereignty of a trial court's judgment. *Id.* (the prosecutorial "misconduct's effect on the trial, not the blameworthiness of the prosecutor, is the crucial inquiry for due process purposes").

Seventh Circuit

In *United States v. Freeman*, the Seventh Circuit affirmed a district court's granting of a defense motion for new trial based on false testimony provided by the government's primary cooperating witness in a drug conspiracy. 650 F.3d 673 (7th Cir. 2011). Similar to the Fourth Circuit's analysis in *Cargill*, the Seventh Circuit picked apart the government's typical arguments. The court stated that the Defendant needed to establish that (1) there was false testimony, (2) the government knew or should have known it was false, and (3) there is a likelihood that the false testimony affected the judgment of the jury. *Id.* at 678.

First, as a threshold matter of determining whether there was false testimony, the government argued that the test requires the defendant to show that the witness's testimony can be verified or refuted—which the defense cannot establish if the testimony is simply a choice between competing inferences. *Id.* In response, the Seventh Circuit stated that "*Napue* does not require that the witness could be successfully prosecuted for perjury." *Id.* at 680 (citing *United States v. Boyd*, 55 F.3d 239, 243 (7th Cir. 1995)). Therefore, "half-truths and vague statements that could be true in a limited, literal sense but give a false impression to the jury" qualify as false. *Id.* As to whether the government should have known about the false testimony, the court relied on a letter defense counsel had sent to the government before trial to warn the prosecutors that their witness could not place the Defendant at the scene of the crime because the Defendant was in prison at the time. *Id.* The court confirmed that the letter put the prosecutors on notice to investigate so they could not ignore evidence that its witness was lying at trial. *Id.* Finally, as in the Fourth and Fifth Circuits, the Seventh Circuit agrees that the "reasonable likelihood" test should be a lower burden for the defendant to meet since false testimony corrupts the truth-seeking function of the trial process. *Id.* at 681.

Second, as in the Fourth and Fifth Circuits, the Seventh Circuit identifies the "reasonable likelihood" standard as setting a "lower threshold for determining materiality." *Id.* at 681. However, as noted above in the *LaPage* discussion, the Seventh Circuit, in its reasonable likelihood analysis, considers whether the defendant had "an adequate opportunity to expose the false testimony on cross-examination." *Id.* In *Freeman*, the court upheld the grant of a new trial for a *Napue* violation despite the Defendant's cross-examination because the prosecutor's objections muted the impact of defense counsel's impeachment. *Id.* at 681–82 (finding the government's case relied heavily on the testimony of the lying witness due to the relative weakness of additional evidence presented at trial).

Eighth Circuit

The Eighth Circuit elaborates on the *Napue* standard in a defendant-friendly manner, placing the duty to correct false testimony of a government witness entirely on the prosecution. *United States v. Foster*, 874 F.2d 491, 495 (8th Cir. 1988). Importantly, defense counsel does not waive the right to relief for a *Napue* violation merely because they were aware of and failed to correct a prosecutor's misrepresentation. *Id.* (the duty to correct false testimony lies with the prosecutor at all times).

In *Foster*, the Eighth Circuit reversed a conviction where the prosecutor failed to correct the testimony of multiple witnesses who stated that the government had not offered any promises in exchange for their testimony. *Id.* Though defense counsel remained silent, despite their awareness of evidence to the contrary, "[t]his did not relieve the prosecutor of her overriding duty of candor to the court, and to seek justice rather than convictions." *Id.* (holding prosecutor's failure to inform the jury of promises made to the witnesses prejudicial because the case "essentially [rested] on the credibility of the witness[es]"); *see also United States v. Begeleisen*, 625 F.2d 203, 208 (8th Cir. 1980) (reversing and remanding conviction in part where government failed to correct a prosecution witness's false testimony denying the existence of any agreement to testify against the Defendant because the witness's testimony was the "linchpin in the government's case" and the existence of such an agreement "was central to the jury's credibility evaluation" of the witness).

Ninth Circuit

In *United States v. LaPage,* the court reversed the Defendant's conviction where a government witness lied, defense counsel cross-examined on the topic, and the prosecutor refused to correct the record until rebuttal summation. 231 F.3d 488 (9th Cir. 2000). This case is helpful because the court expressly rejected the government's argument that *Napue* does not extend to cases where defense counsel had an opportunity to impeach and argue the issue to the jury. The court stated "all perjury pollutes a trial, making it hard for jurors to see the truth." *Id.* at 492. The court insisted that the government had a duty to correct the false testimony during the trial—even when defense counsel had cross-examined on the topic at issue. *Id.* The court reasoned that juries are often skeptical of criminal defense attorneys, who they view as advocates, and also emphasized the prosecutor's special duty to assure that every defendant receives a fair trial. *Id.*; *but see United States v. Renzi*, 769 F.3d 731, 752 (9th Cir. 2014) (rejecting *Napue* claim, in part, because defense counsel effectively attacked the credibility of the government witnesses at issue on cross-examination).

In addition to the defendant-friendly standard applied in *LaPage*, the Ninth Circuit incorporates a reduced burden for defendants when seeking habeas relief. Unlike the majority of the circuits, the Ninth Circuit agrees with the Third Circuit and does not require that defendants meet an additional harmless error standard as applied under *Brecht* when alleging a *Napue* violation. *Hayes v. Brown*, 399 F.3d 972, 984 (9th Cir. 2002). In *Hayes*, the Ninth Circuit, in an *en banc* ruling, observed that the reasonable likelihood standard for determining the materiality of false testimony "necessarily forecloses a *Brecht* harmless error analysis." *Id.* Accordingly, habeas defendants in the Ninth Circuit need not prove any additional prejudice suffered as a result of the presentation of false testimony once the defendant proves the materiality of the *Napue* error. *Id.* at 985; *see also Phillips v. Ornoski*, 673 F.3d 1168, 1196–97 (9th Cir. 2012) (reversing denial of *habeas* relief where prosecution failed to correct witness testimony about the existence of a deal in exchange for testimony because the existence of such an agreement constitutes more than "merely cumulative impeachment" by directly implicating a central witness's credibility, satisfying the materiality standard of *Napue*); *Maxwell v. Roe*, 628 F.3d 486, 508 (9th Cir. 2010).

The Ninth Circuit's opinion in *Hayes* is also helpful because it contains one of the most detailed descriptions of the growth and expansion of *Napue* and its progeny, including a helpful discussion of all the key Supreme Court cases on the topic—from *Mooney* in 1935 to *Bagley* in 1985. 399 F.3d at 983–84.

In *Dickey v. Davis*, the court reversed where the State's primary witness testified falsely regarding his deal with the government and the prosecutor failed to correct the testimony. 69 F.4th 624, 629 (9th Cir. 2023). The witness testified that he had not received anything from the DA's office and that he only spoke to the prosecutor a couple of times—facts that were both false, and the prosecutor knew the testimony was false. *Id.* The court stated "[t]his is an exceptional case in which the prosecutor deliberately elicited, and then failed to correct, false and misleading testimony from the State's star witness, Gene Buchanan." *Id.* at 629. Instead of correcting the false testimony, the prosecutor then "went on to exploit Buchanan's false testimony in his closing argument." *Id.* The court was particularly concerned with the prosecutor's use of leading questions to elicit the witness's false testimony. *Id.* at 645. In addition, the court found that the prosecution's failure to correct the false testimony was material because the witness's "testimony was the centerpiece of the State's case in support of the special-circumstances finding." *Id.* at 644. Ultimately, the court did "not hesitate to conclude there was a reasonable likelihood that the State's failure to correct Buchanan's testimony could have affected the jury's special-circumstances finding" and therefore reversed the district court's ruling as to petitioner's penalty-phase *Napue* claim. *Id.* at 645.

Tenth Circuit

The Tenth Circuit cites *Napue* and *Giglio* when reviewing convictions obtained by the presentation of known false evidence. As a prerequisite, the Tenth Circuit requires the defendant establish (1) perjury by the witness, and (2) the prosecutor's knowledge of the falsity at the time of the testimony. *United States v. Garcia*, 793 F.3d 1194, 1207 (10th Cir. 2015); *United States v. Caballero*, 277 F.3d 1235, 1244 (10th Cir. 2002) (courts will only consider materiality when the defendant sufficiently satisfies the first two elements). Once the prerequisites are met, the Tenth Circuit applies a "more easily satisfied" materiality standard. *Garcia*, 793 F.3d at 1207. In considering the materiality of false testimony, especially when pertaining to a witness's credibility, the court considers the cumulative effect of the potential evidence for omitting facts or failing to correct false testimony. *United States v. Harmon*, 793 F.3d 1194, 1209 (10th Cir. 2015). In addition, the Tenth Circuit is reluctant to find a *Napue* violation where the jury is made aware of the possibility of false testimony that could affect a witness's credibility because issues of credibility are questions for the jury. *United States v. Smalls*, 752 F.3d 1227, 1245 (10th Cir. 2014).

But the Tenth Circuit also abides by the precedent established in *Agurs* that a "prosecutor's knowing use of false testimony involves, not 'just' prosecutorial misconduct, but 'more importantly . . . [the] corruption of the truth-seeking function of the trial process.'" *Douglas v. Workman*, 560 F.3d 1156, 1192 (10th Cir. 2009); *see also Garcia*, 793 F.3d at 1208. In *Douglas*, the Defendant brought a habeas petition alleging the prosecution committed *Brady* (failure to disclose exculpatory evidence), *Napue* (solicitation of false testimony), and *Giglio* (failure to correct testimony known to be false) violations which gave the jury false impressions of witness credibility. *Id.* at 1180–81. The court found that the prosecutor's actions were willful and intentional rather than merely inadvertent, and that the prosecutor's knowing presentation of false testimony "warrant[ed] special condemnation." *Id.* at 1192. The court affirmed the district court's grant of habeas relief from his murder conviction to "censure such willful prosecutorial misconduct." *Id.*

Eleventh Circuit

The Eleventh Circuit generally interprets *Napue* without additional specific considerations except for when false testimony concerns witness bias. In *United States v. Rivera Pedin*, the court stated that a reversal is required for a *Napue* violation when the "estimate of the truthfulness and reliability of the given witness may well be determinative of guilt or innocence." 861 F.2d 1522, 1530 (11th Cir. 1988). Factors that the court considers in such a case are whether the witness's bias becomes irrelevant, or the witness was "thoroughly impeached and proof of [their] bias would be merely cumulative." *Id.*

In *Rivera Pedin*, the court reversed and remanded for a new trial when the prosecution failed to correct the primary witness's testimony that he did not meet with the Defendant to ask for money to not testify. *Id.* at 1529. The court acknowledged that the defense's cross-examination was effective in eroding the witness's credibility, but knowing about the witness's prior extortion attempt would have "introduced a new source of potential bias." *Id.* at 1530.

D.C. Circuit

The D.C. Circuit does not have a circuit-specific test. In this circuit "a conviction obtained by the knowing use of perjured testimony violates the defendant's right to a fair trial mandated by the due process clauses of the Fifth and Fourteenth Amendments." *United States v. Iverson*, 637 F.2d 799, 801 (D.C. Cir. 1980). The prosecutor has an affirmative obligation to correct the record when a prosecution witness testifies falsely. *Id.* In addition, the rule applies both to testimony relating to an essential element of the case and the credibility of a crucial witness. *Id.*

Reversal for *Napue* violations is warranted when "the prosecution relies on testimony which it knows or should know to be false [and] that the conviction must be set aside if there is 'any reasonable likelihood that the false testimony could have affected the judgment of the jury.'" *Id.* at 805 (quoting *Agurs*, 427 U.S. at 103).

In *Iverson*, the government's principal witness, who was awaiting sentence, asserted during cross-examination that she had already been sentenced and the prosecution failed to correct this error. *Id.* at 802. The testimony led to the erroneous conclusion that she could not benefit from cooperating with the government. *Id.* The court determined this constituted reversible error because the testimony was false in a critical aspect and the testimony was the crucial evidence of the Defendant's intent. *Id.* at 805.

The D.C. Circuit emphasized the leniency of the reasonable likelihood test in *United States v. Butler*, 955 F.3d 1052, 1058 (D.C. Cir. 2020) (observing that the "reasonable likelihood test" is "quite easily satisfied" (quoting *United States v. Ausby*, 916 F.3d 1089, 1092 (D.C. Cir. 2019)). In *Butler*, the court reversed and remanded with instructions to vacate the Defendant's sentence where the government introduced false hair microscopy evidence during the trial. *Id.* The court observed that even though the jury "might well have convicted" the Defendant based on testimony from a cornerstone witness—one who had also testified falsely, although such falsities were exposed and corrected on cross-examination—the Defendant was not required to show "that the jury could not (or would not) have convicted him without the false hair evidence." *Id.* at 1058, 1064. The court emphasized that '"even if the false testimony *may* not have affected the jury's verdict, it is material if the evidence reasonably *could* have affected the verdict.'" *Id.* at 1064 (emphasis in original) (quoting *Ausby*, 916 F.3d at 1093 (reversing and vacating sentence where government introduced false hair microscopy evidence)).

CHAPTER 12

Constructive Amendment

12.1 CONSTRUCTIVE AMENDMENT BASICS

A constructive amendment challenge is a lethal weapon in the arsenal of experienced criminal defense lawyers because a violation results in a *per se* reversal of a defendant's conviction. *United States v. Roberts,* 770 F. App'x 563, 566 (11th Cir. 2019) (a constructive amendment is *per se* reversible error); *United States v. Hassan,* 578 F.3d 108, 133–34 (2d Cir. 2008) (constructive amendments are "per se violations of the Grand Jury Clause of the Fifth Amendment that require reversal even without a showing of prejudice to the defendant"); *United States v. Harrill,* 877 F.2d 341, 344 (5th Cir. 1989) (any constructive amendment of the indictment requires reversal and remand for a new trial consistent with the allegations in the indictment); *United States v. Adamson,* 291 F.3d 606, 615 (9th Cir. 2002) (a constructive amendment always requires reversal).

A constructive amendment may happen when prosecutors see their case slipping away because their evidence at trial may not support the specific facts they alleged in the indictment. In response, prosecutors often introduce evidence of uncharged conduct that will generate a conviction under the jury instructions delivered by the court. If an analysis of the evidence, argument, and jury instructions demonstrates that the defendant could have been convicted based on facts or theories not charged in the indictment, you may be entitled to an automatic reversal—even where the evidence was sufficient to convict on the facts and theories actually contained in the indictment. The improper *broadening* of the charges into uncharged conduct triggers a successful constructive amendment challenge.

As the cases from the circuits illustrate, this happens far more frequently than many of us might believe. Thus, it is critical to timely object during trial to both the admission of evidence and any related argument that may constructively amend the indictment. Failure to preserve the issue at trial will result in plain error review on appeal, which will require a showing that the error affected the substantial rights of the defendant. The heightened plain error standard provides the government and appellate court an easy way to avoid the *per se* reversal of the defendant's conviction that should attach when the prosecutor constructively amends the indictment at trial.

This chapter analyzes the historical constitutional underpinning of a constructive amendment challenge, discusses leading cases to help identify what fact patterns yield successful challenges, and compares a constructive amendment to a mere variance because a variance will not result in an automatic reversal of the conviction. The summary of pro-defendant cases discussed below illustrates that successful challenges happen in all kinds of cases—from simple felon-in-possession prosecutions to complex wire fraud and RICO conspiracy prosecutions.

12.2 THE GRAND JURY CLAUSE IN THE FIFTH AMENDMENT

The Grand Jury Clause in the Fifth Amendment states that "no person shall be held to answer for a capital, or other infamous crime, unless on a presentment or indictment of a Grand Jury. . . ." U.S. Const. amend. V. That Fifth Amendment right means that neither the prosecutor nor the trial court can broaden the scope of the alleged crime at trial such that the jury might have convicted on a set of facts or theory that an independent grand jury did not approve.

In 1887, the Supreme Court confirmed that "it is the exclusive prerogative of the grand jury to determine the charges, and once it has done so neither a prosecutor nor a judge can change the indictment to suit [his or her] own notions of what it ought to have been, or what the grand jury would probably have made it if their attention had been called to suggested changes." *Ex Parte Bain*, 121 U.S. 1, 10 (1887). The Supreme Court emphasized that "after the indictment was changed [at trial], it was no longer the indictment of the grand jury who presented it. Any other doctrine would place the rights of the citizen, which were intended to be protected by the constitutional provision, at the mercy or control of the court or prosecuting attorney." *Id.* at 13.

There is also a Sixth Amendment component to a constructive amendment challenge given that the Sixth Amendment protects a defendant's right to be informed about the charges against him and to prevent re-prosecution for the same offense. *United States v. de Leon-De La Rosa*, 17 F.4th 175, 200 (1st Cir. 2021); *United States v. Miller*, 891 F.3d 1220, 1237 (10th Cir. 2018).

12.3 *STIRONE V. UNITED STATES*

The leading Supreme Court decision regarding the constructive amendment doctrine is *Stirone v. United States*, 361 U.S. 212 (1960). In *Stirone*, the Supreme Court confirmed that the Fifth Amendment requires that prosecution begin by indictment before a grand jury. *Id.* at 215. This requirement limits a defendant's jeopardy to offenses actually charged by a group of the defendant's fellow citizens acting independently of either the prosecuting attorney or the trial judge. *Id.* at 218.

In *Stirone*, the government prosecuted a Hobbs Act violation where the indictment alleged that the defendants moved a specific material (sand) through interstate commerce. 361 U.S. at 213. At trial, however, the court permitted the government to introduce evidence showing that the defendants also moved a different material (steel) through interstate commerce. *Id.* at 214. The Supreme Court found that the indictment could not be read as charging interference with movements of steel because the government chose to specifically charge movements of sand—and only movements of sand—in the indictment. *Id.* at 217. The grand jury never approved any charge related to the movement of steel. As a result, the Supreme Court reversed the conviction because the jury could have convicted based on steel, not sand. *Id.* at 218–19. The Supreme Court emphasized that "we cannot know whether the grand jury would have included in its indictment a charge that commerce in steel from a nonexistent steel mill had been interfered with." *Id.*

12.4 IDENTIFYING A CONSTRUCTIVE AMENDMENT

The decisions in *Ex Parte Bain* and *Stirone* provide guidance for how to identify a potential constructive amendment:

- Review the indictment for specific language that limits the alleged criminal conduct in some respect; for example, shipments of a specific material, specific false representations, a specific weapon used in an assault, or stealing the identity of a specific victim.

- Be alert for evidence or closing argument where the government focuses on other uncharged conduct that extends beyond the specific allegations in the indictment—for example, the shipment of a different material, making a different false representation, the use of a different weapon in an assault, or stealing the identity of other victims—such that the proof has impermissibly *broadened* the scope of the indictment.
- Analyze the jury instructions because they will likely not be specific enough to limit the jury's analysis to only the charged conduct.
- If these three elements are present, raise a constructive amendment objection where you cite the Grand Jury Clause and Due Process Clause of the Fifth Amendment, *Stirone*, and any additional controlling circuit level authority cited below.

Of particular importance is the government's choice to file a "speaking indictment" where it alleges specific facts in the indictment it presents to the grand jury, as opposed to using a simple boilerplate indictment that charges the general elements of the offense as those elements appear in the relevant statute and corresponding pattern jury instruction. The government often uses speaking indictments so the prosecutors can issue a detailed press release at the outset of the case to generate media for themselves. This is one area where being media hungry can backfire on the government. Numerous courts have used the fact that the government chose to file a speaking indictment as the basis to reverse a conviction on constructive amendment grounds. As the Supreme Court held in *Stirone,* when the government elects to charge particular facts in its indictment, a conviction must rest on that specific charge and no other. 361 U.S. at 218. In *United States v. Salinas,* the government indicted the Defendant for misapplication of bank funds and specifically alleged that the Defendant had aided and abetted a particular bank principal named Woodul, the president of the bank. 654 F.2d 319, 322 (5th Cir. 1981). At trial, however, the government presented evidence that a different bank principal (a vice president of the bank named Nance) had authorized the loan at issue. *Id.* at 323. The jury instructions did not require that Woodul—and only Woodul—be the principal whom Salinas aided and abetted on the count of conviction. *Id.* Thus, the court's instructions allowed the jury to convict the Defendant for aiding and abetting any principal of the bank, including Nance. *Id.* In reversing, the Fifth Circuit penalized the government for its decision to plead specific facts in its speaking indictment and thereby open the risk of a constructive amendment at trial. The court stated "[t]he grand jury could have named Nance. It could have charged 'unnamed principals.' It chose not to do so." *Id.* at 324; *see also United States v. Miller*, 891 F.3d 1220, 1234–36 (10th Cir. 2018) (emphasizing that the government must be held to the words it chose to include in its indictment); *United States v. Leichtnam*, 948 F.2d 370, 379 (7th Cir. 1991) (same).

Another way to prove a constructive amendment is to contrast the prosecutor's opening statement against his or her closing argument. In opening statement, the prosecutor may stick with the specific facts and theories that appear in the indictment. But then the government encounters proof issues during trial so the prosecutor improperly seeks to broaden the basis to convict during trial and then argues that broader theory or set of facts—the uncharged conduct—in closing argument.

An example is *United States v. Doucet*, 994 F.2d 169, 171 (5th Cir. 1993). In *Doucet*, the government opened its case by accurately summarizing the facts charged in its indictment: the Defendant had previously modified his AR-15 rifle into a fully automatic machine gun. During trial, the prosecutor encountered some proof issues in establishing that the Defendant had actually assembled the rifle into a machine gun so the prosecutor shifted the focus to the Defendant's mere possession of parts that could ultimately be assembled into a machine gun. During closing argument, the government repeatedly emphasized that the Defendant had simply possessed the unassembled parts of the AR-15 for several years, improperly broadening the factual basis for conviction because the mere possession of the unassembled parts of a potential fully automatic weapon would now convict the Defendant. *Id.* at 172.

In reversing, the court emphasized that "the government's opening argument plainly indicated that the government would prove only that Doucet possessed the assembled machine gun." *Id.* The court criticized the government's closing argument, stating "the prosecutor thus invited the jury to convict Doucet of a crime for which he was never indicted: possession of the unassembled parts of a machine gun. That blatant invitation differed materially from what the original indictment called on the jury to do." *Id.* at 173. The court aptly noted that an "indictment is not putty in the government's hands." *Id.*

12.5 CONSTRUCTIVE AMENDMENT VS. MERE VARIANCE

The government will likely respond to any constructive amendment challenge by arguing that the facts amount only to a mere variance of the indictment. The distinction between a constructive amendment and a variance is "significant because, whereas a constructive amendment always requires reversal, 'a variance requires reversal only if it prejudices a defendant's substantial rights.'" *United States v. Adamson*, 291 F. 3d 606, 615 (9th Cir. 2002) (quoting *United States v. Olson*, 925 F.2d 1170, 1175 (9th Cir. 1991)). Thus, there will be fatal and non-fatal variances. A fatal variance still results in reversal because the court finds that the defendant's substantial rights were violated whereas a non-fatal variance does not require reversal because the defendant did not suffer prejudice—similar to a harmless error analysis. *Adamson*, 291 F.3d at 615–16. Once the court finds a variance, the government's batting average for winning on non-fatal variance grounds is very high.

One classic example of a non-fatal variance is a typographical error in the indictment; in other words, an issue of mere semantics. *Russell v. United States*, 369 U.S. 749, 770 (1962); *United States v. Kegler*, 724 F.2d 190, 193–95 (D.C. Cir. 1984); *United States v. Leibowitz*, 857 F.2d 373, 378–79 (7th Cir. 1988); *United States v. Pigee*, 197 F.3d 879, 886 (7th Cir. 1999). The cases also draw a distinction between situations where the bases for conviction are *broadened* during the trial (a constructive amendment) versus *narrowed* (not a constructive amendment). *United States v. Leichtnam*, 948 F.2d 370, 376 (7th Cir. 1991) (collecting cases).

The challenge is trying to draw a clear line between the cases that find a constructive amendment as opposed to a mere variance. As commentators and courts have long recognized, the line between a constructive amendment and a variance is at times difficult to draw. *See, e.g.*, Charles Alan Wright, *Federal Practice and Procedure, Criminal*, Vol. 3, Sec. 516 (2nd ed. 1982) (observing that "[a] rather shadowy distinction has been drawn between an amendment and variance"). For that reason, expect that the government will respond to any constructive amendment challenge with some authority where the court found a non-fatal variance and did not reverse. Many of those pro-government cases are wrongly decided and ignore the actual distinction between a mere variance and a constructive amendment. These decisions typically do not include a thorough analysis of the difference between a constructive amendment and a variance. As a result, hunt for controlling authority in your circuit that compares the two doctrines so that the court applies the appropriate legal test.

In the Ninth Circuit, for example, the court will find a constructive amendment where (1) there is a complex of facts presented at trial distinctly different from those set forth in the charging instrument, or (2) the crime charged in the indictment was substantially altered at trial so that it was impossible to know whether the grand jury would have indicted for the crime actually proved. *Adamson*, 291 F.3d at 615. The court explained how it conducts this analysis in *United States v. Ward*, 747 F.3d 1184, 1191 (9th Cir. 2014). The court emphasized that a constructive amendment, not a variance, occurs when the government's proof at trial includes uncharged conduct and the jury instructions could have allowed the jury to convict based on the uncharged conduct. *Id.* The court analyzes whether there is "some way of assuring that the jury convicted the defendant based solely on the conduct actually charged in the indictment." *Id.* The court reviews the jury instructions to see if they were crafted to specifically capture only the charged conduct and are not so general that the uncharged could get swept into the jury's deliberations. *Id.* If the jury instructions are general enough to permit conviction on uncharged conduct, it is a constructive amendment requiring reversal because it "destroy[s] the defendant's substantial right to be tried only on charges presented in an indictment." *Id.* (quoting *Stirone*, 361 U.S. at 217).

Similarly, in the Fifth Circuit, constructive amendment "occurs when it permits the defendant to be convicted upon a factual basis that effectively modifies an essential element of the offense charged or permits the government to convict the defendant on a materially different theory or set of facts than that with which she was charged." *United States v. Hoover*, 467 F.3d 496, 500–01 (5th Cir. 2006). In making this assessment, the Fifth Circuit also reviews the jury instructions to assess whether the jury could have possibly convicted based on uncharged theories or facts: "we conclude that because the indictment charged Hoover with making one false statement, and the jury instructions allowed the jury to convict him for making a different false statement, the trial court constructively amended Hoover's indictment." *Id.* at 502.

The government will occasionally argue that there is no constructive amendment unless the trial judge committed instructional error by affirmatively altering the essential elements in the jury instructions, thereby suggesting that the trial judge needs to have modified the elements appearing in pattern jury instructions to qualify as a constructive amendment. That is not the law, however. First, an indictment may be constructively amended by either the actions of the court or the prosecutor. *United States v. Doucet*, 994 F.2d 169, 172 (5th Cir. 1993). Second, the government's change in position at trial can be sufficient to work a constructive amendment of the indictment *even where the court does not formally alter the elements of the offense in the jury charge. Id.* (citing *United States v. Beard* 436 F.2d 1084

(5th Cir. 1971)) (emphasis in original). The only question then is whether the government changed its theory during the trial so as to urge the jury to convict on a basis broader than that charged in the indictment. *Id.*; *see also United States v. de Leon-De La Rosa*, 17 F.4th 175, 195 (1st Cir. 2021) (constructive amendment can be brought about by (a) a literal alteration of the words in the indictment, (b) a jury instruction which modifies the offense charged, or (c) the admission of evidence of an offense not charged by the grand jury); *United States v. Simmons*, 11 F.4th 239, 268 (4th Cir. 2021) (a constructive amendment occurs when either the government during its presentation of evidence or argument or the court through its instructions to the jury, or both, broadens the possible bases for conviction beyond those presented by the grand jury); *United States v. Milstein*, 401 F.3d 53, 65 (2d Cir. 2005) (when the trial evidence or jury charge operates to broaden the possible bases for conviction from that which appeared in the indictment, the indictment has been constructively amended).

12.6 *STIRONE*'S PROGENY: HELPFUL CASES

Here is a summary of helpful circuit level opinions, including several that still reversed the conviction when applying a plain error standard:

First Circuit

United States v. de Leon-De La Rosa, 17 F.4th 175 (1st Cir. 2021) (finding constructive amendment under plain error standard where the indictment charged the Defendant with merely intentionally destroying a controlled substance that was subject to forfeiture, but the jury instructions also permitted a conviction for intentionally destroying equipment used for delivering a controlled substance).

Second Circuit

United States v. Hassan, 578 F.3d 108, 133-34 (2nd Cir. 2008) (finding constructive amendment where indictment charged Defendant for importing cathinone, but the jury instructions and trial evidence permitted the jury to convict for importing a different substance, khat, which is not a controlled substance).

United States v. Milstein, 401 F.3d 53 (2nd Cir. 2005) (finding constructive amendment on count that charged distribution of misbranded drugs where trial evidence and jury instruction broadened liability to permit conviction for uncharged conduct—that the drugs were contaminated).

Third Circuit

United States. v. Centeno, 793 F.3d 378, 388 (3rd Cir. 2015) (finding constructive amendment where the prosecutor improperly broadened the potential basis for conviction by arguing in rebuttal summation that the Defendant could be convicted on an accessory after-the-fact theory, which was not charged in the indictment).

United States. v. Syme, 276 F.3d. 131 (3rd Cir. 2002) (finding constructive amendment on plain error review where the district court instructed the jury on a fraud theory that was not alleged in the count of conviction).

Fourth Circuit

United States v. Simmons, 11 F.4th 239, 266–70 (4th Cir. 2021) (finding constructive amendment on plain error review in RICO prosecution where jointly filed jury instructions relied on the wrong state law statute, which thereby permitted conviction on a broader set of underlying predicate acts).

Fifth Circuit

United States v. Tucker, 33 F.4th 739, 743–46 (5th Cir. 2022) (*pro se* Defendant's conviction reversed and vacated under plain error standard where the indictment alleged only that the Defendant had been adjudicated as mentally defective but the trial evidence and jury instructions allowed for conviction if the Defendant had been adjudicated defective *or* had been committed to a mental hospital).

United States v. Hoover, 467 F.3d 496, 497–98 (5th Cir. 2006) (conviction reversed where the government charged the Defendant with falsely stating to an FBI agent that only one person had complained of an illegal practice to him when more than one person had complained, but the government advanced a different theory at trial—that the Defendant knew his statement was false for some other reason).

United States v. Chambers, 408 F.3d 237, 238–41, 247 (5th Cir. 2005) (reversing conviction where the Defendant was indicted for being a felon in possession of 104 rounds of .40 caliber ammunition where the court allowed the government to argue that the components of the ammunition, not the 104 rounds of .40 caliber ammunition, had traveled in interstate commerce).

United States v. Nunez, 180 F.3d 227, 230–32 (5th Cir. 1999) (reversing conviction where the Defendant was indicted on a specific charge—resisting arrest with a fully loaded .40 caliber Berretta semi-automatic pistol—but convicted on a more general charge of resisting arrest without the use of a dangerous weapon).

United States v. Doucet, 994 F.2d 169, 170–73 (5th Cir. 1993) (reversing conviction where the Defendant was indicted for possession of an unregistered firearm already modified to fire as a machine gun but convicted for mere possession of unassembled component parts of a machine gun).

United States v. Harrill, 877 F.2d at 341, 343–44 (5th Cir. 1989) (reversing conviction where the Defendant was specifically charged with submitting false information to a bank regarding requests for "loans and advances," but convicted on the more general allegation of providing false information regarding "any application, advance, commitment, or loan or any extension thereof").

Sixth Circuit

United States v. Hackett, 762 F.3d 493, 502 (6th Cir. 2014) (constructive amendment found in sentencing context of RICO prosecution where Defendant received ten-year sentencing enhancement for discharging a firearm but indictment only charged him with using and carrying a firearm).

Seventh Circuit

United States v. Pigee, 197 F.3d 879, 885–887 (7th Cir. 1999) (constructive amendment in narcotics prosecution found on count where trial evidence and jury instructions broadened basis for conviction but rejected on another count where the trial evidence and argument did not emphasize the discrepancy between the indictment and the jury instructions).

United States v. Ramirez, 182 F.3d 544, 546 (7th Cir. 1999) (constructive amendment found on plain error review where indictment charged carrying a firearm in relation to the distribution of narcotics but evidence did not show any actual distribution, beyond mere possession, of the narcotics).

United States v. Willoughby, 27 F.3d 263, 265 (7th Cir. 1994) (finding constructive amendment on plain error review where indictment charged carrying a firearm in relation to the distribution of narcotics but evidence did not show any actual distribution, beyond mere possession, of the narcotics).

United States v. Leichtnam, 948 F.2d 370 379–81 (7th Cir. 1991) (finding constructive amendment where the indictment specifically charged Defendant with using a Mossberg rifle in relation to drug trafficking but the evidence and instructions permitted conviction based on the possession of two other handguns that were not identified in the indictment).

Eighth Circuit

United States v. Lasley, 917 F.3d 661, 664 (8th Cir. 2019) (finding constructive amendment where trial evidence and closing argument referenced uncharged conduct in an assault prosecution and the jury instructions were not specific enough to eliminate the possibility that the jury convicted due to the uncharged conduct).

United States v. McDill, 871 F.3d 628, 631–32 (8th Cir. 2017) (finding constructive amendment on plain error review where indictment charged Defendant with either harassing or intimidating a forest service officer but evidence included uncharged conduct involving intimidating or threatening the forest service officers).

Ninth Circuit

United States v. Ward, 747 F.3d 1184, 1191–92 (9th Cir. 2014) (reversed two counts of convictions for identity theft where the indictment specifically identified two victims but the evidence at trial involved five victims and the jury instructions failed to identify the two specific victims referenced in the indictment).

United States v. Adamson, 291 F.3d 606, 616 (9th Cir. 2002) (fatal variance found where the misrepresentation specified in the indictment—that servers had been upgraded—was different than the misrepresentation shown at trial—the Defendant misrepresented how the servers had been updated).

United States v. Dipentino, 242 F.3d 1090, 1092–93 (9th Cir. 2001) (finding constructive amendment where the jury was instructed that conviction could be based either on conduct alleged in the indictment or uncharged conduct violating the same federal statute).

United States v. Shipsey, 190 F.3d 1081 (9th Cir. 1999) (finding constructive amendment in Employee Retirement Income Security Act fraud case where the defendant was indicted for making "false and fraudulent pretenses, representations, and promises to certain third parties who relied on those statements," but the instructions permitted conviction if the jury merely found that the Defendant "willfully stole or converted property to his own use" without requiring false representations by the Defendant to third parties who relied on the Defendant's statements).

United States v. Carlson, 616 F.2d 446, 447–48 (9th Cir. 1980) (finding constructive amendment where indictment charged Defendant with misapplying bank funds by causing loan to be made for personal use, but evidence and instructions permitted conviction for misapplying bank funds by causing loan to be made knowing that it was inadequately secured).

Howard v. Dagget, 526 F.2d 1388 (9th Cir. 1975) (finding constructive amendment where indictment charged Defendant with inducing two named women to engage in prostitution, but evidence and instructions allowed jury to convict Defendant of inducing women neither named nor mentioned in indictment).

Tenth Circuit

United States v. Miller, 891 F.3d 1220, 1231–38 (10th Cir. 2018) (finding constructive amendment under plain error review in false statement prosecution of prescribing doctor in an opioid prosecution where trial evidence and closing argument emphasized another false statement not charged in the government's speaking indictment).

Eleventh Circuit

United States v. Roberts, 770 F. App'x 563, 566–67 (11th Cir. 2019) (finding constructive amendment in prostitution of a minor prosecution where the jury instructions permitted conviction for having an opportunity to observe the girl was a minor when the indictment specifically charged only knowingly or recklessly disregarding that the girl was a minor).

United States v. Weissman, 899 F.2d 1111, 1114–16 (11th Cir. 1990) (constructive amendment found in RICO prosecution where the trial judge responded to jury question by instructing the jury that they did not need to find that the DeCavalante Family was the "enterprise"—which was how the indictment charged the enterprise element—and could convict simply if there was "an enterprise proved that meets the definition of the term").

United States v. Keller, 916 F.2d 628 (11th Cir. 1990) (constructive amendment found where indictment alleged that Defendant conspired only with his Co-defendant but jury instructions and evidence permitted conviction for conspiring with other individuals).

D.C. Circuit

United States v. Lawton, 995 F.2d 290 (D.C. Cir. 1993) (constructive amendment found using plain error standard where indictment charged Defendant with embezzling funds from the local American Federation of State, County, and Municipal Employees (AFSCME) union but instructions permitted conviction for embezzling funds from AFSCME's International Union in Washington, D.C.).

CHAPTER 13

Improper Closing Argument

13.1 CLOSING ARGUMENT BASICS

Prosecutors make objectionable comments in opening statement or closing argument in a surprisingly high percentage of criminal trials. There is a large body of cases where convictions have been reversed for a wide variety of improper statements by prosecutors, particularly in rebuttal closing when defense counsel cannot respond. A review of the cases in Chapter 14.5 underscores one troubling reality: you probably have heard prosecutors make similar objectionable arguments in nearly every criminal trial you have defended.

As a result, it is important to know where courts draw the ethical lines in your jurisdiction so you are prepared to object as soon as the prosecutors cross that line. Unlike disputes regarding *Brady* violations or jury instructions—where defense counsel has far more time to anticipate, research, and draft objections before trial—preserving objections during closing argument at trial happens on the fly. As a result, this chapter is structured so you will have helpful authority at your fingertips at trial. We have grouped cases into the most common violations—for example, improper vouching, arguing facts not in evidence, expressing personal opinions—so you can cite both the specific legal error as well as leading pro-defendant cases to appropriately preserve your objection.

Consider keeping a working list of helpful cases from your jurisdiction at the ready during voir dire, opening statement, and closing argument so you are ready to immediately get on your feet and preserve your objections. Also, remain ready to object during rebuttal summation. Defense attorneys are understandably exhausted when they wrap up their closing argument. The natural reaction is to ease up a bit. However, being ready to object during rebuttal closing can save your case because reversible error is likely on the menu. No other aspect of a criminal trial contains more prosecutorial misconduct than rebuttal closing argument.

Our typical approach to making objections during closing argument is to:

- object immediately and cite the legal principle ("vouching," "facts not in evidence," etc.);
- "constitutionalize" the objection by citing the relevant aspect of the Fifth Amendment and/or Sixth Amendment to preserve the most favorable standard of review on appeal;
- although not required, cite a specific case in the relevant jurisdiction where the court reversed a conviction on a similar fact pattern;
- inform the court that the defense is reserving a motion, which allows us to go sidebar either during argument or immediately afterwards so we can add even more depth to our objection on the record and move for a mistrial;
- at sidebar, press for an aggressive curative instruction that expressly lays out why the prosecutor's statement was improper (most courts refuse to give any meaningful curative instruction so forcing the court to consider our proposed instruction will either cure the error or, at a minimum, help our appeal); and/or
- move for either a mistrial or dismissal with prejudice if we can make an "invited mistrial" claim; and
- if the improper comment occurs during rebuttal closing argument, request surrebuttal argument so we can directly respond to the offending statement.

Citing a controlling case from the relevant jurisdiction is not required, but we favor doing it because it signals to the court (and jury) that we know the law better than the prosecutor and may lead the judge to consider the issue much more seriously given that we have demonstrated that the government is inviting reversible error if the judge overrules our objection. Likewise, while it typically is not required to request surrebuttal to preserve an objection during rebuttal closing argument, it has been required in a few jurisdictions over the years. Since the court will typically deny the request for surrebuttal, we raise it to show the appellate court that we took every possible step to try to cure the error during the trial. If the court surprisingly grants our request for surrebuttal closing, we blast the prosecutor's misconduct while still maintaining our objection.

Some defense counsel do not like to object during opening and closing because they are concerned about angering the judge or jury by interrupting the prosecutor. One possible alternative is to get the court and government to agree in advance that you can lodge all your objections on the record at sidebar immediately after opening, initial closing, and rebuttal closing. Some jurisdictions state that an objection is "contemporaneous" and thereby avoids plain error review if it is "made in sufficient time to allow the judge to correct any error if he [or she] had chosen to do so." *United States v. Dorr*, 636 F.2d 117, 120 (5th Cir. 1981); *see generally* Rule 103 of the *Federal Rules of Evidence* and Rule 51(b) of the *Federal Rules of Criminal Procedure.* The goal is to avoid plain error review, so if you pursue this path make sure to get the government's approval of the process on the record and lodge your objection as soon as possible.

13.2 GOVERNING STANDARDS

The *ABA Criminal Justice Standards: Prosecution Function* include several relevant standards that echo the reasoning in the case law where courts have reversed convictions for prosecutorial misconduct during closing argument. Here are the most relevant standards:

- *Standard 3-1.2(b) The Functions and Duties of the Prosecutor* states "the primary duty of the prosecutor is to seek justice within the bounds of the law, not merely to convict. . . ."
- *Standard 3-1.4(a) and (b) The Prosecutor's Heightened Duty of Candor* states "in light of the prosecutor's public responsibilities, broad authority and discretion, the prosecutor has a heightened duty of candor. . . . The prosecutor should not make a statement of fact or law, or offer evidence that the prosecutor does not reasonably believe to be true, to a court, lawyer or third party."
- *Standard 3-6.5(c) Opening Statement at Trial* states "the prosecutor's opening statement should be made without expressions of personal opinion, vouching for witnesses, inappropriate appeals to emotion or personal attacks on opposing counsel. The prosecutor should scrupulously avoid any comment on a defendant's right to remain silent."

- *Standard 3-6.8 Closing Argument at Trial* identifies the specific types of misstatements that yield reversals of convictions, including admonitions that prosecutors should *not*: misstate the evidence in the record; argue inferences that have no good faith support in the record; refer to the defendant's decision to not testify; express personal opinions; imply secret knowledge of the truth or a witness's credibility; make arguments to appeal to improper prejudices of the trier of fact; or present new issues in rebuttal closing.

13.3 *UNITED STATES V. BERGER*

The leading Supreme Court opinion regarding prosecutorial misconduct during closing argument was authored by Justice George Sutherland in *United States v. Berger*, 295 U.S. 78 (1935). In *Berger*, the Defendant was charged with counterfeiting. Witness testimony regarding his identity was key to the government's case. A government witness, who the prosecutor thought could identify the Defendant, had difficulty doing so during trial. *Id.* at 85–86. In closing, the prosecutor argued facts not in evidence and expressed his personal opinion that the witness could identify the Defendant: "you can bet your bottom dollar that she knew Berger . . . I was examining a woman that I knew knew Berger and could identify him, she was standing right here looking at him, and I couldn't say, 'Isn't that the man?' Now imagine that? But that is the rules of the game and I have to play within those rules." *Id.* at 86.

The Court reversed because "the jury was thus invited to conclude that the witness knew Berger well but pretended otherwise; and that this was within the personal knowledge of the prosecuting attorney." *Id.* Justice Sutherland then penned the most quoted passage in cases where courts reverse convictions for prosecutorial misconduct:

> [T]he prosecutor's role transcends that of an adversary: he [or she] 'is the representative not of an ordinary party to a controversy but of a sovereignty . . . whose interest . . . in a criminal prosecution is not that it shall win a case, but that justice shall be done. As such, he [and she] is in a peculiar and very definite sense the servant of the law, the twofold aim of which is that guilt shall not escape or innocence suffer. He [or she] may prosecute with earnestness and vigor—indeed, he [or she] should do so. But, while he [or she] may strike hard blows, he [or she] is not at liberty to strike foul ones.

> It is as much his [or her] duty to refrain from improper methods calculated to produce a wrongful conviction as it is to use every legitimate means to bring about a just one.
>
> *Id.* at 88.

13.4 LEGAL STANDARDS OF REVIEW IN THE CIRCUITS

The following summarizes the legal standard a defendant needs to pass in each circuit to reverse a conviction due to improper closing argument. The standards are very similar, but not identical. It helps to have the applicable standard in mind as you object during trial because it will sharpen the issue on any subsequent appeal. For example, your objection can memorialize the severity of the prejudice or why the court's proposed curative instruction fails to solve that prejudice.

First Circuit

The test for granting a new trial in the First Circuit, like most circuits, contains two parts. First, the court determines whether the prosecutor's arguments amounted to prosecutorial misconduct. *United States v. Ayala-Garcia*, 574 F.3d 5, 16 (1st Cir. 2009). Second, whether the misconduct has "so poisoned the well" that a defendant must be given a new trial. *Id.* In making that determination, the court considers several factors: (1) the severity the misconduct; (2) whether it was deliberate or accidental; (3) the context in which it occurred; (4) whether the judge gave any curative instructions and their likely effect; and (5) the strength of the evidence against the defendant. *Id.* at 19.

Second Circuit

The Second Circuit will reverse for prosecutorial misconduct during the government's opening statement or closing arguments "if the misconduct caused substantial prejudice by so infecting the trial with unfairness as to make the resulting conviction a denial of due process." *United States v. Certified Environmental Services, Inc.*, 753 F.3d 72,

95 (2d Cir. 2014) (quoting *United States v. Elias*, 285 F.3d 183, 190 (2d Cir. 2002) (quotations omitted)). Substantial prejudice is determined by evaluating three factors: (1) "the severity of the misconduct"; (2) "the measures adopted to cure the misconduct"; and (3) "the certainty of conviction absent the misconduct." *Id.* While the Second Circuit test is quite onerous, it does recognize a cumulative prejudice argument regarding prosecutorial misconduct. *Id.*

Third Circuit

The leading case in the Third Circuit is *U.S. v. Liburd*, 607 F.3d 339, 342–45 (3rd Cir. 2010). In *Liburd,* the Court employed a two-part analysis: (1) determine whether prosecutor's remarks constituted misconduct, and (2) evaluate whether that misconduct so infected the trial with unfairness as to make the resulting conviction a denial of due process in light of the entire proceeding. (citation omitted). In making the determination as to whether there is a resulting denial of due process, the court examines the curative instructions, if any, given by the trial court; the weight of the properly admitted evidence against the defendant; and the prosecutor's improper actions. In this case specifically the court noted that the improper statements occurred in the opening statement and, despite the fact that the evidence in the case was strong, the impropriety in the case may have caused the Defendant to alter his defense and thus it affected the entire trial.

Fourth Circuit

In the Fourth Circuit, prosecutorial misconduct warrants reversal of a conviction when the prosecutor's conduct "so infected the trial with unfairness as to make the resulting conviction a denial of due process." *United States v. Benson*, 957 F.3d 218, 234 (4th Cir. 2020) (quoting *United States v. Caro*, 597 F.3d 608, 624 (4th Cir. 2010)). The circuit's test for reversible error has two parts. *Id.* The defendant must establish that "'(1) the prosecutor's remarks or conduct were improper and (2) that such remarks or conduct prejudicially affected his substantial rights so as to deprive him of a fair trial.'" *Id.* (quoting *Caro*, 597 F.3d at 624). In determining whether the prosecutor's improper conduct prejudicially affected the defendant's substantial rights, the Fourth Circuit considers six factors: (1) the degree to which the prosecutor's remarks had a tendency to mislead the jury and to prejudice the defendant; (2) whether the remarks were isolated or extensive; (3) absent the remarks, the strength of competent proof introduced to establish the guilt of the defendant; (4) whether the comments were deliberately placed before the jury to divert attention to extraneous matters; (5) whether the prosecutor's remarks were invited by improper conduct of defense counsel; and (6) whether curative instructions were given to the jury. *United States v. Lazo*, 816 F. App'x 752, 768 (4th Cir. 2020) (quoting *United States v. Scheetz*, 293 F.3d 175, 186 (4th Cir. 2002)). The circuit provides that no single factor is dispositive, and these factors should be "'examined in the context of the entire trial.'" *Id.* (quoting *United States v. Lighty*, 616 F.3d 321, 361 (4th Cir. 2010)).

Fifth Circuit

In the Fifth Circuit, improper prosecutorial statements during closing argument warrant reversing a conviction when "the prosecutor's remarks cast serious doubt on the correctness of the jury's verdict." *United States v. Beaulieu*, 973 F.3d 354, 360–61 (5th Cir. 2020). That assessment is made by evaluating "(1) the magnitude of the prejudicial effect of the statements, (2) the efficacy of any cautionary instructions, and (3) the strength of the evidence of defendant's guilt." *Id.*

Sixth Circuit

The Sixth Circuit implements a two-step inquiry to determine whether prosecutorial misconduct rises to the level of unconstitutionality. *Simpson v. Warren*, 475 F. App'x 51, 59

(6th Cir. 2012). The conduct must be both improper and flagrant. *Id.* If improper, the court reviews four factors to assess whether the impropriety was flagrant: (1) whether the conduct and remarks of the prosecutor tended to mislead the jury or prejudice the defendant; (2) whether the conduct or remarks were isolated or extensive; (3) whether the remarks were deliberately or accidentally made; and (4) whether the evidence against the defendant was strong. *Id.* In addition, if the statements were not flagrant, the court will still find prosecutorial misconduct "if (1) the proof against the defendant was not overwhelming, (2) opposing counsel objected to the conduct, and (3) the trial court failed to give a curative instruction." *Id.*

Seventh Circuit

The Seventh Circuit evaluates prosecutorial misconduct via a two-step process: (1) whether the challenged remark was improper; and (2) whether it prejudiced the defendant. *United States v. Klebig*, 600 F.3d 700, 716–21 (7th Cir. 2009). There are several factors to consider in the prejudice evaluation: (1) the nature and seriousness of the prosecutorial misconduct, (2) whether the prosecutors' statements were invited by the conduct of defense counsel, (3) whether the district court sufficiently instructed the jury to disregard the statements, (4) whether the defense was able to counter the improper arguments through rebuttal, and (5) whether the weight of the evidence was against the defendant. *Id.* at 720–21.

Eighth Circuit

The Eighth Circuit "has set forth a two-part test for reversible prosecutorial misconduct: (1) the prosecutor's remarks or conduct must in fact have been improper, and (2) such remarks or conduct must have prejudicially affected the defendant's substantial rights so as to deprive the defendant of a fair trial." *United States v. Beckman*, 222 F.3d 512, 527 (8th Cir. 2000). In determining whether such remarks are prejudicial, the "court considers three factors: (1) the cumulative effect of such misconduct; (2) the strength of the properly admitted evidence of the defendant's guilt; and (3) the curative actions taken by the trial court." *Id.*

Ninth Circuit

The Ninth Circuit analyzes a claim of prosecutorial misconduct in closing argument by focusing on its asserted impropriety and substantial prejudicial effect. *United States v. Weatherspoon*, 410 F.3d 1142, 1145–46 (9th Cir. 2005). If the comment was improper and defense counsel timely objected, the court will reverse if the error is not harmless; that is, if the court concludes it is more likely than not that the misconduct materially affected the fairness of the trial. *United States v. Reyes*, 577 F.3d 1069, 1078 (9th Cir. 2009). If defense counsel did not timely object, reversal is warranted under plain error review "only if the prosecutor's improper conduct so affected the jury's ability to consider the totality of the evidence fairly that it tainted the verdict and deprived [the defendant] of a fair trial." *Weatherspoon*, 410 F.3d at 1151.

Tenth Circuit

In a case where the Tenth Circuit affirmed the conviction, it stated "the test for whether a defendant's trial was fundamentally unfair based on a prosecutor's comments proceeds in two steps: (1) the court first decides whether the prosecutor's comments were improper, and (2) if so, it examines their likely effect on the jury's verdict." *United States v. Christy*, 916 F.3d 814, 824 (10th Cir. 2019). This analysis of the effect of such conduct proceeds under three standards of review: *de novo*, abuse of discretion, and plain error. To obtain *de novo* review, the trial court must have overruled defendant's objection. Abuse of discretion is available if the trial court "takes curative action" following an initial objection but the defendant objects to the sufficiency of that action. Finally, plain error review is available in two circumstances: (1) defendant objects, the court sustains, and defendant does not object to the sufficiency of the "curative action"; or (2) defendant fails to object "at trial but raises the issue on appeal." *Id.* at 826.

Eleventh Circuit

In a case where the Eleventh Circuit affirmed the conviction, it stated that the standard for a claim of prosecutorial misconduct during closing argument is the "argument must be improper and prejudicial to a substantial right of the defendant." *United States v. Bailey*, 123 F.3d 1381, 1400 (11th Cir. 1997). And a curative instruction, taken in light of the context of the entire trial, may render an otherwise reversible prejudicial remark by the prosecutor harmless. *Id.*

D.C. Circuit

In the D.C. Circuit, a new trial based on prosecutorial misconduct during closing arguments is warranted when the defendant has "suffered sufficient prejudice." The test for sufficient prejudice consists of three factors: "(1) the severity of the prosecutor's misconduct; (2) the measures adopted to cure the misconduct; and (3) the certainty of conviction absent the improper remarks." *United States v. Earle*, 375 F.3d 1159, 1165 (D.C. Cir. 2004) (quoting *United States v. Gartmon*, 146 F.3d 1015, 1026 (D.C. Cir. 1998)). Notably, this standard of review applies whether it is harmless error or plain error review. *Gartmon*, 146 F.3d at 1026.

13.5 *BERGER'S* PROGENY: HELPFUL CASES

The following list of cases is grouped by topic and organized by circuit so you can quickly find relevant cases on each topic in your jurisdiction. All these cases resulted in reversed convictions unless specifically noted.

13.5.1. Improper Vouching and Bolstering

Improper vouching, bolstering, and expressions of personal belief are similar concepts—the prosecutor makes a statement to place the credibility and reputation of the prosecutor's behind the government's theory of the case. The Supreme Court identified two dangers with this type of improper argument: (1) such comments convey the impression that evidence not presented to the jury but known to the prosecutor supports the charges, and (2) the prosecutor's opinion carries with it the imprimatur of the government and may induce the jury to trust the government's judgment rather than its own view of the evidence. *United States v. Young*, 470 U.S. 1, 19 (1985). Numerous decisions below cite *Young* to support reversing convictions due to improper vouching, but the Court in *Young* did not reverse the defendant's conviction.

The Sixth Circuit describes these concepts in detail—defining vouching as when a prosecutor expresses a personal belief in the witness's credibility and improper bolstering as when the prosecutor implies that the witness's testimony is corroborated by evidence known to the government but not known to the jury. *United States v. Acosta*, 924 F.3d 288, 300–01 (6th Cir. 2019).

Here is a summary of helpful circuit level opinions on improper vouching and bolstering:

First Circuit

United States v. Canty, 37 F.4th 775, 789 (1st Cir. 2022) (improper for a prosecutor to bolster the credibility of law enforcement witnesses by stating "we" had put in three years of hard and serious work on the case by carefully talking with others, spending time with them, and emphasizing that law enforcement made sure their testimony had corroborative evidence).

United States v. Manning, 23 F.3d 570, 572–73 (1st Cir. 1994) (improper vouching where prosecutor stated that detectives could not possibly lie to the jury because detectives are bound by the truth and an oath of honesty).

Second Circuit

United States v. Certified Environmental Services, Inc., 753 F.3d 72, 86, 94–95 (2d Cir. 2014) (during opening statement, it was improper for prosecutor to vouch for cooperating witness's commitment to tell the truth or discuss the conditions of the pleas and/or what punishments will occur if witnesses fail to be truthful. In rebuttal, improper vouching for the prosecutor to comment that the agents and AUSAs were from the local community).

United States v. Burse, 531 F.2d 1151, 1155 (2d Cir. 1976) (improper vouching where prosecutor repeatedly stated "we know [certain testimony] is true.").

Third Circuit

United States v. Molina-Guevara, 96 F.3d. 698, 703–704 (3d Cir. 1996) (impermissible vouching during rebuttal where prosecutor said that an uncalled U.S. Customs Agent would have corroborated the testimony of another agent who testified and whose credibility was at issue. Prosecutor argued it was "insulting" and "ridiculous" to think that the government would put a witness on the stand who would lie).

Fifth Circuit

United States v. Smith, 814 F.3d 268 (5th Cir. 2016) (conviction for possession for child pornography reversed where the prosecutor vouched for the credibility of witnesses and offered his own integrity as a prosecutor against the alibi witnesses during closing arguments).

United States v. Aguilar, 645 F.3d 319, 325 (5th Cir. 2011) (impermissible vouching of a government agent witness by referring to their position as a government agent, saying it would be alarming if they lied, that they strive to be ethical, and making an emotional appeal that agents risk their lives for "us and our children" and that it is a "sad deal" for them to be called liars).

United States v. Gracia, 522 F.3d 597, 601 (5th Cir. 2008) (impermissible expression of a personal opinion where prosecutor offered personal assurances to the jury that government witnesses are telling the truth and that law enforcement witnesses should be believed simply because they were doing their job).

United States v. Garza, 608 F.2d 659, 661–66 (5th Cir. 1979). (impermissible expression of a personal opinion where, among other errors, prosecutor stated that investigating agent was "a professional man" whose "motives are pure as the driven snow," and "if I thought that I had ever framed an innocent man and sent him to the penitentiary, I would quit." The court reversed, stating "if you throw a skunk into the jury box, you can't instruct the jury not to smell it.").

Sixth Circuit

Stermer v. Warren, 959 F.3d 704, 730–41 (6th Cir. 2020) (improper expression of a personal opinion when the state prosecutor repeatedly referred to the defendant as a liar: "[w]e know she is a liar. There is no question but that she's a liar and will lie when it suits her . . . we have to take a cautious view of a statement by someone who is accused of a very serious crime." The court emphasized that the prosecutor "failed to support this claim by reference to lies in the evidence" in a case where the Defendant did not testify and "the prosecution introduced the transcript of her interviews.").

United States v. Acosta, 924 F.3d 288, 300–01 (6th Cir. 2019) (conviction reversed on plain error review where prosecutor bolstered the credibility of a detective by arguing "he testified very well, he understood and remembered everything he did" and stating detective was "a fine young man" and another did "fine work." Court defines improper vouching as "when a prosecutor supports the credibility of a witness by indicating a personal belief in the witness's credibility" and improper bolstering as "when the prosecutor implies that the witness's testimony is corroborated by evidence known to the government but not known to the jury.").

Walker v. Morrow, 458 F. App'x 475, 489–91 (6th Cir. 2012) (improper bolstering where prosecutor argued that investigator "would have been happy to fold his case file up . . . if [the victim's] death had been a suicide" because it is always improper for a prosecutor to suggest that a defendant is guilty merely because he is being prosecuted or has been indicted).

United States v. Francis, 170 F.3d 546, 550–51 (6th Cir. 1999) (improper vouching in prosecutor's description of testifying cooperator's plea agreement where prosecutor informed jury that prosecutor would have to recommend sentence reduction to court because "it is easy for a prosecutor to imply, either intentionally or inadvertently, that the prosecutor is in a special position to ascertain whether the witness was, in fact, testifying truthfully." Prosecutor also improperly bolstered investigating agent's testimony by failing to introduce evidence to establish that agent had actually corroborated facts that the agent claimed he had corroborated. Bolstering occurred because "prosecutor was implying a guarantee of truthfulness based on facts outside the record.").

Eighth Circuit

United States v. Cruz-Padilla, 227 F.3d 1064, 1069–70 (8th Cir. 2000) (improper expression of racially motivated personal belief of guilt where prosecutor, in an drug conspiracy prosecution, argued that "once you start living a lie as illegal aliens do or are forced to do, it is easier to lie when you get into trouble the next time" because the comment shifted from evidence to emotion and the Constitution prohibits racially biased prosecutorial arguments).

Ninth Circuit

United States v. Asencio-De Leon, 828 F. App'x 393, 396 (9th Cir. 2020) (improper vouching found under plain error standard where prosecutor argued that government agent witnesses had "no real motive" to lie in prosecution for assaulting federal officer. Prosecutor also committed error during cross-examination of Defendant by asking if the agents had testified untruthfully in their trial testimony).

United States v. Preston, 873 F.3d 829, 843–44 (9th Cir. 2017) (improper for prosecutor to vouch for victim of child abuse in closing to suggest that the witness' testimony must be true. [Conviction reversed based on cumulative impact of multiple instances of prosecutorial misconduct.]).

United States v. Alcantara-Castillo, 788 F.3d 1186 (9th Cir. 2015) (conviction reversed due to prosecutor's improper vouching of a border patrol agent's testimony citing evidence not in the record).

United States v. Weatherspoon, 410 F.3d 1142, 1146–48 (9th Cir. 2005) (reversible error for the prosecutor to state that witnesses "had no reason to come in here and not tell you the truth. And they took the stand and they told you the truth.").

United States v. Combs, 379 F.3d 564, 574–76 (9th Cir. 2004) (improper vouching in rebuttal closing where the prosecutor "plainly implied that she knew [an agent] would be fired for committing perjury and that she believed that no reasonable agent in his shoes would take such a risk.").

United States v. Kerr, 981 F.2d 1050 (9th Cir. 1992) (conviction reversed on plain error review where prosecutor introduced his personal opinion regarding the government's key witnesses' credibility).

United States v. Molina, 934 F.2d 1440, 1446 (9th Cir. 1991) (improper expression of personal belief for prosecutor to argue defendant is guilty because there was additional inculpatory evidence not produced at trial. Ten to twelve agents were available to testify but only three testified).

Tenth Circuit

United States v. Starks, 34 F.4th 1142, 1173–74 (10th Cir. 2022) (improper bolstering of government cooperator whose credibility was at issue where prosecutor argued that "nobody [had] ever told [the witness] to do anything other than tell the truth. And she sat there and she told you the absolute truth.").

United States v. Rios, 611 F.2d 1335, 1343 (10th Cir. 1979) (improper expression of prosecutor's personal belief that defendant was guilty for prosecutor to argue "I think you have sitting before you a genuine certified Mr. Big in the heroin business, and he is the Defendant." Also, improper inference that defendant threatened two cooperating witnesses without any link to the evidence at trial).

Eleventh Circuit

United States v. Hands, 184 F.3d 1322, 1333–34 (11th Cir. 1999) (improper vouching where the prosecutor argued that an uncalled witness would have corroborated a witness's trial testimony, especially because the prosecutor alluded to the uncalled witness in opening but never called the witness at trial).

13.5.2 Improper Comment on Defendant's Right Not to Testify

These cases involve situations where the prosecutor violated a defendant's Fifth Amendment right not to testify by suggesting the defendant should have testified or improperly shifted the burden of proof to the defense—a burden that always resides with the government. This often happens in rebuttal closing where the prosecutor responds to defense counsel's attack on the credibility of the government's witnesses and evidence.

Here is a summary of helpful Supreme Court and circuit level opinions on improper comments on the Defendant's right not to testify:

Supreme Court

Griffin v. State of California, 380 U.S. 609, 611–13 (1965) (Supreme Court reverses conviction pursuant to self-incrimination clause of the Fifth Amendment where prosecutor commented on Defendant's failure to testify).

First Circuit

United States v. Roberts, 119 F.3d 1006, 1014–15 (1st Cir. 1997) (improper for prosecutor to comment that the Defendant has no obligation to testify, but then states the Defendant has to put on a compelling case).

Ninth Circuit

United States v. Preston, 873 F.3d 829, 842-43 (9th Cir. 2017) (improper for prosecutor to comment on Defendant's decision not to testify where prosecutor stated that "there was no testimony in this case that contradicts [the victim's] testimony" because the Defendant was the only person who could have provided contrary testimony. [Conviction reversed based on cumulative impact of multiple instances of prosecutorial misconduct.]).

United States v. Hill, 953 F.2d 452, 460 (9th Cir. 1991) (a prosecutor may not comment on a Defendant's failure to present witnesses if it calls attention to the Defendant's own failure to testify or violates another person's privilege).

Eleventh Circuit

United States v. Foster, 626 F. App'x 820, 824 (11th Cir. 2015) (improper for a prosecutor to comment on Defendant's invocation of his Fifth Amendment right not to testify because it urges "the jury to draw the inference from silence that he [was] guilty.").

13.5.3 Lack of Candor

This objection includes three related fact patterns, all of which violate a prosecutor's duty of candor: (1) the prosecutor misrepresents the evidence submitted into the record at trial; (2) the prosecutor makes a statement that he or she knows is false based on information not in the trial record; or (3) the prosecutor refers to facts outside the trial record to plug evidentiary holes needed to convict.

Here is a summary of helpful circuit level opinions on lack of candor:

First Circuit

United States v. Canty, 37 F.4th 775, 789 (1st Cir. 2022) (improper for prosecutor to make a statement unsupported by evidence that assumed motivations in applying a tourniquet to another's arm).

United States v. Azubike, 504 F.3d 30, 38 (1st Cir. 2007) (improper for the prosecutor to assert a telephone recording showed the Defendant knew a drug kingpin when the evidence did not support that assertion).

United States v. Roberts, 119 F.3d 1006, 1015 (1st Cir. 1997) (improper for a prosecutor to comment on the Defendant's participation in a motorcycle club and suggest it is a gang despite failing to introduce any evidence of the Defendant's involvement in a gang).

Second Circuit

United States v. Certified Environmental Services, Inc., 753 F.3d 72, 95 (2d Cir. 2014) (improper for prosecutor to reference "circumstances that [the jury doesn't] know anything about," as those are not facts in evidence).

United States v. Forlorma, 94 F.3d 91, 94 (2d Cir. 1996) (improper for prosecutor to argue that a suit found in a suitcase with narcotics fit the Defendant to suggest Defendant was aware of the narcotics when there was no evidence that the suit fit the Defendant).

United States v. Modica, 663 F.2d 1173, 1179–80 (2d Cir. 1981) (improper for a prosecutor to (a) argue a cooperating witness felt scared when the witness never admitted to such a feeling, and (b) use information in the investigative file to make an argument about a witness's demeanor).

United States v. Burse, 531 F.2d 1151, 1154 (2d Cir. 1976) (improper for the prosecutor to refer to documents not in evidence and comment on a general increase in bank robberies to invite the inference that this trend is evidence of the Defendant's guilt. Prosecution also argued that the government's chief cooperating witness served jail term when he was, in fact, still awaiting sentencing, and that a defense witness was drunk during the alleged crime and while testifying on the stand).

Third Circuit

United States v. Brown, 765 F.3d 278, 296–97 (3d Cir. 2014) (conviction reversed where the prosecutor indicated during rebuttal that attempting to get fingerprints from a firearm would have been futile because the retrieving detective had covered up any identifiable prints when no such testimony was elicited, and prosecutor did not even call a fingerprint expert to show any attempt at getting prints off the firearm).

Fifth Circuit

United States v. Beaulieu, 973 F.3d 354, 358–59 (5th Cir. 2020) (improper for prosecutor to make arguments based on facts not in evidence that (a) Defendant refused to testify as a compelled witness in another matter because "he feared being called a rat"; and (b) that AUSA never said he would not prosecute Defendant for refusing to testify).

United States v. Kang, 934 F.2d 621, 626–27 (5th Cir. 1991) (improper for prosecutor to argue the Defendant was predisposed to cheating on his taxes based on hearsay evidence admitted for a limited purpose and that the prosecutor then used in closing for the truth of the matter asserted to prove intent).

United States v. McPhee, 731 F.2d 1150, 1153 (5th Cir. 1984) (improper for the prosecutor to seek conviction by implying the Defendant was involved in other, unindicted criminal conduct: "we want you to find him guilty for a bunch of other reasons.").

Sixth Circuit

Washington v. Hofbauer, 228 F.3d 689, 709 (6th Cir. 2000) (improper for a prosecutor to characterize victim's story as having been consistent over time when there was no evidence supporting that factual assertion. This misconduct and improper emphasis on Defendant's "bad character" led to reversal).

Seventh Circuit

Evans v. Jones, 996 F.3d 766, 775–81 (7th Cir. 2021) (improper for state prosecutor to argue during rebuttal that a trial witness recanted his identification of the Defendant in a homicide prosecution only after an investigator working for the Co-defendant interviewed the witness before trial—thereby confirming that the Defendants could also find and intimidate the witness—because there was "no evidence in the record from which the prosecutor could reasonably infer" that the witness met with a defense investigator).

United States v. Farinella, 558 F.3d 695, 701 (7th Cir. 2009) (improper for prosecutor to exaggerate the safety issues caused by Defendant's changing the "best when purchased by" labels on bottles of salad dressing when the government had not submitted any evidence that the dressing was "rotten," would make anyone ill, or was past its expiration date).

United States v. Klebig, 600 F.3d 700, 716–19 (7th Cir. 2009) (improper for the prosecutor to conduct a demonstration during closing argument and claim that the markings of an uncharged homemade silencer fit the markings on a sawed-off rifle when no witness testified to that issue).

Eighth Circuit

United States v. Beckman, 222 F.3d 512, 527 (8th Cir. 2000) (improper for a prosecutor to assert that the Defendant lost his job because of a failed drug test when "the only evidence regarding a drug test in relation to [Defendant's] employment [was Defendant's] denial that he lost his job due to such test.").

Ninth Circuit

United States v. Preston, 873 F.3d 844 (9th Cir. 2017) (improper for prosecutor to misstate the evidence by arguing that either the victim was telling the truth or the victim was an evil liar when the defense offered no evidence suggesting the victim was an evil liar. [Conviction reversed based on cumulative impact of multiple instances of prosecutorial misconduct.]).

United States v. Reyes, 577 F.3d 1069 (9th Cir. 2009) (improper for prosecutor to argue in rebuttal summation that company's finance department "did not have any idea" that backdating of stock options had occurred where prosecutor knew the SEC had brought separate civil suits against the company CFO and other finance department executives alleging that the finance department knew about the alleged backdating).

United States v. Kojayan, 8 F.3d 1315, 1318–22 (9th Cir. 1993) (improper for prosecutor to suggest the government was powerless to call an absent witness and claim the witness invokes his Fifth Amendment rights after being arrested when the prosecutor knew that the absent witness had not invoked his Fifth Amendment rights but instead had entered a plea agreement with the government promising to cooperate and testify if called by the prosecutor).

Eleventh Circuit

United States v. Foster, 626 F. App'x 820, 824–25 (11th Cir. 2015) (improper for prosecutor to argue that the defendant "traded meth for sex with a white female" when the testimony was inaccurate).

D.C. Circuit

United States v. Davis, 863 F.3d 894, 902–03 (D.C. Cir. 2017) (improper for prosecutor to incorrectly claim (a) that Defendant continued to willfully file fraudulent tax returns while working as a tax preparer despite being aware of the government's investigation into his allegedly illegal behavior; and (b) Defendant knew of and engaged in part of the conspiracy even though the Defendant was not employed as a tax preparer during that portion of the conspiracy).

United States v. Watson, 171 F.3d 695, 699 (D.C. Cir. 1999) (improper for prosecutor to misquote a witness's testimony during closing in a way that tied the Defendant more tightly to the charged conduct).

13.5.4 Misstating the Evidence and Law

This objection does not appear in as many reported cases as the other issues, but prosecutors do sometimes make statements that directly contradict the jury instructions or the defendant's constitutional rights.

Here is a summary of helpful circuit level opinions on misstating the evidence and law:

First Circuit

United States v. Roberts, 119 F.3d 1006, 1015 (1st Cir. 1997) (improper for prosecutor to tell the jury that the Defendant has the same responsibility as the government and must present a compelling case).

Second Circuit

United States v. Burse, 531 F.2d 1151, 1154 (2d Cir. 1976) (improper for prosecutor to insinuate that Defendant's failure to provide proof of his innocence is evidence of his guilt).

Fifth Circuit

United States v. Cantu, 876 F.2d 1134 (5th Cir. 1989) (improper for prosecutor to instruct the jury that in order to find the Defendant not guilty, the jury has to find that government witnesses lied).

Sixth Circuit

United States v. Carter, 236 F.3d 777 (6th Cir. 2001) (conviction reversed under plain error review when the prosecutor intentionally misstated a key witness's testimony and attacked the defense counsel's truthfulness four times in his rebuttal argument using the phrases "a bold fabrication," "an absolutely whole lie," and a "tremendous colossal lie.").

Seventh Circuit

United States v. Fenzl, 670 F.3d 778, 783 (7th Cir. 2012) (improper misstatement of law when prosecutor conflated an allegation of fraud with breach of contract by arguing "[Defendant's] failure to subcontract any of the . . . work to a minority business enterprise was fraud" because the decision not to use a minority business was made after the contract was signed and not during the bidding process).

United States v. Vargas, 583 F.2d 380, 387 (7th Cir. 1978) (improper for prosecutor to mischaracterize the burden and standards of proof by stating that the jury had to decide between finding the Defendant guilty or finding that government agents lied under oath: "if you find the defendant not guilty, I want you to write on there that all of those people [agents] lied. Ricevuto is a liar. Garcia is a liar. Collins is a liar. Kowalski is a liar. Fanter is a liar.").

Ninth Circuit

United States v. Velazquez, 1 F.4th 1132, 1134–41 (9th Cir. 2021) (a "flagrant distortion of the law" where the prosecutor compared the reasonable doubt standard to making everyday decisions like the certainty that a familiar meal "is not going to make you sick" or the certainty that you will not get into an accident when going for a routine drive).

United States v. Sandoval-Gonzalez, 642 F.3d 717, 726 (9th Cir. 2011) (in an illegal re-entry case, improper for prosecutor to imply that the defendant's evidence was not sufficient to establish all the elements of derivative citizenship and incorrectly state that there was a presumption of alienage for those born outside of the United States).

Tenth Circuit

United States v. Starks, 34 F.4th 1142, 1154–59 (10th Cir. 2022) (improper for the prosecutor to advise the jury that the substantial evidence presented at trial "changed" the presumption of innocence and revealed "the naked truth" about the Defendant).

D.C. Circuit

United States v. Williams, 836 F.3d 1, 13 (D.C. Cir. 2016) (in a prosecution for second degree murder, it was improper for prosecutor to argue that the jury could not consider the deceased victim's consent to a ritual beating to inform its opinion of the Defendant's state of mind).

13.5.5 Sandbagging in Rebuttal Closing

This objection applies when the prosecutor raises a new argument—a new theory or new facts—that the prosecutor held back from his or her initial closing to prevent defense counsel from being able to shoot it down in the defense closing. Rebuttal closing is a huge hammer for prosecutors, and many wield that hammer far too aggressively, particularly in cases where the government lacks compelling evidence. While few reported cases have reversed convictions solely due to sandbagging in rebuttal closing, it happens fairly frequently, particularly in close cases where an aggressive prosecutor pushes the limits in rebuttal to try to win a losing case.

One source to cite is the Advisory Committee note to Rule 29.1 of the *Federal Rules of Criminal Procedure*, which addresses closing argument and states that "the fair and effective administration of justice is best served if the defendant knows the arguments made by the prosecution [o]n behalf of conviction before the defendant is faced with the decision whether to reply and what to reply." In addition, Section 3-6.8 of The *ABA Criminal Justice Standards: Prosecution Function* expressly states that the prosecutor "should not present or raise new issues" in rebuttal closing.

The government will likely respond to any challenge about their inappropriate statements in rebuttal closing by asserting that the prosecutor was merely responding to improper comments made by defense counsel in the defendant's closing argument. The cases, however, state that "two wrongs do not make a right." *Plymail v. Mirandy,* 8 F.4th 308, 319–20 (4th Cir. 2021). Defense counsel's misconduct during closing argument does not grant the prosecutor a license to make otherwise improper arguments. *United States v. Young,* 470 U.S. 1, 8 (1985). The prosecutor must object to improper arguments from defense counsel, not merely respond in kind. *Id.* But in weighing the impact of the prosecutor's improper remarks in rebuttal closing, the reviewing court can also take into account defense counsel's opening salvo in the defense closing argument. *Id.*

Here is a summary of helpful circuit level opinions on sandbagging in rebuttal closing:

Third Circuit

United States v. Brown, 765 F.3d 278, 296 (3d Cir. 2014) (conviction reversed because it was improper for prosecutor to develop new arguments during rebuttal. Here, in response to a defense argument regarding the lack of forensic fingerprint evidence, the prosecutor argued that fingerprints could not been extracted from a firearm in question, but the prosecutor had not introduced evidence to support that argument).

Fourth Circuit

United States v. Smith, 962 F.3d 755, 770, 771 (4th Cir. 2020) (when the government waived initial closing argument, it had the effect of sandbagging the Defendant by setting him up to avoid a subject in his closing argument, only to learn that it was too late to reply to the prosecutor's side of the story. This violates Rule 29.1 of the *Federal Rules of Criminal Procedure,* but the error was held to be harmless due to the evidence of guilt).

Ninth Circuit

United States v. Maloney, 755 F.3d 1044 (9th Cir. 2014) (improper for prosecutor to argue that the Defendant must be lying because he had no luggage with him while allegedly on a trip from Riverside to Las Vegas because prosecutor never introduced any evidence regarding luggage).

13.5.6 Impugning the Defense

This group of cases relates to improper attacks that prosecutors launch against both Defendants and defense counsel, often accusing the defendant of cheating in some fashion, such as hiring a high-priced defense attorney to "buy" an acquittal.

Here is a summary of helpful circuit level opinions on impugning the defense:

Second Circuit

United States v. Burse, 531 F.2d 1151, 1154 (2d Cir. 1976) (improper for the prosecutor to imply that defense counsel was pressuring witness into delivering testimony favorable to the Defendant).

United States v. Friedman, 909 F.2d 705, 708 (2d Cir. 1990) (improper for the prosecutor to attack the defense team by suggesting a Defendant can buy an acquittal by hiring a defense attorney. Nor can the prosecutor state that the defense counsel will "make any argument he can to get [his client] off.").

Fifth Circuit

United States v. Murrah, 888 F.2d 24, 26–27 (5th Cir. 1989) (improper for a prosecutor to imply a Defendant and his counsel are unethical by accusing them of hiding witnesses or evidence since "no counsel is to throw verbal rocks at opposing counsel" and "prosecutors do not have a hunting license exempt from the ethical constraints on advocacy.").

Sixth Circuit

United States v. Acosta, 924 F.3d 288, 300–01 (6th Cir. 2019) (conviction reversed on plain error standard in narcotics case where, among other misconduct, prosecutor improperly commented on the credibility of defense witnesses by expressing his personal belief that the witnesses were lying. The improper comments included "he's lying—he's lying about taking that stuff over [to the apartment]," "should he be entitled to any credibility whatsoever? Not at all. Zero," "Barnes is a proven liar, don't believe anything he had to say," and "is he entitled to any credibility for what he said? No, not at all.").

United States v. Francis, 170 F.3d 546, 552 (6th Cir. 1999) (improper for prosecutor to attack testifying Defendant by arguing "he lied to to you . . . if there was a con artist who took the stand at trial, it wasn't [government cooperator], it was Lewis Francis. I submit to you that the reason he took the stand is he thought he could charm his way in your hearts and minds and somehow convince you that he's this nice, charming banker who would never . . . engage in such activity." The court drew a line between situations where the prosecutor fails to link his statements to trial evidence (improper) and where the prosecutor concludes the Defendant lied in his testimony by analyzing the trial evidence that demonstrates the lie (proper)).

Seventh Circuit

United States v. Farinella, 558 F.3d 695, 700 (7th Cir. 2009) (improper for the prosecutor to state "don't let the defendant and his high-priced lawyer buy his way out of this . . . you have to earn justice, you can't buy it.").

Ninth Circuit

United States v. Charley, 1 F.4th 637, 651–52 (9th Cir. 2021) (improper for prosecution to denigrate the Defendant's character in closing argument by making numerous implications regarding the Defendant's violent nature by repeatedly recounting the character evidence presented by various witnesses, arguing that their stories "showed that [the Defendant] did not have the same demeanor that she had here on the stand.").

United States v. Weatherspoon, 410 F.3d 1142, 1150 (9th Cir. 2005) (improper for prosecutor to offer an opinion regarding the character of the defense counsel, denigrate the defense counsel's strategy as a scam, or categorize the role of defense counsel, "even in response to similar tactics by the defense.").

United States v. Sanchez, 176 F.3d 1214, 1224 (9th Cir. 1999) (improper to criticize the defense counsel's strategy by stating "ladies and gentlemen, I'm going to ask you not to credit that scam that has been perpetrated on you here.").

Sechrest v. Ignacio, 549 F.3d 789, 811 (9th Cir. 2008) (improper for a prosecutor to call the defense a "fraud" and that society would be at risk if the jurors fell for the fraud).

D.C. Circuit

United States v. Earle, 375 F.3d 1159, 1163–65 (D.C. Cir. 2004) (improper for a prosecutor to make an argument, without support, that defense counsel investigated the case prior to his retention, lied about the date of retention, and encouraged false testimony from defense witnesses).

13.5.7 Improper Appeals to Jurors' Emotions

This cluster of cases involves prosecutors making comments designed to inflame the jurors' emotions, passions, and prejudices, which is improper because jurors are supposed to simply focus on the admitted evidence and analyze that evidence against the elements of the charged offense. "Court proceedings are held for the solemn purpose of endeavoring to ascertain the truth which is the *sine qua non* of a fair trial." *Estes v. State of Tex.* 381 U.S. 532, 540 (1965). Prosecutors who tell the jury to "send a message to the community" or to "place themselves in the victim's shoes" violate this principle (and the Due Process Clause of the Fifth Amendment) by intentionally taking the jury's focus off the elements of the alleged crime and the evidence at trial.

Here is a summary of helpful circuit level opinions on improper appeals to jurors' emotions:

First Circuit

United States v. Canty, 37 F.4th 775, 787 (1st Cir. 2022) (improper to appeal to jurors' emotions by characterizing Defendants as greedy individuals who came to make easy money off the backs of addicted local community members).

United States v. Ayala-Garcia, 574 F.3d 5, 17–18 (1st Cir. 2009) (improper for the prosecutor to suggest the defendants were killers and that the jury had a duty to convict to protect the public: "do your job, find the Defendants guilty.").

United States v. Manning, 23 F.3d 570, 572–73 (1st Cir. 1994) (improper for prosecutor to instruct jury to "take responsibility for your community" and "[c]onvict the Defendant because justice compels conviction.").

Second Circuit

United States v. Certified Environmental Services, Inc., 753 F.3d 72, 95 (2d Cir. 2014) (improper for a prosecutor to argue that the jury should consider the "consequences" of their verdict).

United States v. Modica, 663 F.2d 1173, 1180 (2d Cir. 1981) (improper for the prosecutor to tell the jury to make sure they "don't let [the Defendant] walk out of [the] room laughing at [them].").

Fourth Circuit

Plymail v. Mirandy, 8 F.4th 308, 317–18 (4th Cir. 2021) (improper for prosecutor to encourage jury to send a message against men with the "sweet tooth of sadomasochism" by finding Defendant guilty and to render a guilty verdict "for all of us, for womankind, for all of us.").

Sixth Circuit

Simpson v. Warren, 475 F. App'x 51, 61–62 (6th Cir. 2012) (improper for a prosecutor to inflame the passions and prejudices of the jury by implying that the government had met its burden and now the jury must discharge its duty. The prosecutor twice stated that "'dumping' and 'throwing' [the officer's] 'dead body' before the jury should not be a prerequisite to convicting" Defendant. Moreover, the prosecutor argued that the "nice looking fellow" before the jury looked different than when he was pointing a gun at the victim).

Ninth Circuit

United States v. Weatherspoon, 410 F.3d 1142, 1149 (9th Cir. 2005) (improper to tell the jury that a conviction will make the community safer, because such an argument is designed to appeal to the passions, fears, and vulnerabilities of the jury).

United States v. Sanchez, 659 F.3d 1252, 1256–57 (9th Cir. 2011) (improper for prosecutor to state that a conviction will "send a memo to all drug traffickers, to all persons south of the border and in Imperial County and in California. . . .").

Eleventh Circuit

United States v. Hands, 184 F.3d 1322, 1333 (11th Cir. 1999) (improper for the prosecutor to repeatedly call the Defendant a "wicked and vicious drug dealer" because the statements were calculated to inflame the jury and persuade them to convict based on emotion rather than evidence).

CHAPTER 14

Motion for Terminating Sanctions

14.1 DEVELOPING A MOTION FOR TERMINATING SANCTIONS

The sequence of this book is designed to illustrate that prosecutors commit misconduct at every stage of a criminal prosecution: during the pre-indictment investigation, grand jury, pre-trial discovery, and throughout every phase of the trial (voir dire, opening statement, witness exams, and closing argument). Defense counsel should preserve objections to every act of misconduct because any single act of misconduct might result in a reversal of a conviction on appeal. A *Franks* violation, a *Brady* violation, a *Napue* violation, and improper statements in voir dire or closing argument can each lead to reversal on appeal.

It is exceptionally rare, however, for a trial judge to grant a motion to terminate a criminal case based on a single, isolated act of prosecutorial misconduct. As a result, defense counsel needs to build a case for terminating sanctions in a deliberate fashion. Even the most reasonable and skilled trial judges typically need to witness multiple acts of intentional prosecutorial misconduct in several phases of the case before they will seriously entertain a motion that would take the case away from the jury, and some trial judges will never consider granting such a motion. The best course then may be to hold off on filing a motion to terminate until you have established multiple acts of blatant misconduct to demonstrate that the cumulative effect of all the misconduct justifies dismissing the indictment.

As demonstrated below, the most helpful pro-defendant jurisprudence on this topic comes out of the Ninth Circuit, particularly *United States v. Chapman* (524 F.3d 1073 (9th Cir. 2008)) and *United States v. Bundy* (968 F.3d 1019 (9th Cir. 2020)). Most circuits have opinions that lay out the applicable legal standard to evaluate a motion for terminating sanctions. *See, e.g., United States v. Rosario-Pérez*, 957 F.3d 277, 299 (1st Cir. 2020); *United States v. Walters*, 910 F.3d 11, 20–23 (2d Cir. 2018); *United States v. Wright*, 913 F.3d 364, 371 (3d Cir. 2019); *Plymail v. Mirandy*, 8 F.4th 308, 317–20 (4th Cir. 2021) and *United States v. Smith*, 687 F.2d 147, 152–53 (6th Cir. 1982).

14.2 FIFTH AMENDMENT DUE PROCESS VS. THE COURT'S SUPERVISORY POWERS

For matters on direct review from a federal district court, an appellate court may dismiss an indictment with prejudice based on prosecutorial misconduct under one of two theories: a violation of the Due Process Clause of the Fifth Amendment or by invoking the court's supervisory powers. As explained by the Ninth Circuit, "[F]irst, a district court may dismiss an indictment on the ground of outrageous government conduct if the conduct amounts to a due process violation. Second, if the conduct does not rise to the level of a due process violation, the court may nonetheless dismiss under its supervisory powers." *Chapman*, 524 F.3d at 1084. It is harder to establish a due process violation because the defendant must show that the government's conduct was "so outrageous that common notions of fairness and decency would be offended were judicial process invoked to obtain a conviction." *Walters*, 910 F.3d at 27. However, courts are receptive to cumulative effect style challenges in the context of due process arguments. *United States v. Preston*, 873 F.3d 829, 834 (9th Cir. 2017) ("the cumulative effect of multiple trial errors can violate due process even where no single error . . . would independently warrant reversal"). If the court decides that the defendant has proven either theory, it need not consider the other theory. *Bundy*, 968 F.3d at 1030.

However, if the matter is on habeas review, the federal court lacks any broad supervisory power and can only consider whether the state prosecutor committed a due process violation. *Plymail v. Mirandy*, 8 F.4th 308, 317 (4th Cir. 2021) (citing *Donnelly v. DeChristoforo*, 416 U.S. 637, 642 (1974)).

14.2.1 Proving a Due Process Violation

To meet "the very heavy burden of establishing a due process violation to dismiss an indictment for outrageous governmental misconduct, a defendant must show that the Government's conduct was 'so outrageous that common notions of fairness and decency would be offended were judicial process invoked to obtain a conviction.'" *Walters*, 910 F.3d at 27 (quoting *United States v. Al Kassar*, 660 F.2d 108, 121 (2d Cir. 2011)). To make this determination, the government conduct must be "so offensive that it shocks the conscience," which normally involves "coercion or a violation of the defendant's person." *Id.* at 27. The due process standard can be met where the government's conduct "involves extreme physical or mental brutality or where the crime is manufactured by the government from whole cloth." *Bundy*, 968 F.3d at 1030 (citing *United States v. Green*, 962 F.2d 938, 942 (9th Cir. 1992)); *see also United States v. Butler*, 828 F. App'x 602, 606 (11th Cir. 2020) ("A constitutional violation occurs when law enforcement's technique is so outrageous that it is fundamentally unfair and shocking to the universal sense of justice mandated by the Due Process Clause of the Fifth Amendment"); *United States v. Black*, 733 F.3d 294, 302 (9th Cir. 2013) (holding that dismissal for outrageous government conduct is limited to "extreme cases in which . . . the government's conduct violates fundamental fairness and is so grossly shocking and so outrageous as to violate the universal sense of justice").

Cumulative effect typically arises in the context of due process violations. In *Preston,* the Ninth Circuit stated that "[T]he cumulative effect of multiple trial errors can violate due process even where no single error . . . would independently warrant reversal." 873 F.3d at 834. The misconduct at issue in *Preston* included improper witness testimony, prejudicial propensity evidence, witness vouching, commenting on the Defendant's decision not to testify, and misstating the evidence in closing argument. The court also laid out its cumulative effect analysis, which begins by first asking whether the cumulative effect prejudiced the defendant. When prejudice to the defendant is clear, the court need not decide the individual prejudice of any of the individual errors. When the errors are not isolated but instead stand in "unique symmetry such that they amplify each other," then the court will look for a cumulative effect. *Id.* at 845–46 (citing *Ybarra v. McDaniel*, 656 F.3d 984, 1001 (9th Cir. 2011)).

14.2.2 The District Court's Supervisory Power

A district court "may exercise its supervisory power to implement a remedy for the violation of a recognized statutory or constitutional right; to preserve judicial integrity by ensuring that a conviction rests on appropriate considerations validly before a jury; and to deter future illegal conduct." *United States v. Hastings*, 461 U.S. 599, 505 (1983). While the circuit courts explain the legal standard for a supervisory powers style attack a bit differently, they typically require that the defendant meet three elements: (1) flagrant prosecutorial misconduct, (2) substantial prejudice suffered by the defendant, and (3) no lesser remedial action is available. *Chapman*, 524 F.3d at 1085.

First, to establish flagrant misconduct, defendants do not need to show willfulness or bad faith. *Id.* Instead, mere reckless disregard for a prosecutor's constitutional obligations is sufficient. *Id.* The court may find flagrant misconduct more readily where the government also fails to accept responsibility for its wrongdoing. *See United States v. Kojayan,* 8 F.3d 1315, 1322–23 (9th Cir. 1993) (highlighting government's failure to accept responsibility for its wrongdoing in finding flagrant misconduct).

Second, defendants also bear the burden to establish that they suffered prejudice. *Bundy*, 968 F.3d at 1037 (holding that Defendants "specifically suffered prejudice in not being able to prepare their case fully, refine their voir dire strategy and make stronger opening statements"). In *Chapman,* the Defendant would have been prejudiced in any retrial because the defense had shown its hand to the government such that the government would unjustly be receiving a mulligan to fix the tactical mistakes it had made in the initial trial. The Ninth Circuit emphasized that granting a mistrial "would advantage the government, probably allowing it to salvage what the district court viewed as a poorly conducted prosecution." *Chapman*, 524 F.3d at 1087.

Third, regarding the lesser remedy factor, courts look at many of the same facts that inform the prejudice analysis—issues such as the impact on the cost of defense, fading witness memories, and the possible advantages to the prosecutor if the courts remands for retrial. *Schoenauer v. United States*, 759 F. Supp. 2d 1090, 1106 (S.D. Iowa 2010) (holding retrial inappropriate given the passage of time and undue hardship on Defendant who has already incurred significant expense); *Bundy*, 968 F.3d at 1043 (holding district court must conclude a lesser remedy will not fully address the damage caused by the government's misconduct and ask "if any lesser remedy will put the defense at a greater disadvantage").

14.3 DOUBLE JEOPARDY

The government will likely get the opportunity to appeal the trial court's dismissal because the dismissal is based on misconduct, not a factual determination that the government failed to come forward with sufficient facts to convict.

The Supreme Court has repeatedly held that "jeopardy attaches when the jury is empaneled and sworn." *Martinez v. Illinois*, 572 U.S. 833, 834 (2014) (quoting *Crist v. Bretz*, 437 U.S. 28, 35 (1978)). Jeopardy terminates, thus triggering the Double Jeopardy Clause, as a result of "only an actual judgment of acquittal, or an unreversed conviction." *United States v. Miller*, 952 F.2d 866, 872 (5th Cir. 1992) (quoting *Richardson v. United States*, 468 U.S. 317, 327 (1984) (Brennan, J., concurring in part)). By contrast, the "vitally important interest" of "finality of judgments" embodied in the Double Jeopardy Clause does not apply to mistrials or trial errors that prevent a sustained verdict. *Yeager v. United States*, 557 U.S. 110, 118 (2009) (quoting *Crist*, 437 U.S. at 33). Whereas an acquittal signifies that the fact finder necessarily decided that the government failed to prove at least one element of the offense beyond a reasonable doubt, a mistrial or trial error means that the fact finder made no such decision at all. *See Martinez*, 572 U.S. at 842; *United States v. Hoeffner*, 626 F.3d 857, 866–67 (5th Cir. 2010). In short, by pressing for dismissal with prejudice, defense counsel is likely allowing the government to revisit the trial court's ruling on the prosecutorial misconduct on appeal.

An appellate court should review the dismissal of an indictment under the abuse of discretion of standard. *Chapman*, 524 F.3d at 1086. Any legal issues predicating the district court's dismissal receive *de novo* review while the district court's findings of fact are reviewed for clear error. *United States v. Velarde-Gavarrete*, 975 F.2d 672, 674 (9th Cir. 1992). Chapter 15 contains a more detailed discussion on the various standards of appellate review. Given that the appellate court will show deference to the factual findings of the trial court, defense counsel should present a detailed factual record to the trial judge so the court can adopt those facts in its final order.

Topics to consider raising to the trial judge include every example of prosecutorial misconduct and all the related prejudice inflicted on the defense:

- All the facts supporting every instance of prosecutorial misconduct throughout the entire case.

- Every possible way that the government could improve its case on retrial after seeing your opening statement and any key cross-examinations.
- Every possible way that you would have pursued a different trial strategy but for the misconduct: in your opening, cross-examination of witnesses, voir dire, and jury selection.
- How a delay or recess in the trial won't cure the problem because of the inconvenience to the jury and their inability to re-engage with the facts after taking any time away from trial.
- The financial burden to the defense to have to do a retrial.
- Fading memories, sick witnesses, or evidence that might be unavailable due to any delay in a retrial.
- Any evidence suggesting that the government invited the mistrial for tactical reasons, such as seeking a fresh start in a second trial after seeing the defense in the initial trial.
- The government's lack of contrition for its misconduct.

14.4 MOTION FOR TERMINATING SANCTIONS: HELPFUL CASES

United States v. Chapman, 524 F.3d 1073 (9th Cir. 2008) (court invokes supervisory powers to affirm district court's dismissal of indictment with prejudice where prosecutor failed to provide defense counsel with *Brady/Giglio* information related to prior criminal history of numerous government witnesses).

United States v. Bundy, 968 F.3d 1019 (9th Cir. 2020) (district court's dismissal of obstructing federal law enforcement charges upheld as an appropriate exercise of its supervisory powers where government withheld a series of *Brady/Giglio* evidence related to the Defendant's core defense at trial—that FBI snipers had taken positions to surveil the Defendant's cattle farm, thereby leading Defendant to seek assistance and protection from local militia groups).

United States v. Preston, 873 F.3d 829 (9th Cir. 2017) (conviction reversed for violation of Due Process Clause where cumulative effect of prosecutorial misconduct during closing argument and other trial errors deprived the Defendant of a fair trial).

United States v. Kohring, 637 F. 3d 895 (9th Cir. 2011) (conviction in public corruption case reversed where prosecutors improperly withheld *Brady/Giglio* information related to a cooperating Defendant who testified for the prosecution).

United States v. Kojayan, 8 F.3d 1315 (9th Cir. 1993) (conviction reversed where prosecutor lied to the jury, the trial court, and the appellate court about the existence of a cooperation agreement with a witness the Defendant elected not to call at trial because the defense was under the misimpression that the witness could invoke the Fifth Amendment and refuse to testify).

Plymail v. Mirandy, 8 F.4th 308 (4th Cir. 2021), as amended (Sept. 7, 2021) (reversing grant of summary judgment against the Defendant's habeas petition claim that the government's improper statements "exhorting the jury to protect women and send a message to the community and to 'sadomasochistic' persons" during closing argument was so fundamentally unfair that it constituted a due process violation).

United States v. Pisoni, No. 15-20339-CR (S.D. Fla. Nov. 18, 2022) (Order Granting New Trial, ECF No. 767 at 2, 17–18) (granting new trial where the government violated the Defendants' Sixth Amendment right to effective assistance of counsel by invading the defense camp via a cooperating Co-defendant and deliberately displayed a lack of candor with the court by lying about their possession of privileged materials).

United States v. Nejad, 521 F. Supp. 3d 438 (S.D.N.Y. 2021) (dismissing all charges with prejudice following a guilty jury verdict because the government determined that "further prosecution of the case would not be in the interests of justice" after the government repeatedly failed to disclose exculpatory evidence, attempted to bury late disclosures among previously disclosed documents, made misrepresentations to the court to evade responsibility for the late disclosures, and FBI agents misused raw search warrant returns in violation of Defendants' Fourth Amendment rights).

In re Special Proc., 825 F. Supp. 2d 203 (D.D.C. 2011) (investigating the government in their prosecution of Senator Ted Stevens in Alaska in response to: (1) "the significance of the government's decision to dismiss the indictment and not to seek a retrial"; (2) *Brady* violations and misrepresentations the government admitted to; (3) prosecutorial misconduct "to a degree and extent" the judge had not seen in twenty-five years on the bench; and (4) a likelihood that the government may have committed "additional constitutional and procedural violations" that were yet to be discovered or addressed).

CHAPTER 15

Preserving Objections for Appeal

The reported cases demonstrate that the government has a rather poor history of accepting any responsibility when it commits prosecutorial misconduct. Instead of consenting to some form of reasonable relief to cure the issue they created, prosecutors often respond by aggressively arguing that defense counsel either waived or failed to timely object to their misconduct. The government seeks to win by procedural default to avoid having to answer on the merits for the prosecutor's serious violations of your client's constitutional rights.

In addition, there are countless appellate decisions where courts have ignored serious prosecutorial misconduct—knowingly suborning perjury from trial witnesses, willfully withholding exculpatory evidence, intentionally misrepresenting evidence during closing—by applying the plain error standard because defense counsel did not properly preserve an objection to the prosecutor's misconduct. Compare *United States v. Modena*, 302 F.3d 626, 634-36 (6th Cir. 2002) (affirming conviction under plain error standard where prosecutor improperly vouched for government witness by stating that witness had converted into a "law-abiding man" and prosecutor improperly pressured the jury to convict by arguing that "[w]e're not finished until this verdict is returned") with *United States v. Francis*, 170 F.3d 546, 550–51 (6th Cir. 1999) (conviction reversed under *de novo* standard for improper vouching where prosecutor described plea agreement of cooperating witness by indicating that prosecutor would have to recommend a sentence reduction to the court for witness to receive a reduced sentence).

As a result, this chapter aims to provide helpful guidance on how and when to object to misconduct. At a high level, consider using a belt and suspenders approach to preserving objections: object in writing with pre-trial motions and again at trial where possible; raise every potential rule of evidence that might apply to an issue; "constitutionalize" your objection; object on the record so your objection is memorialized in the trial transcript; and move for mistrial when appropriate.

15.1 MAKING A TIMELY OBJECTION

The timeliness of a trial objection is governed by the Contemporaneous Objection Rule, in *Federal Rules of Criminal Procedure* 51(b) and *Federal Rules of Evidence* 103. FRE 103(a)(1) applies to defense objections to the *admission* of government evidence. Defense counsel needs to timely object and state the specific ground for the objection (unless it is apparent from the context) to preserve the objection. As a result, consider using pre-trial motions *in limine* or written offers of proof at trial to get your objections on the record before the government even attempts to introduce the offending evidence at trial. If you can't object in writing before the prosecutor seeks to introduce the evidence, object immediately when the issue arises.

By contrast, FRE 103(a)(2) applies when defense counsel opposes the prosecutor's request to *exclude* defense evidence. Defense counsel properly preserves their position by informing the court via a proffer or where the substance of the evidence sought to be elicited was apparent to the court. *United States v. Kay*, 513 F.3d 432, 455–56 (5th Cir. 2007) (informal pre-trial offer of proof sufficient under Rule 103 and no further objections needed at trial); *United States v. Lucas*, 849 F.3d 638, 642 (5th Cir. 2017) (same). As a result, when the government seeks to exclude your evidence, provide a detailed offer of proof where you also cite both the applicable rule(s) of evidence and any constitutional hook for the evidence; for example, right to confront, right to compulsory process, right to present a complete defense, or right to due process. The exclusion of evidence that would support a defendant's theory of defense is a leading basis to reverse a conviction on appeal because it prevents the defendant from presenting a complete defense. *Crane v. Kentucky*, 476 U.S. 683, 690 (1986) (confirming that the Constitution guarantees criminal defendants "a meaningful opportunity to present a complete defense"); *Washington v. Texas*, 388 U.S. 14, 19 (1967) (confirming that the Constitution provides criminal defendants the right "to present the defendant's version of the facts as well as the prosecution's to the jury so that [the jury] may decide where the truth lies"); *United States v. Lowery*, 135 F.3d 957, 959 (5th Cir. 1998) (reversing conviction because the district court excluded evidence related to the Defendant's theory of defense: "it is well established that a criminal defendant is entitled to present his theory of defense, including witnesses, testimony and exhibits"). As a result, be active if the government ever seeks to exclude any defense evidence at trial.

Given the pace and unpredictability of most criminal trials, there will be situations where you may realize that you should have lodged an objection to something that happened earlier in the trial. Raise your objection at that point or at the next break in trial and move to strike the prior introduction of the government's evidence. While certain circuit courts are stricter than others (see Section 15.5), many do provide a little leeway when defense counsel failed to immediately raise an objection. The point of the Contemporaneous Objection Rule is to provide the trial judge enough notice to fix the issue. In closing argument, for example, a contemporaneous objection in some jurisdictions is one "made in sufficient time to allow the judge to correct any error if he had chosen to do so," including "at the first possible moment after the jury ha[s] left the courtroom." *United States v. Dorr*, 636 F.2d 117, 120 (5th Cir. Unit A Feb. 1981); *see also United States v. Appolon*, 695 F.3d 44, 66 (1st Cir. 2012) (holding an objection made the next day timely because closing arguments had not yet concluded and the district court "could have taken any necessary corrective action"). If you should object a little late during trial and the government complains, focus the discussion on the fact that the court still has sufficient time to remedy the issue. If the court still overrules your objection, you may have made a strong enough record to avoid plain error review on appeal.

In addition, trial judges often respond to defense objections with boilerplate and meaningless curative instructions that never cure the prejudice ("the jury will remember the evidence" or "what the lawyers say is not evidence"). When this happens, some jurisdictions require that defense counsel must also object to the court's curative instruction to preserve the entire issue for appeal. Failing to object to the curative instruction waives the objection to the underlying issue. *United States v. Taylor*, 514 F.3d 1092, 1096 (10th Cir. 2008) (holding that defense counsel failed to preserve an issue at trial when he failed to either object or move for mistrial following the court's curative instruction). As a result, object to any curative instruction and renew all your objections on the underlying issue.

15.2 MAKING A SPECIFIC OBJECTION

Defense counsel should be specific about what they are objecting to and the basis of their objection or they may confront plain error review on appeal. *See United States v. Burton*, 126 F.3d 666, 671–673 (5th Cir. 1997) (objecting under FRE 801(d)(2)(E) does not provide a specific enough basis); *United States v. Eagle*, 515 F.3d 794, 803–804 (8th Cir. 2008) (objecting to "relevance" is not sufficient to preserve objection). However, defense counsel should not need to cite a particular case or mention "magic words" to support the objection. *See United States v. Rashad*, 396 F.3d 398, 401 (D.C. Cir. 2005) (holding that defendant objecting under ineffective assistance of counsel grounds was enough to preserve error); *United States v. Massey*, 443 F.3d 814, 819 (11th Cir. 2006) (holding that defense attorney not saying "*mens rea*" or "intent" did not bar preservation of mental state issue); *Ferguson v. Sec'y for Dep't of Corr.*, 580 F.3d 1183, 1212–13 (11th Cir. 2009) (although "'magic words are not needed to make a proper objection,' counsel must articulate his concern with sufficient specificity 'to inform the trial judge of the alleged error'").

Our preferred approach is to cite to every specific rule of evidence that might possibly apply. For example, when trying to exclude irrelevant evidence, object under FRE 401 through 403, not simply FRE 401. Or, if you seek to exclude some aspect of expert testimony, object under FRE 701 through 704 and FRE 401 through 403, not simply FRE 701. You can narrow the scope of your objection on appeal after having more time to review the relevant cases, but you will have covered the landscape at trial and preserved all of your options.

While citing case law is not required to preserve an objection, we like to cite cases to support objections on issues we anticipated before trial; for example, *Stirone* for any constructive amendment issue, *Berger* for improper closing argument, and *Napue* for challenges to the introduction of false testimony. We typically keep a roster of controlling circuit level cases on a laminated "play sheet" that we draft before trial that includes the key Supreme Court and circuit level authority on common issues like *Brady/Giglio*, *Napue*, constructive amendment, FRE 401/403, hearsay, and improper voir dire/opening statement/closing argument. Having the ability to immediately cite controlling case law signals to the trial judge that you know your stuff and may elevate the court's respect for the positions you take throughout the trial.

If the defense moves for a mistrial, re-prosecution is ordinarily not barred by double jeopardy. *Oregon v. Kennedy*, 456 U.S. 667, 673 (1982).

However, under the "invited mistrial" doctrine, double jeopardy rights will attach when the prosecutor intentionally provoked a mistrial. *Id.* at 676. The public policy point is that the government should not be allowed a second trial if it intentionally sabotaged the first trial after it saw the defense strategy and realized that it needed a mulligan if it had any chance at obtaining a conviction.

Proving an "invited mistrial" is a very difficult standard to meet. *Id.* at 688. Mere prosecutorial overreaching or prejudicial conduct without the relevant intent will not bar retrial based on double jeopardy grounds. *Id.* at 675–76. However, where the prosecutorial misconduct at issue is sufficiently severe, consider raising the "invited mistrial" doctrine when you move for mistrial to try to influence the double jeopardy analysis if the district court agrees to grant the mistrial. If the trial judge makes a factual finding that the prosecutors intentionally sabotaged the first trial to gain an advantage in a re-trial, you might be able to invoke double jeopardy to avoid the second trial.

15.3 CONSTITUTIONALIZE YOUR OBJECTIONS

"Constitutionalize" every possible objection because constitutional errors typically receive a far more favorable standard of review on appeal. When an evidentiary error possesses a constitutional dimension, the government must demonstrate that the error was "harmless beyond a reasonable doubt." *Chapman v. California*, 386 U.S. 18, 24 (1967). On the other hand, for non-constitutional errors—such as abuses of discretion involving a rule of evidence—the government only needs to demonstrate that it was "highly probable" that the defendant was not prejudiced by the error. *Id.* This is a significant difference on appeal and justifies attempting to constitutionalize every defense objection at trial.

As a result, think about raising constitutional concerns on all evidentiary objections. For example, if the government moves to exclude some of your cross-examination of a government witness, don't merely argue that your proposed questioning is relevant under FRE 401—also challenge the exclusion of evidence under the Fifth and Sixth Amendments by raising objections tied to the Due Process Clause, the Confrontation Clause, and the right to present a complete defense. *See, e.g., Delaware v. Van Arsdall*, 475 U.S. 673, 678 (1986) (the Confrontation Clause of the Sixth Amendment guarantees the defendant the opportunity to cross-examine the government's witnesses); *United States v. Haischer*, 780 F.3d 1277, 1284

(9th Cir. 2015) (an evidentiary error violates a defendant's due process rights when it excludes (1) the main piece of evidence (2) for the defendant's main defense to (3) a critical element of the government's case).

Likewise, if the prosecutor seeks to exclude any of your evidence or witnesses, make your FRE 401 proffer but also object that the government's position violates both the Fifth and Sixth Amendments—the Due Process Clause, the Compulsory Process Clause, and the right to present a complete defense. *Crane v. Kentucky*, 476 U.S. 683, 690 (1986) (the Constitution, through the Due Process Clause of the Fifth Amendment and the Compulsory Process and Confrontation Clauses of the Sixth Amendment, guarantees criminal defendants "a meaningful opportunity to present a complete defense"). As another example, if the prosecutor argues facts that constructively amend the indictment, specifically refer to both the Grand Jury Clause and Due Process Clause in the Fifth Amendment. *United States v. Lloyd*, 807 F.3d 1128, 1164 (9th Cir. 2015) (constructive amendment challenge reviewed *de novo* because it is grounded in the Fifth Amendment's Grand Jury Clause).

Common constitutional challenges under the Fifth Amendment include due process violations, violations of the Grand Jury clause, the right to not incriminate yourself, and an accused's protection against double jeopardy. Common Sixth Amendment challenges involve the Confrontation Clause, the Compulsory Process Clause, the right to present a complete defense (regarding any potential exclusion of theory of defense evidence), the right to a speedy trial, the right to counsel, and the right to an impartial jury.

15.4 APPLICABLE STANDARDS OF REVIEW ON APPEAL: FROM *DE NOVO* TO PLAIN ERROR

Appellate courts use varying standards of review depending on the issue on appeal—*de novo*, clearly erroneous, substantial evidence, abuse of discretion, and plain error. Understanding the differences between the various standards demonstrates why it is so important to frame objections properly.

15.4.1 *De Novo* Standard

Under *de novo* review, the appellate court gives no deference to the district court's decision—the appellate court simply reviews the issue like the trial court never ruled on it. This is the most defendant friendly standard of review on appeal. *De novo* review applies to legal issues, not factual issues.

An example of legal issues receiving *de novo* review on appeal are violations of a defendant's Fifth and Sixth Amendment rights. *United States v. Jimenez*, 464 F.3d 555, 558 (5th Cir. 2006). This underscores the importance of "constitutionalizing" every possible objection at trial.

De novo review is sometimes used for mixed questions of law and fact: "The standard of review for a mixed question all depends on whether answering it entails primarily legal or factual work." *United States Bank Natl. Ass'n ex rel. CWCapital Asset Management, LLC v. Village at Lakeridge, LLC*, 138 S. Ct. 960, 967 (2018). Some circuit courts have established certain guidelines to answer this question. For example, in the Sixth Circuit, mixed questions are reviewed *de novo*. *United States v. Kennedy*, 61 F.3d 494, 497 (6th Cir. 1995). In the Ninth Circuit, "mixed questions are typically reviewed *de novo*, but, depending on the nature of the inquiry involved, may be reviewed under a more deferential clearly erroneous standard." *United States v. Lang*, 149 F.3d 1044, 1047 (9th Cir. 1998).

15.4.2 Clearly Erroneous Standard

The "clearly erroneous" standard is more pro-government because the appellate court must give more deference to the district court's ruling. To satisfy the clearly erroneous standard, the appellate court must conclude that although there is evidence to support the trial court's ruling, the appellate court is left with the "definite and firm conviction" that the lower court committed a mistake based on looking at all of the evidence. *United States v. United States Gypsum Co.*, 333 U.S. 364, 395 (1948). Appellate courts apply the clearly erroneous standard when reviewing a question of fact found by the trial judge. For example, the court's factual findings regarding a vindictive prosecution motion would be reviewed under the clearly erroneous standard. *United States v. Leathers*, 354 F.3d 955, 962(8th Cir. 2004). Or, in the context of a motion to suppress, the clearly erroneous standard applies to whether officers had "reasonable suspicion" for a traffic stop or any other factual finding underlying the motion to suppress. *United States v. Phillips*, 71 F.4th 817, 822 (10th Cir. 2023).

A question of fact found by the jury, not the court, will be reviewed under the substantial evidence standard. Like the clearly erroneous standard, appellate courts apply significant deference to decisions made by the jury. An example would be a jury finding of guilt on any count in the indictment. The appellate court will only reverse a decision made by the jury if no "rational trier of fact could have found the essential elements of the crime beyond a reasonable doubt." *Jackson v. Virginia*, 443 U.S. 307, 319 (1979).

15.4.3 Abuse of Discretion Standard

The "abuse of discretion standard" is another highly deferential standard that applies when the appellate court reviews discretionary decisions made by the trial court. Examples include the court placing time limits on defense counsel's opening statement or witness exams. *United States v. Larson,* 495 F.3d 1094, 1101 (9th Cir. 2007) (applying *de novo* review to a Confrontation Clause challenge based on the exclusion of an area of inquiry but applying the abuse of discretion standard to the limitation on the scope of questioning within a given area). Appellate courts will find abuse of discretion only when the district court "has acted arbitrarily or irrationally, has failed to consider judicially recognized factors constraining its exercise of discretion, or when it has relied on erroneous factual or legal premises." *United States v. Welsh*, 879 F.3d 530, 536 (4th Cir. 2018).

15.4.4 Plain Error Standard

The worst standard from the defense perspective is the "plain error" standard. If defense counsel did not adequately preserve an issue at trial, the appellate court will apply the plain error standard. Per Rule 52(b) of the *Federal Rules of Criminal Procedure*: "Plain errors or defects affecting substantial rights may be noticed although they were not brought to the attention of the court." The Supreme Court has recognized plain error as "an 'error' that is 'plain' and that 'affect[s] substantial rights.'" *United States v. Olano*, 507 U.S. 725, 732 (1993). The appellate court has discretion to correct the error but should only do so if the error "seriously affect[s] the fairness, integrity, or public reputation of judicial proceedings." *Id.* In practice, if the appellate court thinks that the jury may have still convicted the defendant given the strength of the remaining evidence, the plain error standard gives the appellate court the ability to ignore severe prosecutorial misconduct and affirm the conviction. Plain error review is the Mt. Everest of legal hurdles facing criminal defendants on appeal—it is the highest bar to clear. No single factor kills more viable prosecutorial misconduct claims than plain error review. You can avoid the plain error standard by making timely, specific objections that include every possible evidentiary and constitutional basis that potentially supports your position.

15.5 PRESERVING OBJECTIONS: HELPFUL CASES

First Circuit

To properly object to error and preserve the issue for appeal, defense counsel must lodge a timely objection. What constitutes timeliness "var[ies] with the circumstances" but generally means while the court still can take any necessary corrective action in response. *United States v. Ayala-Garcia*, 574 F.3d 5, 20 n.13 (1st Cir. 2009); *United States v. Appolon*, 695 F.3d 44, 66 (1st Cir. 2012) (holding an objection made the next day timely because closing arguments had not yet concluded and the district court "could have taken any necessary corrective action"); *United States v. Azubike*, 504 F.3d 30, 39 (1st Cir. 2007) (holding an objection timely when it occurred at sidebar following closing argument conclusion and emphasizing that a "stricture governing the timing of objections should not be employed woodenly"). Regardless, the defendant holds the burden "to take his objection at the earliest possible opportunity when, by so doing he can enable the trial judge to take the most efficacious action." *Holden v. United States*, 388 F.2d 240, 242–43 (1st Cir. 1968).

Second Circuit

To properly object to error and preserve the issue for appeal, defense counsel must lodge a contemporaneous objection and should move for mistrial or "request specific curative instructions." *United States v. Oquendo*, 192 F. App'x 77, 81 (2d Cir. 2006); *United States v. Aquart*, 912 F.3d 1, 35–36 (2d Cir. 2018) ("[W]here, as here, the defense neither sought further instructions nor moved for a mistrial after objection to the vouching question was sustained, that is 'some indication' that the defense itself did not perceive the improper question 'as rendering the trial unfair'" (quoting *United States v. Melendez*, 57 F.3d 238, 243

(2d Cir. 1995)); *Melendez*, 57 F.3d at 242–43 ("Although no federal rule of procedure requires a mistrial motion in order to preserve the issue of prosecutorial misconduct for appeal, the absence of such a motion provides some indication that the improper remark was not perceived as rendering the trial unfair").

Third Circuit

To properly object to error and preserve the issue for appeal, defense counsel must lodge a timely objection to avoid plain error review. A timely objection must be sufficient to call the trial judge's attention to the error. *United States v. Colletti*, 984 F.2d 1339, 1344 (3d Cir. 1992). It must also provide opportunity for remedial action to be taken. *United States v. Somers*, 496 F.2d 723, 742 (3d Cir. 1974) ("[H]ad a timely objection been made, remedial action, if appropriate, could have been taken"). This requirement means objections should be raised immediately. *Id.* at 738 n.28 ("We agree . . . that requiring immediate objections to improprieties in openings serves the dual purpose of forestalling further improprieties and 'curing' improper remarks"). Otherwise, "the incident was not nearly as significant as [an argument on appeal] would suggest." *Id.* Making the objection sufficiently specific at the time of the incident, and lodging a general objection by moving for mistrial, preserves the issue for appeal. *See Gov't of Virgin Islands v. Joseph*, 770 F.2d 343, 348 (3d Cir. 1985) ("[W]e note that [defense counsel] specifically objected to the prosecutor's comments on his trial conduct . . . and took a general objection by moving for a mistrial at the close of the summation").

Fourth Circuit

To properly object to error and preserve the issue for appeal, defense counsel must lodge a timely objection to avoid plain error review. An objection is not contemporaneous or timely when it comes at the conclusion of an argument. *United States v. Polytarides*, 584 F.2d 1350,

1353–54 (4th Cir. 1978); *United States v. Elmore*, 423 F.2d 775, 781 (4th Cir. 1970) ("We think that the concern for judicial efficiency and adversary fairness . . . requires defense counsel promptly to make his objection known so that the district judge can quickly caution the jury and prevent further prosecutorial intemperance"). Moving for a mistrial at the conclusion of a prosecutor's statement is not sufficient to preserve an objection for review. *Polytarides*, 584 F.2d at 1354. Defense counsel should object *and move for mistrial. United States v. Taylor*, 900 F.2d 779, 782 (4th Cir. 1990) (holding that where "there was no contemporaneous motion for a mistrial" the court may not consider prosecutor witness vouching in a closing statement on appeal); *United States v. McGill*, 3 F. App'x 181, 183 (4th Cir. 2001) ("Moreover, absent plain error, an improper closing argument is not grounds for reversal where the defendant has not objected *and moved for a mistrial*"); *United States v. Rhodes*, 779 F.2d 1019, 1030 (4th Cir. 1985) (holding an objection to an allegedly improper closing argument "not reversible error because there was no motion for a mistrial").

Fifth Circuit

A "sufficiently contemporaneous objection" that preserves an error for appeal is one made in time for the trial judge to "correct any possible mistaken impressions that might have been left in the minds of the jurors," including "at the first possible moment after the jury [has] left the courtroom." *United States v. Dorr*, 636 F.2d 117, 120 (5th Cir. 1981).

Sixth Circuit

"In order to preserve a claim of error, the objecting party must 'inform[] the court . . . of the action the party wishes the court to take, or the party's objection to the court's action and the grounds for that objection'" *United States v. Bradley*, 917 F.3d 493, 505 (6th Cir. 2019) (quoting Federal Rules of Criminal Procedure, 51(b)).

Seventh Circuit

To preserve an objection for appeal, the objecting party should "make a timely and specific objection" so that "the court has the opportunity to rectify the error, if indeed there has been error, at the time." *United States v. Johnson*, 26 F.3d 669, 677 (7th Cir. 1994) (citing *United States v. Lewis*, 954 F.2d 1386, 1391 (7th Cir. 1992)). Raising an objection "some time after the alleged error has occurred and after the opportunity to address the error has passed obviously defeats the purpose of the requirement of timeliness. In addition to being timely, the objection must also specify the precise nature of the alleged error." *Id.* (citing *United States v. Wynn*, 845 F.2d 1439, 1442 (7th Cir. 1988)). Moreover, "defense counsel is well-advised to request a prompt cautionary instruction from the trial court." *Id.*

Eighth Circuit

To preserve an error of prosecutorial misconduct for review, "the better practice is to make objection at the time of the asserted prejudicial utterances. This will afford the court an opportunity to properly warn the prosecutor that improper argument will not be tolerated, and to promptly take action designed to more effectively remove from the minds of the jury the sting or poison of the prejudicial statement." *Birnbaum v. United States*, 356 F.2d 856, 866 (8th Cir. 1966) (quoting *Isaacs v. United States*, 301 F.2d 706, 736 (8th Cir. 1962)).

Ninth Circuit

To preserve an objection for appeal, counsel "must *timely* object and state the *specific* grounds for his objection." *See, e.g., United States v. Gomez-Norena*, 908 F.2d 497, 500 (9th Cir. 1990) (emphasis added). As to the specification requirement, an objection will not be preserved for appeal if a party fails to "make a specific objection" or makes "the wrong specific objection." *United States v. Del Toro-Barboza*, 673 F.3d 1136, 1152 (9th Cir. 2012) (quoting

Gomez-Norena, 908 F.2d at 500) (holding defendant failed to preserve objection where counsel objected on "vouching" grounds, rather than on grounds of "prosecutorial misconduct"). As for the timely requirement, an objection must be contemporaneous to the alleged misconduct. *See, e.g.*, *Kaiser Steel Corp. v. Frank Coluccio Constr. Co.*, 785 F.2d 656, 658 (9th Cir.1986). A failure to bring a contemporaneous objection "firmly bars relief for misconduct." *Id.*

Tenth Circuit

To preserve an issue for appeal, a party "must make a timely and proper objection." *United States v. Lonedog*, 929 F.2d 568, 570 (10th Cir. 1991); *see also United States v. Beckman*, 662 F.2d 661, 662 (10th Cir. 1981) (holding that, absent a contemporaneous objection, the issue of prosecutorial misconduct will be reviewed under the plain error standard). If a party objects to prosecutorial misconduct and the court subsequently issues curative instruction, the initial objection is not preserved for appeal. *United States v. Taylor*, 514 F.3d 1092, 1096 (10th Cir. 2008). In such a case, it is assumed that the court's instruction cured the initial objection. *See id.* Thus, if the party disagrees with the court's curative instruction—or if issues remain—the party must advance a second contemporaneous, proper objection. *See id.* (holding that defense counsel failed to preserve an issue at trial when he failed to either object or move for mistrial following the court's curative instruction).

Eleventh Circuit

Generally, "to preserve an issue at trial for appeal, a party must raise an objection 'that is sufficient to apprise the trial court and the opposing party of the particular grounds upon which appellate relief will later be sought.'" *United States v. Parker*, 816 F. App'x 377, 379 (11th Cir. 2020) (quoting *United States v. Dennis*, 786 F.2d 1029, 1042 (11th Cir. 1986), modified on other grounds by *United States v. Dennis*, 804 F.2d 1208 (11th Cir. 1986)). In other words, counsel must raise the specific grounds on which appellate relief will be sought. *See, e.g.*, *United States v. Ward*, 796 F. App'x 591, 597 (11th Cir. 2019) (holding counsel did not preserve an issue for appeal because, during his objection, counsel failed to bring attention to the specific statute at issue). The Eleventh Circuit has explained that although "'magic words are not needed to make a proper objection,' counsel must articulate his concern with sufficient specificity 'to inform the trial judge of the alleged error.'" *Ferguson v. Sec'y for Dep't of Corr.*, 580 F.3d 1183, 1212–13 (11th Cir. 2009) (quoting *Williams v. State*, 414 So.2d 509, 512 (Fla. 1982)). Finally, counsel's objection must be contemporaneous to the alleged prosecutorial error. *See, e.g.*, *United States v. Newton*, 44 F.3d 913, 920 (11th Cir. 1994) ("Absent a contemporaneous objection, the propriety of the Government's closing argument and alleged prosecutorial misconduct in improperly vouching . . . are reviewed under a plain error standard").

D.C. Circuit

Generally, to preserve an issue for appeal, counsel's objection must be timely and specific. *See, e.g.*, *United States v. Wilson*, 605 F.3d 985, 1022 (D.C. Cir. 2010). A specific objection is one in which counsel explains the grounds on which he is objecting. *See id.* The specificity requirement may be overcome if counsel "can demonstrate on appeal that the ground for the objection was obvious from the context in which it was made." *United States v. Boyd*, 54 F.3d 868, 872 (D.C. Cir. 1995).

Index